MW01601401

To Amjad Bahman,
a pioneer ... the
community

M Tahir
10/15/04

Please provide feedback

508 - 898 - 2789

ama_tahir @ yahoo.com

The Muslim Vote:

Counts and Recounts

by Tahir Ali

The Muslim Vote:
Counts and Recounts

by Tahir Ali

The Rhodes-Fulbright Library

ISBN: 1-55605-353-3 (Soft Cover)

ISBN: 1-55605-369-X (Hard Cover)

Library of Congress Control Number: 2004107912

WYNDHAM HALL PRESS
Lima, Ohio 45806
www.wyndhamhallpress.com

Printed in The United States of America

TABLE OF CONTENTS

DEDICATED TO:

In memory of my son: Yaser Ali

No one talks about his or her

death experience.

Front Cover Comments
[Judge this book by its' cover].

Each of the three pictures on the front cover represents a milestone in the path of American Muslims toward political empowerment. The pictures placed inside the book depict a significant historical moment, as well.

The picture in the middle shows Hillary Rodham Clinton holding a plaque presented to her at the controversial Boston fundraiser on June 13, 2000. The presenter, the author of this book, Tahir Ali, is standing next to the Former First Lady.
Photo credit: Dr. Malik Masood Khan

The picture on the bottom shows the American Muslim leadership taking a covenant from an audience of 10,000 people, who endorsed the bloc vote, at the ISNA convention on September 3, 2000.
From left to right: Sayyid Syeed, secretary general of the Islamic Society of North America (ISNA); Nihad Awad, national director of the Council on American-Islamic Relations (CAIR); Muzammil Siddiqi, president of ISNA; Yahya Basha, president of the American Muslim Council (AMC); Agha Saeed, founder-chairman of the American Muslim Alliance (AMA); Aly Abuzaakouk, executive director of the AMC.
Photo credit: ISNA Administration

The picture on the top shows President George W. Bush speaking at the Islamic center in Washington D.C. on September 17, 2001.

PREFACE

The saga of American Muslims' emergence into mainstream U.S. politics is a compelling one. More important still to me is that, for the first time in our history, Muslims in America organized a bloc vote to help elect George W. Bush the forty-third president of the United States of America.

This book should appeal not only to the early Muslim immigrants but also to any newly arrived ethnic or religious group. In more ways than one, it is a record of the struggle to mold a political identity. The challenges and difficulties American Muslims have been facing are no different from those the American Irish, Italians or Jews have gone through. Dean Murphy of *The New York Times* articulated this point well on October 27, 2000:

> **For American Muslims,**
> **Influence in American Politics Comes Hard**
> When Salam Al-Marayati read yesterday that Hillary Rodham Clinton would return $50,000 in political contributions from members of the American Muslim Alliance, he got a sinking feeling. It was happening again, Mr. Al-Marayati said. A prominent Muslim-American — in this case, Agha Saeed, who is president of the alliance — was being punished for pushing Muslim-Americans into the political mainstream, he said. "Agha Saeed was successful in unifying the Muslim vote and, for the first time, in creating a voting bloc."

This became the turning point for the American Muslim. The New York Senate race between Hillary Clinton and Rick Lazio left no stone unturned, and left American Muslims caught between a rock and a hard place. Anti-Muslim bigotry got ugly, pushing the Muslims into an embarrassing position. But the Muslims stood their ground. If the measure for maturity is the ability to deal with complexity, American Muslims measured up. This also, was a moment of truth for America as an open society and Hillary as a main stream politician. At stake was the freedom of speech, on one hand, and equal access on the other. This episode is better understood in terms of the unintended rather than the intended consequences. If the intention was to stigmatize some Muslim organizations and to seek their exclusion from the political process, the unintended consequences led to 1) further isolation and ultimate defeat of Rick Lazio, 2) brought national attention to Muslim voters and organizations which showed them to be quite modern, moderate and mainstream, and 3) refocused the question of equal access to politics.

Hillary Rodham Clinton did indeed return the money raised by the Muslim community in Boston. In the wake of that embarrassing moment, Muslims in America got both national and international attention.

Major newspapers, magazines and television stations around the world — the Associated Press, the New York Times, the New York Daily News, the Boston Globe, the Christian Science Monitor, BBC, ABC, NBC, CBS, FOX, CNN, L'Alsace Monde in France, Al-Ahram in Egypt, the Dawn in Pakistan, the Jerusalem Post, Middle East Quarterly, the Washington Post, the Detroit Times, the Washington Times, the L.A. Times, etceteras. — reported the Hillary Clinton/Rick Lazio blowup involving diametrically opposite approaches of inclusion and exclusion.

The news media remained predominantly focused on the New York Senate race, propelled by Rick Lazio's racist remarks against Muslims which put Hillary Clinton in a defensive position, on the run. However, every time the Senate race was mentioned, the Muslim bloc vote and the endorsement for George Bush got a mention as well. This was the good part; otherwise the Muslim endorsement probably would have gone unnoticed, hence the $50,000 given to Hillary Clinton got the American Muslims $50 million worth of publicity.

Admittedly Muslim leadership's main concern at that point was not how to deal with the bigotry issue; there was plenty of time to respond to that. The main concern was how to make sure things did not reach a level where President George Bush would consider returning our endorsement. It was actually more an issue of dealing with the conditions and responding in a manner that showed our mainstream credentials, our ability to affect things and then to change them. It was also necessary to make available to them the totality of our political positions – to rectify the distortions through communication of what we actually had said, what we stood for, what we were doing and what our organizations were all about. His campaign office had reportedly returned donations from a notable Muslim-American leader, Abdurahman Alamoudi, the president of the American Muslim Council (AMC), a lobbying and grassroots group headquartered in Washington, D.C.

Was Hillary Clinton truly oblivious to the identity of the fundraiser's sponsors? The answer to that question and the circumstances that may have led the former First Lady to return the Boston Muslim community's money are included in a chapter in this book.

There are many Muslims living in the United States who have served as role models for communities. They are exemplary people. They are people who come from different backgrounds and are seen here as ordinary citizens, but yet Americans and their neighbors have not discovered their talents as citizens, doctors, engineers and academics by profession. They are seen as ordinary by the fact of their immigration, but actually they are extraordinary and outstanding people. A great number of American Muslims may have had some material reasons for coming to America: to adopt a glamorous life style, attain higher education or get rich. But, as years went by, some also realized there was more to life in America than the obvious and tangible. These were the people who inadvertently became community activists, leaders of Islamic centers; they took on responsibilities and delivered more than they had promised. These were the few who had a vision in life, a selfless plan.

I have met most of them and have known some for more than a decade. In these pages, some will emerge as extraordinary minds, activists and community leaders, others as ordinary people whose character developed over the years. Consequently, some were invited to the White House to meet with President George Bush on September 11, 2001. But, as the tragic events of that day started to unfold, the meeting had to be postponed. It was in such later meetings that the president was advised to use the word *terrorist* in place of the phrase *Islamic terrorist* in describing the campaign against the September 11 perpetrators and Osama Bin Laden, and not to label this as "campaign infinite justice". Similarly, the word *crusade* was dropped because it carries painful historical memories that could only invoke passions and anger around the Muslim world. One of the most remarkable things that happened was that contact was made with the White House shortly after the incident. During this period of crisis, the White House remained interactively involved with the

Muslim community and respectfully sensitive to their needs.

This book will help you become familiar with American Muslim activists. Getting to know these community leaders, and acquiring a better understanding of the visions and aspirations they hold for the American Muslims, could provide readers with some of the answers as to what led to the tragic events on September 11, 2001.

I have lived more than 23 years in the United States, mostly in Massachusetts. I may have unknowingly *met* the Boston "Bin Ladens." While the intent and focus here is not on September's shocking actions, I have found that the fallout remains the same: anti-Muslim bigotry, a McCarthy mentality, hate crimes and attacks on civil liberties.

As the dust settles, these shadows reappear on the altered horizon. The events of the Hillary/Lazio Senate race and the attack on the World Trade Towers and the Pentagon can all be seen as a transforming moment for the self-imaging of Muslims.

It is my belief — and others will agree — that the expertise American Muslims possess can be very useful for the long-term security of the United States of America. This book will, I hope, conform to the taste of the American population. It is not fiction and it is not a novel. The style, however, is designed to make you think otherwise, to make it more interesting to read. Each person and every incident mentioned is true. These are real people. This story may be told in many ways, by people of varying ethnicities. It is the story of every population new to our country.

A lot of people mentioned in this book have in one way or another contributed to it.

Acknowledgments are due to Katherine Shaw of *the Worcester Telegram & Gazette*; Iqbal Hussain, a leading activist and academician from Toronto, Canada; and Ms. Uzma Ali, a student at Harvard and an employee at the Harvard School of Public Health in Cambridge. They have been instrumental in the development of this text. Their timely suggestions and valuable changes enhanced the material immensely.

I thank the news media, for allowing the "fair use" of their articles, specifically, *the Worcester Telegram & Gazette, MetroWest Daily* and *the Washington Report on Middle East Affairs*. These and other related articles in their entirety, a glossary of Islamic terms and acronyms used in the book have been included for reference only.

And, last of all but certainly not least, a special thanks to my wife Labiba Ali for putting up with me during the time it took to complete the book. She, in the wake of the tragic events of September 11, 2001, even suggested an alternate title for the book: "Allah Bless America."

CHAPTER 1   *Internal Debates and Uneasy Transformations*

[Status report about dilemmas of self-definition – how to understand one's self in a new context. Challenges for immigrant Muslims combined with the challenge of how the immigrant and indigenous Muslims can become a unified community].

"Takbir"
"Allah-O-Akbar"
"Takbir"
"Allah-O-Akbar"
Chanted the crowd at the Islamic center in Cambridge, Massachusetts, as the Imam of the Islamic center, Sheikh Basuni Mohammad Nahela, continued to deliver his remarks in Arabic.

"I agree with brother Tahir: it is obvious that if there were a Muslim candidate running for a political office, we would all be behind him. But we are not there yet, so the next best thing to do is to seek out and support those candidates or incumbents who have the Muslim interest at heart. Seek out those who have historically paid attention to Muslim concerns and have supported us."

"But *Ya-Akhi* (dear brother) isn't it *haram* (forbidden) in Islam to support non-Muslims?" shouted a disgruntled member of the audience.

As I struggled whether or not to dignify that comment with a response, to my utter relief, Walid Sallam—the moderator of the panel—sensed my discomfort came to my rescue. "... just wait for the *fatwa* (religious decree)..." is all that I could hear the man saying. Although I have my reservations regarding the authenticity of some of these *"fatwas,"* I was content with this particular peaceful outcome. People want to make sure that participation in politics was consistent with their ethical and moral beliefs – *fatwa* was one among many ways to gain that certitude. One sample of such a *fatwa* is included in the apendices.

The crowd remained cautious, some nodding with approval and others remaining skeptical. I could sense feelings of discontent and apprehension in some of my Muslim brothers as I tried to explain the importance of involvement and participation of American Muslims in mainstream United States politics.

"This year the estimated 7 million Muslims across the States can make a difference in the forthcoming U.S. elections, more specifically in the presidential election. If we decide to vote in large numbers for a specific agenda, we can create a bloc vote and get behind one candidate in this election; I don't see why we Muslims cannot get ourselves on the political map."

Sheikh Basuni Mohammad Nahela, a Ph.D. student at the renowned Al-Azhar University in Cairo, majoring in Islamic studies, originally came from Egypt. Of a slim build, he stood a couple of inches shy of six feet, his ruddy complexion mostly hidden behind the well-groomed black beard and penetrating eyes. The Sheikh was probably in his early forties, or at least he appeared to be. He had a way of communicating effectively with the anxious and curious crowd. You could see his eyes light up as he jumped in and tried to explain further in his native Arab language. I always felt uncomfortable that I did not speak or fully understand the language in which our holy book, the Qu'ran, was revealed to Prophet Mohammad (Peace be upon him [pbuh]). Maybe it was a mistake to make available translated copies of the Qu'ran. But, on the other hand, it is because of the translated English copies that many non-Arabic-speaking Muslims like myself have been conducting the Qu'ran study session in Islamic centers similar to the Bible study program held in churches.

There was a distinctly noticeable contrast between this Cambridge audience and me, their invited guest. Most, if not all of them, spoke and understood Arabic very well and most, unlike me, had long black beards. Lack of a beard or the knowledge of the Arabic language does not make one a lesser Muslim, although some would like you to believe so.

I knew the message had finally sunk in. Members of the audience started thanking me and shaking my hands, and began to ask related questions. I started to cast my eyes about the room to find Abdul Wahab Khoshafa. He knew what my look meant, and before any time was wasted, a table was set for "voter registration by mail" cards to be distributed and filled in right there.

"All of you who are U.S. citizens and have not yet registered to vote, please fill out the forms, and we will put the stamp on it and mail it for you," Abdul Wahab, originally from Yemen, shouted across the room.

That day, I was surprised to learn, more than a hundred men

and women registered to vote here for the first time. Most of them had been citizens of the United States for a period covering at least two U.S. presidents, but had completely ignored voting.

This year we all shall vote and exercise our full citizenship rights, I thought proudly as I was leaving the building.

Even today I can l feel the warmth, kindness and hospitality that was bestowed upon me by members of the Islamic Society in Cambridge. This meeting, the first of its kind, took place on the warm evening of August 25, 2000. Similar meetings took place at various other locations in Massachusetts and, soon thereafter, across most of the other states.

It came as no surprise that the media picked up on this activity. *The MetroWest Daily News*, for example, ran a story by Nicole Simons in its September 18th issue, just 25 days after the first meeting in Cambridge. The top headline in this front-page story said it all:

American Muslims form voting bloc.

> After carefully weighing the merits of both sides, American Muslims from MetroWest and across the nation plan to form a voting bloc to influence this year's presidential election.

David Caruso's article followed, in the October 30 issue:

Muslims hope to gain more political power.

> For decades they have been ignored by politicians, and in turn have defiantly avoided the ballot box on election day, feeling their votes are worth little in a nation that unfairly regards them with suspicion.

> But 7 million American Muslims are hoping they can finally make some sort of impact on their country's political culture this year, by banding together to vote for George W. Bush.

American Muslims' impact on the presidential race was made visible in another heading, **"Poll: Bush won support from first-time Muslim voters"** in a November 18th report by Michael Kunzelman of the same newspaper.

> A record number of Muslim first-time voters may have tipped the presidential election in George Bush's favor, ac-

cording to a poll released yesterday by the Massachusetts Chapter of the American Muslim Alliance.

"In the past," Ali added, "we would vote every which way and cancel each other out."

Raindrops Keep Falling on my Head

The scattered rain showers didn't seem to dampen the spirit of the thousands of people who stood in the rain while George Walker Bush was sworn in as the forty-third president of the United States of America on the 25th of January, 2001.

It was a proud moment for him, for the Bush family, for the Republican party—and for the American Muslim community. In November of 2000, Muslims all across the country voted in large numbers for George W. Bush.

President Bush appeared well rehearsed as he delivered his inaugural address. The president stood, confident and completely oblivious to the raindrops falling on his head, saying, "With a single oath, we affirm old traditions and make new beginnings…"

In his speech I found the theme "build and reach out." — "And this is my solemn pledge: I will work to build a single nation of justice and opportunity."

The catch phrase "America, at its best" was well placed, repeated through his entire address. "America, at its best, matches a commitment to principle with a concern for civility." Then "America, at its best, is also courageous." Or "America, at its best, is a place where personal responsibility is valued and expected." And my favorite, "America, at its best, is compassionate." It was in this context that the president went on to add the words that caught the attention of many Muslims: "Church and charity, synagogue and mosque lend our communities their humanity, and they will have an honored place in our plans and laws."

It came as no surprise to Muslims when the *Pittsburgh Post-Gazette,* the day after the inauguration, observed: "With just one word — *mosque* — Bush opened the door for an increased role for American Muslims, a growing community in both size and influence that solidly backed Bush in his quest for the White House."

Nor were we surprised by Ralph Z. Hallow's article, a day later in *The Washington Times*, when we read "Republican National Committee Chairman James S. Gilmore III, and other party and conservative leaders are expected to meet again with leaders of the American Muslim community, whose vote went overwhelmingly for George W. Bush in November."

These words reflected what the national chairman of the American Muslim Alliance (AMA), Dr. Agha Saeed, has been stressing all along, "In this year's election, not only have 7 million Muslims crossed the Rubicon, we have played a decisive role in the formation of a new national coalition of voters. It won't be long before political analysts realize that Muslim voters have played a historic role."

In my opinion, America, at its best, can be very accommodating.

The sun may not have been shining on George Walker Bush as he waved at the passing parade (as I like to say, even though it was raining on his parade that day), the president's words were illuminating.

And, as for the American Muslims, this was just the beginning. When it rains, it pours.

The news items reproduced below in their entirety depict a broader picture from journalists view point:

September 18, 2000
American Muslims form voting bloc
By Nicole Simons CNC STAFF WRITER
WAYLAND—Presidential hopefuls Al Gore and George W. Bush may need to rethink their campaign strategies.

After carefully weighing the merits of both sides, American Muslims from MetroWest and across the nation plan to form a voting bloc to influence this year's presidential election.

"It's a unity of purpose," said Tahir Ali, a member of the Islamic center in Wayland, the chairman of the Massachusetts of the American Muslim Alliance.

Of approximately 7 million American Muslims, only about 1 million voted in the last presidential election, Ali said. The AMA hopes to rally its members and boost that number to 4 million.

"We are going to vote as a bloc," he said.

Local centers and mosques have launched voter registration drives, encouraging their members to become involved, first in the national election, and eventually, in local politics.

About 700 members of the Islamic center registered to vote

this weekend, according to Ali. At least 3,000 Muslims registered to vote throughout eastern Massachusetts.

Although Ali doesn't know which politician the majority of the country's Muslims supports, he hopes to find out before Nov. 7.

"At this point it's very difficult to say that," he said.

The AMA will distribute a questionnaire to American Muslims through its Web site (www.amaweb.org), local chapters, and e-mail soliciting opinions on local, state and national candidates and issues.

The AMA will learn as much as it can about each candidate, including voting records and credentials. It will use that information to determine who is more sensitive to the needs of American Muslims.

"None of the candidates is going to be 100 percent for the Muslim interest," Ali said.

Some of the topics Ali said were important to the American Muslim community include foreign policy, particularly with such countries as Kosovo, Bosnia and Kashmir. The Middle East peace process is a concern as is the use of secret evidence.

Currently, the Immigration and Naturalization Service can arrest, detain or deport non-citizens on the basis of secret evidence without telling the person what that evidence is.

When the questionnaire responses are tallied, the AMA will release an election advisory, informing American Muslims of which candidate they should endorse.

"In order for us to maximize our influence," the AMA Web site says, "we must vote together to support the issues and candidates that help us achieve our goals."

That's not to say American Muslims can't exercise their right to vote and choose who they want. But for those who wouldn't have voted or who aren't sure who to support, the AMA's advisory will help, Ali said.

The advisory may also help educate politicians who have little knowledge of the American Muslim agenda.

"It is our task to educate and make sure the Muslim viewpoint is put into the politicians' hands," Ali said.

To get their voices heard — and as a sort of litmus test to see which candidate responds — Ali said the AMA may sponsor a walk to Washington, D.C., before the election, where the candidates will be invited to speak.

The reaction to the potential invitation may be enough to indicate the candidate's attitude toward American Muslims, Ali said.

Muslim groups such as AMA and AMC may eventually form a coalition with other groups such as Hispanics or African-Americans to form an even larger voting bloc, Ali added.

Voter registration, however, is at the top of the list for now. The clock is ticking closer to the Oct. 18 registration deadline, and Ali wants to see every eligible American Muslim voter at the polls in November.

October 30, 2000
Muslims hope to gain more political power
By David B. Caruso NEWS STAFF WRITER

For decades they have been ignored by politicians, and in turn have defiantly avoided the ballot box on election day, feeling their votes are worth little in a nation that unfairly regards them with suspicion.

But 7 million American Muslims are hoping they can finally make some sort of impact on their country's political culture this year, by banding together to vote for George W. Bush.

The American Muslim Alliance voted last week to endorse Bush for president after reviewing his policy positions and evaluating his performance in three debates with Democrat Al Gore.

Tahir Ali of Westborough, the alliance's Massachusetts representative, said the vote went to Bush partly because of his opposition to U.S. immigration policies which many Muslims believe are racist, and partly because of his pledge to make the United States an unbiased arbitrator in the Middle East peace process.

"Whereas Al Gore is 100 percent for Israel, we believe Mr. Bush when he says that any lasting peace is going to have to be a peace that is good for both sides." Ali said.

The choice is not without controversy.

A statement released by the alliance said the endorsement for Bush was at least partly based on the presence of U.S.

Senator Joseph Lieberman, a Jew, on the Democratic ticket.

In a nation that has, at least in theory, held religion at an arm's length from politics, Muslim opposition to Lieberman's run for vice president is likely to be criticized by some who say a candidate's religious beliefs should not be an issue.

But Ali said the senator's involvement with the campaign, and the campaign cash he has received from pro-Israeli groups, is a legitimate concern.

"I am uncomfortable with the level of Jewish donations to Gore and Lieberman," he said. "I worry that they cannot be as objective."

He also stressed that Gore and Lieberman's likely positions on Israel were only one factor in the endorsement decision.

Bush, he said, has a better record of meeting with Muslim groups. His position that the United States should forgive some Third World debt would benefit several Islamic nations.

Bush has also made a point of voicing his opposition to an anti-terrorism act that allows federal agents to detain immigrants indefinitely on the basis of "secret evidence" they are not obligated to present in court.

In the second presidential debate, Bush called that practice a form of racial profiling and said he believed it unfairly targeted Muslims.

The goal of the American Muslim Alliance this year is to boost turnout at the polls, and turn the nation's Muslim population into a more powerful voting bloc.

It could be a tall order. Muslims have traditionally not voted as a bloc in the United States. Demographically, they tend to split their vote much like the rest of the country, with slightly more than half voting Democratic and slightly less than half voting Republican.

They also often lack unifying issues to rally around, partly because they are a group split along hundreds of ethnic lines that includes Arabs, Africans, Slavs, Turks, Pakistanis and black Americans.

Some conservative Muslims also believe their religion prohibits them from voting in a country that is not governed by Islamic law.

Ali said a year's worth of organizing, though, should overcome many of those obstacles and turn the group into a potent and unified voting force.

"I think what we are doing is, hopefully, getting the word out that the candidates should be listening to us too," he said. "We want to make this country a better country."

November 18, 2000
Poll: Bush won support from first-time Muslim voters
By Michael Kunzelman NEWS STAFF WRITER

WAYLAND—A record number of Muslim first-time voters may have tipped the presidential election in George Bush's favor, according to a poll released yesterday by the Massachusetts of the American Muslim Alliance.

About 91 percent of Muslims in Florida cast ballots for Bush as part of an alliance-endorsed voting bloc, said chapter chairman Tahir Ali, of Westborough.

"The Muslims in America did have an impact in the presidential election this year," Ali said during an interview at the Islamic center of Wayland. "If we had voted like we did in previous elections, guess who would be president right now? Al Gore."

This was the first time the alliance, in conjunction with the American Muslim Political Coordinating Council, has encouraged its members to vote for the same presidential candidate.

"In the past," Ali added, "we would vote every which way and cancel each other out."

Ali said the alliance endorsed Bush, in part, because it believes he will remain an unbiased arbitrator in the Middle East peace process. The alliance also says Bush has been more willing to meet with Muslims and hear their concerns.

"He has definitely made an effort to communicate with Muslims," agreed alliance member Ruheena Razvi, 25, of Weston. "Al Gore just dismissed us from the beginning."

Ali downplayed the notion that Gore's selection of a Jewish running mate, U.S. Senator Joseph Lieberman, may have played a part in its endorsement of Bush.

"I'm sure it played a role for some American Muslims, but we're very open-minded," he said. "I don't think it mattered in this case."

In a national, post-election telephone poll of Muslim voters, the alliance found that more than 80 percent of them voted for Bush, compared to 10 percent for Ralph Nader and 9 percent for Gore. An even larger percentage of Florida's 60,000 eligible Muslim voters supported Bush, according to the survey.

Even though Gore notched an easy victory in Massachusetts, he didn't get much help from the estimated 10,000 Muslims who live in the commonwealth. A statewide poll of 700 Muslim voters found that 76 percent voted for Bush, according to Ali.

The alliance's survey also found that 40 percent of Muslims who voted in the presidential election were doing so for the first time. Ali said a record number of Muslims voted last week, a trend he attributed to a nationwide voting drive.

"We wanted to send a message: We are here, we're here to stay, and we have a voice," said Dr. A. Karim Khudairi, an alliance member and Northeastern University biology professor.

Muslims tended to vote according to issues and not along party lines, Ali said. The alliance may have endorsed a Republican presidential candidate, but it also supported Democrats like Hillary Clinton in New York, David Bonior in Michigan and Maxine Waters in Michigan.

"If there's a candidate who will serve the interests of the Muslim community, then that's the candidate we'll be voting for in the future," Khudairi said.
Dr. Zafar Cheema, a Sudbury resident and alliance member, said the survey shows that the country's 7 million Muslims are a demographic that politicians can't afford to ignore.

"It's an evolutionary process," Cheema added. "We're going through the first stages of that process.

CHAPTER 2   *the man from the West*

[*Contemplating new strategies and institutions. The Internal debates were beginning to congeal into specific strategies and blueprints for new institutions*].

So the real question becomes: how did American Muslims become politically savvy "overnight"? Actually, it took them roughly ten years to realize the power of the vote. It all started in 1991. Dr. Agha Saeed, then a visiting professor at Harvard University, believed that his time in Massachusetts would be well spent inculcating in local Muslims the importance of their involvement in the U.S. political system.

Dr. Saeed was born in Quetta, Pakistan, in 1948, one year after that country became independent. He lives in California with his wife Ameena and 16-year old daughter Mariam. At nearly six feet in height and weighing close to 200 pounds, Dr. Saeed always gave the impression of self-confidence and authority. He was very articulate and perfectly aware of his thought processes. The doctor chose his words carefully and delivered them effectively. These attributes enabled him to completely mesmerize his listeners, make his point and galvanize people into action.

Agha Saeed started by explaining to a handful of Muslims in the community the importance of their participation in mainstream U.S. politics. It took a series of such meetings before the community resolved to have a combined political entity. This gave birth to the first political Muslim organization—the American Muslim Political Alliance of Massachusetts (AMPAM). In the first election, Mohammad Khusro of Andover was chosen to serve as president. His tenure would be followed by that of Farooq Ansari of Westborough.

AMPAM was busy sponsoring breakfast and dinner meetings with elected officials such as state senators Matthew Amorello and Arthur Chase, and Congressman Peter Blute. AMPAM was building momentum. But with this came growing pains. We were not careful enough in observing proper protocol within our own community so, unable to find ways to cope with this new experience, the politically enlightened Muslim organization in Massachusetts soon broke apart. In the midst of all this activity my son Yaser was diagnosed with leukemia – a bitter experience that caused my family and I to drift away from political activities.

Yaser was admitted to Richland Memorial Hospital in Columbia, South Carolina for treatment. Our family found the Muslim community in South Carolina to be very helpful in our tragic situation.
A newcomer and a complete stranger to Columbia, I decided to pay
a visit to its only Islamic center, near the hospital. There I found
myself joining in a discussion with the members of the Islamic community. It was lead by Dr. Mirza Baig then a chief engineer at Co-
lumbia-based Duratek, Inc., a company that developed technology
and systems to manage and treat radioactive and other hazardous
waste.

Although they were not sure who I was, the group greeted me
cordially when they found out why I was in Columbia. They had
already heard that a family from Massachusetts had arrived for their
son's cancer treatment.

In an attempt to organize the community politically, a meeting
was arranged where Baig introduced me to the eager members of
the community: Irfan and Shahnaz Alvi, Aziz-uddin, the late Anwar
Shaikh and other physicians. Lest they too drift apart, I set the tone
of the meeting to focus on the high mortality rate such endeavors
face. The meeting had to take place in Richland Hospital's bone
marrow unit, and the first task for the community was to take a
delegation to meet with the governor. The meeting was successful
and a liaison committee led by Baig was created. The Columbia community was on its way politically.

A few months later, after burying Yaser in Columbia on February 25, 1994 in the holy month of *Ramadan* (a month that Muslims
all over the world observe by fasting from sunrise to sunset, abstaining from any food or water, and sensuous pleasure), we returned to
Massachusetts.

Meanwhile, in Massachusetts AMPAM had gone dormant. There
were far too many painful memories associated with AMPAM now.
To revive the political organization would only bring back the bitter
memories. But the political entity had to be maintained somehow.
On my request, a few activists in the community got together and
realized the necessity of forming an umbrella organization with leaders of various religious and cultural organizations in Massachusetts,
and getting them on one platform. The purpose was to bring coher-
ence and harmony among organizations. The Muslim Coalition of
Massachusetts (MCM) was thus created. Dr. Mian Ashraf, an activ-

ist acknowledged by the community for his service, and Ziad Sandakli, then president of the Islamic Society of Greater Worcester proposed my name as the MCM's first chairman, since I had conceived it.

Meanwhile, Attorney John Mattson of Westborough was challenging democratic state Senator Bob Duran for his seat. Governor William Weld had come to town to help fellow republican John Mattson in his bid for the state senate seat. Members of the MCM did their part and made their presence known by joining in the campaign for Mattson. The Muslim coalition arranged for a debate between the challenger and the incumbent senator. This was broadcast on *WCATV* in the Westborough district. I used my local access television certificate to facilitate the debate, and ended up as its producer/director. The *Worcester Telegram and Gazette* carried the debate story next day, giving credit to MCM for sponsoring the first-ever televised debate between Duran and Mattson.

Since the Muslim community in South Carolina already had a taste of political success from their advantageous meeting with the governor's official in Columbia, all it took was a call to the community and the Muslim Coalition of South Carolina was born. At this rate it would not have been too long before the Muslim coalition idea would catch on in neighboring states, paving the way to a national coalition: The Muslim Coalition of the United States of America (MCUSA).

AMPAM admittedly was dormant, however Agha Saeed was still busy building the political infrastructure on the West Coast, the Muslim political machine that he created and nurtured so carefully.

By this time, the movement's headquarters was established in Freemont, California, under the banner of the American Muslim Alliance. None other than Dr. Saeed himself headed the national organization. Under his leadership and guidance, the AMA managed to form political organizations similar to AMPAM in other states.

Dr. Saeed now had the added task of bringing these groups together under the national organization. In a letter that was received by some of us in Massachusetts, Dr. Agha Saeed wrote, "The state of Massachusetts is special to the AMA in a unique sense, it is the birthplace. The journey of the thousands steps began here. Once I had introduced the basic idea of a national Muslim organization dedicated to political self-empowerment, the first steps were taken together by Dr. Mohammed Saeed, Dr. Abrar Syed, Dr. Siddiq Abdullah, Mr. Tahir Ali, Mr. Farooq Ansari, Dr. Mansoor Khan, Dr. Omar Khalidi, Dr. Tanveer Hussain, Dr. Punjawani, Mr. Mahboob Sultan, Mr. Mohammed Khusro, Dr. Riaz Khan, sister Shereda Hosein, Dr. Waseem Khan, Dr. Aleem Khan, Dr. Riaz Ahmed, Mr. Khalid Arif and sister Pamela Taylor, to name a few only. We all came together and AMPAM was formed as the foundation stone of a national organization. Our collective dream — called the AMA — that began in the single state of Massachusetts now finds itself a reality by having emerged as a truly national organization, in Arizona, California, Colorado, Florida, Illinois, Michigan, Missouri, New Jersey, New York, Ohio, Oregon, Pennsylvania, Texas, Washington and Wisconsin. Our organizational network in Connecticut, New Hampshire and Vermont, although dormant for a while, is also currently being revived."

One of the effective ways of getting a message across is by making sure that the message goes out to each one of its intended recipients. Dr. Agha Saeed sent a copy of this letter to me and reportedly to others on the list. This was his way to ensure that the message got through–and that each one of the recipients realized the importance of that message so they were all "on the same page."

The doctor concluded by saying, "Now we are asking AMPAM to formally join the national organization, in essence to join itself. After all, AMA is AMPAM made national."

Muslims in Massachusetts realized that this blend of autonomy and coordination would enable them to become a recognized political force in 1996 and years to follow. They found this invitation and the program for unity and success desirable. Consequently, the AMPAM was dissolved and became a chapter of the AMA. The MCM was also completely dissolved – there was no need to duplicate efforts. The Massachusetts Chapter of the AMA was headed by Dr. Mohammad Saeed of Lynnfield, who was followed by Dr. Kimet Gul Khattak of Hadley. I became its fifth chairman during the 2000-01 term.

Fortunately, Dr. Agha Saeed was still in town, teaching at Harvard University where he could see the beginnings of the success of his work.

On a fine Saturday morning in 1991, about 46 registered Muslim Republicans arrived at Worcester's Sheraton-Lincoln Inn (now the Holiday Inn). This was the caucus where delegates for the 1992 Republican Convention from the Third Congressional District were to be elected. It was here that Massachusetts Muslims first showed their united political resolve. Their votes counted, and Mr. Farooq Ansari of Westborough was elected, along with Mrs. Barbara Khan, as Delegate and Alternate, respectively. It was amusing when Mrs. Robbi Blute, wife of Former Congressman Peter Blute who was presiding over the caucus, said, "I was surprised to see all these names ending with a vowel; I said to myself, 'there are a lot of Italians here today.' " Looking at the voter list—Farooq Ansari, Yasmeen Ansari, Tahir Ali, Labiba Ali, Hannah Bahnassi, Amjad Bahnassi—it's easy to understand Mrs. Blute's comic remarks. What came as a pleasant surprise was the fact that Mrs. Blute, a resident of Shrewsbury, and others were also rejoicing in our victory. "This is the first time someone from outside Worcester won," a caucus attendee revealed to Mrs. Khan and Mr. Ansari. To our utter amazement, the xenophobic hysteria was not to be found here.

Mrs. Barbara Khan, born in America, had embraced Islam in the early stages of her life. Her husband Kamal Khan, a physicist by profession, was a Muslim originally from Pakistan. Mr. Khan was born in a region in the north of the country, neighboring Afghanistan. Both husband and wife found it hard that day to wipe the smiles from their faces. The area's American Muslims had every right to be proud of and to celebrate this victory."There is no success like success," reported an excited and cheerful Dr. M. Riaz Khan, as we all gathered at Mr. Ansari's house, to capture and celebrate this moment of success.

Dr. Khan, a professor of business administration at the UMass Lowell, was never hesitant in offering words of encouragement and sound advice on matters that were important and dear to the Muslim community. He said, "We need to be cautious, because the committee has in the past, according to Agha Saeed, disqualified delegates—for whatever criteria they have for disqualifying a delegate."

Dr. Mohammad Mushtaque, an anesthetist at Memorial Hospital in Worcester added, "Let's not break open the bottle of champagne yet," he added, jokingly in the humorous style that our community members have always enjoyed.

But this was just the beginning. Agha Saeed was not done yet; his job had just begun and he was very much aware of that. While we were all in a festive mood and completely caught up in this victory, Agha Saeed was already many steps ahead of us in his thought process.

"Mind you, not all the delegates are elected at the caucus," he said. Everyone was silent, as we waited for the punch line. After realizing that Agha Saeed *had* no punch line, Mr. Rasheed Khan — brother-in-law of Farooq Ansari and a respected member of the Muslim community — was brave enough to break the silence and ask the obvious: "So what does that mean?"

"Let that be a topic of discussion for some other time. However, in the interim, let's keep that thought in mind," Dr. Saeed said, sounding rather tired as he glanced at his wristwatch.

It was Barbara Khan who found out that delegates-at-large, also known as "super delegates," were scheduled to be elected few weeks later, on May 21, 1992. The caucus were to be held at the Sheraton Tara hotel in Framingham in Massachusetts.

After spending some more time in Boston, Dr. Agha Saeed returned to his home in California, but not without leaving a road map for the area's jubilant Muslims to follow. It was Barbara Khan and Kamal Khan who researched what super delegates were all about. "It is payback time. This is where the state committee elects either those who have been heavy contributors or elected officials like state senators, state representatives, mayors," reported Barbara Khan.

That particular year, State Republican Committee members had the option to choose a slate of pre-selected candidates for the positions of delegates and alternates. The state committee chairman presented the candidates' names to the voters with his recommendation to vote for the entire slate. However, as always, write-ins and any nominations from the floor were accepted.

That year the slate included well-known political personalities like Governor William F. Weld, Lieutenant Governor Paul Argeo Cellucci and State Treasurer Joseph Malone. The write-in list was also revealed. These were candidates who had requested to be considered for one of the delegate- or alternate-at-large positions. A handout was passed out to each committee member that read:

PERSONS REQUESTING CONSIDERATION FOR
DELEGATE- OR ALTERNATE-AT-LARGE
Mayor Theodore D. Mann
Executive Councillor John P. Harris
Andrew Brennan
Mayor Kevin J. Sullivan

Neil L. Chayet
James W. Rappaport
Alexander Spaulding
Alexander Ellis, III
Edmund DelPrete
William C. Sawyer
Senator Matthew J. Amorello
Senator Arthur E. Chase
William Ryan
Alfred A. Fondacaro, Jr.
James M. Coyle
David Gallo
William F. Hoffmann, III
Tahir Ali
Mark Enoch
Cheryl Belknap
William Belknap
Arthur Larrivee
William F. Arrigal, Jr.

I admit it was exciting to see my name included among the ranks of senators and mayors—and a cause for worry. It appeared to be a difficult task to accomplish: here I was, a nobody, completely at the mercy of the state committee, running against the governor's slate, and then all of us competing for the same seat. Even the write-ins were very well known at that time. The ones I was aware of at the time included mayor of Newton, Theodore Mann—to compete against a mayor of a rich town like Newton, also predominantly Jewish, looked to me like certain disaster. Then, who did not know Senators Amorello and Chase? Not to mention Neil Chayet, whom I remembered from and enjoyed on his show "Neil Chayet Looking at the Law," aired—and still does—on a popular Boston radio station, WBZ. And then there was James Rappaport, who would become the chairman of the Republican State Committee, currently a contestant in the primaries for the Lieutenant Governor's spot.

The process was not particularly easy. First, a committee member must nominate you for the write-in, then the nomination must be seconded by another committee member. Once over that hurdle, a candidate is given an opportunity to make his/her pitch for the position in a 5-minute speech before the state committee. After that process, the voting starts. The majority may have liked you enough to vote for you by writing in your name and striking a name from the slate. But guess what? Unless they all struck off the same name, you still would not have enough votes. I had delivered a short speech while my wife Labiba handed my bio-data out to each of the committee members.

"For America to retain the mantle of leadership in the next decade, we must improve the education that our children are receiving," I told the potential voters. I was saying that because I honestly believed that the standards in mathematics and science were not on a par with those of Pakistan or India. I arrived at that conclusion after I spent time helping my children in these subjects. I myself had been very good at mathematics and science, and could contrast the countries' systems. I promised the committee members in the audience that I would work toward ensuring that the education plank was prominently featured in the Republican platform. I pointed out to them that the South Asian countries could play a major role in the coming 'new world order.' And I could make a difference in the Republican party, "because I bring a unique perspective and understanding of that part of the world to the party. I can relate to the thinking processes of the leaders and people of that part of the world."

Shahid Mahmood, a well-known cricketer in Pakistan, was an activist in New Jersey. He had been involved in the Republican party quite early. Shahid was a member of the host committee for a fund-raising dinner where the guest of honor was the president's daughter, Dorothy Bush. Mr. Mahmood was also a member of the organizing committee for the Bush/Quayle victory '88 parade that was hailed by Congressman Guy Molinari as one of the highlights of the campaign. The former cricketer had hosted fund-raising events for candidates and incumbents alike. It was Shahid who instructed me to generate a list of my own activities in the community and put that on a piece of paper, along with my credentials.

The first round of voting was over, and, for some reason, the counting was taking longer than usual. Farooq Ansari approached me and said, "You did well; it looks like you may have won." I must admit my feelings were mixed — more optimistic than pessimistic.

"Keep your fingers crossed. You know 'it's not over until the fat lady sings,' " I quickly responded. As Farooq retreated to the visitors' gallery, Labiba and I were approached by a neatly and quite elegantly dressed lady with a wrinkled but radiant face that seemed familiar. She commended me for delivering a fine speech, then introduced herself as Nancy Bush Ellis. She was the sister of the president of the United States! No wonder the face looked familiar; she had a striking resemblance to her brother. I vaguely recall her saying something about diversity being important for the Republican party.

Republican state committee member Stanley Tyliszczak, who lived in the same town as I and was then a member of the Westborough Historical Commission, joined us and told us, "President Bush has always had a special relationship with Westborough. After all, he is descended from one of the founding families, the Fays." Stanley paused for a moment, maybe to read the expression on our faces. The expression on my face, if any, was probably one that asked: "Fays who?"

Stanley, then a member of the Westborough Historical Commission, started to make more sense to me as he continued, "She [Nancy Bush] and her brother are in direct line from one of the town fathers, Captain Jonathan Fay." Captain Fay was born in Westborough in 1724, and is buried in the town's memorial cemetery.

We were still rejoicing and cherishing the moment when one of the officials announced, "This was a very close race, and for the first time in history, we thought that the slate had been broken." Someone in the crowd was saying that the slate was indeed broken and I had been elected. At any rate, a delegate was removed and I was named the alternate-at-large.

I was astonished: how did that happen? There were no Muslim voters here. My friends and fellow Muslims were anxious to know the secret.

It's no secret: this is the United States of America. Anything is possible here, if there is a genuine determination to reach your goal. This country welcomes you with open arms, but nothing is achieved without determination and hard work. Meanwhile, back in New Jersey, Shahid Mahmood got elected alternate-at-large as well.

Barbara Khan and her husband Kamal Khan were rightfully proud of this victory, because it was they who had done their homework. Mrs. Khan had a strategy that I adopted without hesitation. She provided me with the state committee member list. I had called each person on that list, asking them for their support and also their vote. State committee member Tom Mason had assured me that he would nominate me from the floor, and he had lived up to his word. Republican state committee member Stanley Tyliszczak later told me that once he and his member friends, [Robbi Blute, Ralph Lespasio, Debbie Messier and Ed Bertorelli] decided to vote for me, they worked on a winning strategy. They all reviewed the names on the list one by one until they found a person that they could all agree to strike off on their ballots, then all would enter my name as the write-in.

Later that week Stanley introduced Farooq and me to the members of the Westborough Republican Committee. Stanley asked us both to share with the committee members our experience in politics. This exercise apparently would help the committee to decide whether or not either or both of us could qualify for membership.

"When did you register to become a Republican? And why did you decide to become a Republican?" a committee member asked Farooq during his speech.

It was a good question. Farooq was struggling to find an appropriate response. He found the words and managed to give an acceptable reply, not easy to do when he had been thrown off guard.

As a matter of fact, one of the reasons we decided to pick the Republican party was because it appeared to be the smart thing to do at the time. All this was new territory to us, and, frankly, we were not that many in numbers to make much impact. Massachusetts, historically, remains a predominantly Democratic state and, therefore, it is relatively less competitive to become a Republican delegate than a Democratic one. I doubt if any of us even knew what either party's platform was or what it stood for. Agha Saeed was registered as a Democrat and not a Republican, at that.

I spoke next. As I finished, before anyone had a chance to ask questions, I turned to the gentleman who had asked Farooq the "why Republican?" question and told him that *I had voted for Ronald Reagan*. The committee members broke into laughter. Amidst that laughter I heard someone say, "You will do all right." Farooq and I were then inducted into the Westborough Republican Committee.

After that, there was no stopping either of us. Farooq Ansari and I headed for Houston to attend the 1992 Republican National Convention. Barbara Khan had decided to stay behind in Massachusetts for personal reasons. Governor Weld led our delegation.

For the Muslim community in Houston, this was a proud moment as well; they came from all across the town to meet with us. To some, the mere fact that they were in the company of the first American Muslims to attain this position was reason enough to celebrate, and celebrate they did. Dr. Agha Saeed, although a registered Democrat, was also in a celebrating mood, but with a purpose in mind. He knew it was as good a time as any to harness this energy and form a political entity. The rest of us had not yet realized that, by just one word, we would be able to convert our political success into a community asset.

Agha Saeed called me from California to inform me that he had booked a hospitality suite in the same hotel where the Massachusetts delegates were staying. At the time I had no idea what the reason was for a hospitality suite. I relayed Dr. Saeed's message to Mr. Ansari, and his question—for which I had no answer—was "what exactly do you mean by a hospitality suite?"

Our hospitality suite was set up in a room overlooking the front lobby in the hotel where most of the members of the Massachusetts delegation were staying. The Muslim community of Houston had really done a fine makeover of the suite; it was like a window opening into the Arabian world. The bird's-eye view of the Holy Site *Kaaba* in the sacred city of Mecca was just one of the huge posters on the walls to fascinate visitors. It caught the eyes of every soul entering the suite, the huge black square surrounded by limitless devotees, all wearing white.

Books on Muslim culture were neatly placed on the tables, along with artifacts that depicted the Eastern culture and the Islamic way of life. Middle Eastern cuisine was set on one of the tables. All of this left an exotic taste in the mouths *and* food for thought in the minds of the visitors. Among the distinguished visitors were Bosnian U.N. Ambassador Sacirbey, Lieutenant Governor Paul Argeo Cellucci, State Treasurer Joseph Malone and Governor William Weld. It was an honor to introduce Governor Weld to the Muslim community.

"Tahir, you know my wife Susan can relate to this; she speaks some Arabic," the governor said as he reviewed the Islamic books on display. The following day Mrs. Weld stopped by the hospitality suite and, sure enough, she spoke the Arabic language. "The first lady will recite from memory the first chapter of the Holy Book, the Qu'ran," I told the community as the governor's wife protested silently. The first chapter *"Surah Fatiha"* comprise a few verses, and she delivered those in Arabic as we all listened in awe. Someone shouted *"Takbir,"* and the community responded with the appropriate chant *"Allah-O-Akbar."*

By the end of the day, the hospitality suite had seen a large number of guests, ranging from delegates to congressmen and the governor. This was the last day of the convention, and, as the sun was setting in Houston, Agha Saeed rose to address the Muslim community present. "Did you all feel how much energy there was in this room today? Don't you think we should do something about it—or should we just let this energy fade away?"

Soon thereafter, Agha Saeed, Farooq Ansari and I were successful in harnessing the talent in the community to form a chapter of AMPAM in Houston. Surprisingly enough, most of our time was spent outside the convention center, either speaking at rallies held in support of Bosnia or entertaining guests at the hospitality suite. It was very clear in my mind that attending the convention was secondary, after all. The priority had shifted toward the empowerment and mobilization of the Muslim community, and bringing its members into mainstream U.S. politics. As I retired to bed late that night, completely exhausted, reflecting on what we had accomplished in such a short time helped me relax. But then, this was not simply an event to rest on, but also one to build upon.

CHAPTER 3   *The Governor and I*

[Strategy in application and confirmation by consequences – new activist, turn personal contact into community assets, community begins to buy in as they see positive results].

William Weld was elected governor of Massachusetts in 1990 with 51 percent of the vote. As governor, Weld had restored fiscal stability to Massachusetts government.

Born on July 31, 1945, in Smithtown, New York, Weld graduated summa cum laude from Harvard College in 1966. The following year, from Oxford University; then in 1970, William Weld graduated cum laude from Harvard Law School.

In 1990, hardly any American Muslims in Massachusetts were paying much attention to the gubernatorial race, but this was to change in the years to come. The impact on the Muslim community that began with Governor Weld's visit to the 1992 Houston hospitality suite was a beneficial one. Abdurahman Alamoudi, the secretary of the American Muslim Council (AMC), was very much impressed by Weld, and called me to see if I could arrange a Muslim delegation to meet with the governor. I did, the governor agreed, and so we met a few months later.

At that meeting, Weld said, "Tahir, why don't you sit next to me?" I was happy and proud to oblige, and sat at the head of the table to his right. I first introduced Abdurahman Allamoudi to Weld. He spoke at length to the governor, explaining the charter and mission of the American Muslim Council. Mohammad Khusro talked about AMPAM, its goals and its efforts at the grass roots level for Muslim empowerment. Dr. Kimet Gul Khattak expressed his disappointment with the media and its negative stereotyping of Muslims. Dr. Yaser Najjar, then president of the Islamic Society of Greater Worcester and a professor of geography at Framingham State College, stressed the need for the commonwealth to recognize two major Muslim *Eid*, or holidays.

Four of the executive members of the Pakistan Association of Greater Boston were also present, including the association's president, Dr. Siddiq Abdullah, a professor at Pine Manor College, and its vice president, Saghir Tahir, who was elected to the New Hampshire State Assembly in 2000. Hameed, the nephew of one of the champions of the U.S. civil rights movement, Al-Haaj Malik Shabaaz, formerly known as Malcolm X, appeared to be as articulate as his uncle. We all praised and thanked the governor for taking time out of his busy schedule to meet with us and to lend an ear to Muslim concerns.

"I believe today we may have even made history," Barbara Khan reflected as a dozen of us came out of the governor's chamber after what we all felt was a phenomenal and very productive meeting.

That day's meeting resulted in the creation of a Muslim liaison committee, to follow up on the Muslim community's concerns and issues that had been pointed out to the governor. After this, some members of the community worked with their local school committees and libraries, to correct any misconceptions about Islam in textbooks. Muslims were now encouraged to seek state jobs, while others were appointed to state-recognized commissions.

Muslim students were no longer marked tardy for showing up late — or not showing up at all — on their religious holidays. The meeting with the governor gave the Muslim community the boost it needed to actively participate in — and reap rewards from — the political process. In the months to follow various meetings were arranged with elected officials at the local and state levels. The Muslim community had learned how to get their foot in the door.

Weld was re-elected to a second term as governor in 1994, but this time with 71 percent of the votes cast. The Muslim community in Massachusetts voted overwhelmingly for Weld. However, since it was not a close race, the Muslim vote may not have made much of a difference. But Muslims were voting, and that itself was difference enough.

Meanwhile, Muslims all across the States were outraged, disgusted and appalled with world's ambivalence towards the pathetic situation in Bosnia. History recalls that the rampant killing of innocent men, women and children in mind-boggling numbers has been given various names: the U.S. Civil War tore a country apart, and as Margaret Mitchell aptly put it, the South became a civilization "Gone with the Wind." World War II saw "ethnic cleansing" of the worst kind, even today remembered as the "Holocaust."

The few survivors of Holocaust horrors were to witness more atrocities being carried out mercilessly, even in this modern age. Ethnic annihilation was once more systematically carried out, this time with Bosnian Muslims as the target. Bosnian Muslim women, including girls who had yet to reach puberty were being raped daily in the camps, by members of the Serbian army. The media used the correct phrase, *rape camps,* to describe what was happening in Bosnia.

The world was apparently angry at what was going on, yet nothing was being done about it. Those nations that had said "no more," in reference to the Holocaust, were silent. As the Jews and gypsies had suffered, so now did the Muslims. Perhaps the world's people thought: "Islam was and still is the fastest growing religion; the world can do with a few Muslims wiped out."

Back in Houston, when I asked the Bosnian U.N. Ambassador Nadreb Sacirbey what message he wanted me to relay to the president, he replied emphatically, "Tell him we do not want American soldiers to fight for us; we can fight our own war. Give us weapons so that we can fight and defend ourselves." The world was watching, but no one did much to lift the arms embargo against Bosnia.

The American Muslims decided that it was up to them to prick the conscience of the world. The news about the first Muslim victory in Massachusetts, followed by Muslim participation in the National Republican Convention in Houston, had already planted the seeds of hope and initiative in the minds of the American Muslims across the States. The time had come to put the Muslim unity to the test, once again, this time for a humanitarian cause.

The Bosnia Task Force had been formed in Chicago for the same purpose. The task force team, with the help of American Muslim Council in addition to various Islamic centers across the States, decided to rally on May 15, 1993. The rally was to be held in front of the White House, with the hope that United States will use its influence in NATO to help lift the arms embargo against Bosnia.

Boxing legend Muhammad Ali, formerly Cassius Clay, and Yusuf Islam, better known as the popular '70s singer-songwriter Cat Stevens, were among the list of invitees.

Governor Weld was unable to attend, but he had asked me if I could go in his stead and represent him at the rally. It was an honor to represent the governor of Massachusetts, so I did, bearing the following letter addressed to Mr. Abdul Malik Mujahid, the chairman of the Bosnia Task Force, U.S.A. One of the organizers of the rally read the governor's message aloud on the stage for the crowd of thousands, mostly Muslims, gathered at Lafayette Park. Former Governor Weld wrote:

I very much regret that I am not able to join you this weekend for the Bosnia Rally that you are organizing in Washington, D.C., in conjunction with other Islamic centers across the United States.

I have asked my friend Mr. Tahir Ali, a national delegate and the New England representative of the American Muslim Council, to represent me at the rally. He is carrying a brief message from me reflecting my thoughts on the tragic situation in Bosnia.

Recent events in Bosnia are a tragedy of the first magnitude. The world watches in disbelief at the atrocities that are occurring there. I know I represent the sentiments of all Massachusetts citizens in deploring the treatment of Bosnian Muslims. Many of you attending this weekend's rally no doubt have friends or relatives caught in the middle of this tragic conflict. We share your outrage at the atrocities and ethnic violence occurring in the former Yugoslav republics, particularly Bosnia, and our hearts go out to the victims of this genocidal violence as they confront the daily struggles for survival.

Similar messages from other elected officials were read that day, and each served as a morale booster for the attending Muslims. Gestures like these went a long way in the minds of the Muslim listeners. At least they knew they were not alone in the fight against that inhumanity.

Thousands started to pour into Washington, D.C., that day. Before noon, close to 50,000 Muslims from all across the United States had gathered in the Mall, in front of the White House on that warm Saturday. Chants of "U.S.A., U.S.A., have a heart; U.S.A., U.S.A., do your part" and "Lift the arms embargo; end the genocide" rose across the Mall. The crowd hoped that day to accomplish two things: first, they wanted President Clinton to lift the arms embargo, and second, they hoped that he would take appropriate action and order air strikes against Serbian military positions.

Yusuf Islam, Nadreb Sacirbey, Virginian Congressman Jim Moran and other leaders outlined strategic and moral reasons why the United States must act immediately. The speakers warned that if the United States failed to check Serbian aggression, repression would spread its chilling shadow across the region, possibly triggering World War III. The third World War may not have started, but the world did see Slobodan Milosevic and his war machine range into Kosova, to finish what he had started.

I met Yusuf Islam for the first time in 1991. It had been a long time since the U.S. media had covered him, as I learned later from Sarah Edwards of NBC. "Mr. Ali," she said, "I would like to set an interview with Yusuf Islam. There are many that wonder what happened to Cat Stevens. Now that he has surfaced after such a long absence, it will make a lot of people happy to hear from him again."

She apparently was disappointed when I told her that he was on his way to England. But I offered her the videotape of the interview that I had produced in the WCAT TV studio in Westborough, which had also aired on Worcester's. Channel 3. I told her she was welcome to use that footage and sent it to her.

"Next time when he comes, please call me." Sarah requested.

Yusuf Islam stayed at my neighbor's house, across the street from my Westborough home. He was here to address the members of the Islamic Society of Greater Worcester, to talk about the Islamic school "Islamia" that he had established in England.

"I want the Muslims here to take a covenant in establishing an Islamic school here, as well." Yusuf Islam's tone was firm.

Sound advice soon became a reality. The members of the Islamic Society of Greater Worcester took his words to heart. A few years later the first full-time Islamic school, Al-Hamra Academy, was established, largely due to the efforts of Dr. Mohamed Lazounni, originally from Algiers, and Sadia Khan, who came to the States from Pakistan.

Unfortunately, Islam is one of the most misunderstood religions in the West. It has been wrongly associated with violence, either out of ignorance or by design of those who might profit from its negative image. There are those who would want you to believe that it may even pose a threat to Western society. Then someone like Yusuf Islam comes along. He reveals to the World how Islam has changed his life, from drugs and confusion to piety and righteousness. The Qu'ran says "...Allah guides those whom he wishes." Another misconception many people in the West have centers around the role of the women in Islam. To the Western eye, Islam defines women in derogatory terms. They see *Hijab* (the head covering for Muslim women) as sign of oppression imposed on women by men. Iqbal Hussain, an activist in Toronto, noted that even his teenage son, Aleem had an explanation, "women in Islam wear the *Hijab* for the same reason a Sikh wears a turban, because it's part of his faith."

The Qu'ran again is very clear on the "equal" status of women in Islam. I thoroughly enjoyed reading Michael Paulson's article "The draw of Islam" in the May 13, 2001 issue of the *Boston Globe*:

> Sara Graziano's father was a lapsed Catholic, her mother an active Pentecostal, and she was confused. So at 14, torn between her father's atheism and her mother's fundamentalism, she dragged herself to the library and started reading about Buddhism, Hinduism, Judaism and Islam. She found herself drawn to Islam, which she believed rang truer than her mother's Christianity. On March 8, the Wellesley College junior recited one sentence: "I bear witness that there is no God but Allah, and I bear witness that Muhammad is his messenger." [This is *shahada* to accept Islam]

Islam is a religion of peace. It is a universal religion. However, the occasional rampant acts of some of its followers — due, perhaps, to their own emotional overload — can give Islam a bad name, as would happen with any religion whose individual members may occasionally take an action not preached, condoned or supported with that religion's tenets. Bombs are blasted in civilian areas killing women and children in the name of Islam. No thank you! This is not Islam, but a repugnant display of criminal behavior. Reportedly, some of these crimes may have been carried out in the name of Islam by non-Muslims to raise bad feelings about Muslims; that has yet to be proven. In some attacks, though, before the blood of the victims has even dried, Hamas — or some such organization — claims responsibility, and the suicide mission is justified as an act of retaliation. Heard that before, and it won't be the last time, either. The bloody saga continues.

Regardless of what happened in the Muslim world, particularly in places like the Middle East, our Muslim-American struggle for recognition as a political force continued. The name *AMA* soon became synonymous with "Muslim political machine." Governor Weld and his administration were cognizant of this fact, as is indicated to the following letter sent to my attention on January 19, 1996:

> On behalf of the Weld-Cellucci Administration, I commend you for your extraordinary contribution of time and energy to the Massachusetts Republican party. Since meeting you as

a National Delegate-at-Large at the Republican National Convention in 1992, I have been delighted to work with you to advance the goals of our administration and the GOP.

Your success in creating a liaison committee composed of various Muslim leaders in Massachusetts has been vital to strengthening the bond between our administration and the Muslim community. As an accomplished television producer, you have heightened political participation across the Commonwealth by producing programs of interest to American Muslims in particular, as well as to the general viewing audience.

I am pleased to note that the increased political involvement among American Muslims that you have helped inspire in Massachusetts has evolved into the American Muslim Alliance (AMA), a national organization working toward the empowerment and mobilization of this vibrant community. Indeed, the AMA would do well to cultivate such outstanding role models as yourself in its development as a decisive political force.

Lieutenant Governor Cellucci and I look forward to continuing to work closely with you in the coming months and years.

Sincerely,

William F. Weld

"Tahir, were your ears burning?" Yvonne Boyle said in an excited tone, picking up on my call to the governor's office one day. I was not quite sure why Yvonne said that, but explained why I was calling. I simply wanted to see if the governor would be willing to give us a proclamation for an event that we Muslims were planning to hold.

"Bill Weld and we all were just talking about you," Yvonne continued. As the director of scheduling for the governor, Yvonne Boyle had always been very helpful in getting me through to the governor, whenever I needed to speak with him. She was also instrumental in facilitating the meeting with Governor Weld and the Muslim community. In my letter of thanks to the governor, I had specifically mentioned and acknowledged her efforts.

On that day, Yvonne wanted to tell me that Governor Weld had decided to run for U.S. Senate. He was counting on support from the Muslim community, among others. A few weeks later, William Weld announced his resignation as governor, and became Citizen Weld in order to begin his campaign for the Senate.

Muslims loyalties were divided between Senator John Kerry and Former Governor William Weld in this race for the Senate seat. I was unable to harness full Muslim support. Despite my protests and to my utter disappointment, certain members of the Muslim community conducted a fund-raiser for the incumbent senator. The architect behind this fund-raiser was reportedly a businessman from New York, who was successful in persuading that year's chairman of the AMA and others to put their support behind Kerry. Rumor had it that he was a close friend of the Clintons.

The Muslim vote in the Senate race was thus divided, and in such a close race, each vote counted. Although the community later discovered that they had been manipulated by the apparently selfish motives of one of their own brethren, the damage was already done. Although I never met the man in question until much later, I found that some things I had heard about him may not have necessarily been true. I still feel remorse, because we really did let a friend down in not lending our support to a man who had recognized our organization and encouraged our work. After that setback, Weld was headed for another political disaster, when President Clinton nominated him for the position of Ambassador to Mexico. Unfortunately, that appointment never materialized. Senator Jesse Helms, the chairman of the Foreign Relations Committee, made his objections loud and clear. The gentleman from North Carolina, vehemently opposed the appointment and never put Weld's nomination on the committee's agenda. Soon thereafter, Weld was to disappear from the public eye.

As fate would have it, on June 6, 2001, Jesse Helms was no longer to chair the Foreign Relations Committee. He had gained a reputation for blocking any of President Clinton's ambassadorial nominees who did not meet his personal approval; Weld was just one of many. Joseph Biden of Delaware replaced Jesse Helms and the insider's perception was that he would not give President George Bush such a hard time as Helms had pugnaciously given to Clinton.

This turn of events was the result of the defection of Senator James Jeffords of Vermont from the Republican party. With that, on June 6,

2001, Democrats won control of the Senate. After the Jeffords announcement, that he was going to leave the GOP and become an independent, the Republicans had lost their Senate majority.

From there, the domino effect was evident: Senator Trent Lott of Mississippi had to relinquish the Senate majority leadership to Thomas Daschle of South Dakota. Edward Kennedy of Massachusetts took over from Jeffords the Health, Education, Labor and Pension Committee leadership. One defection caused 18 Republicans to relinquish their chairmanships to the Democrats. The Senate scales now became precariously balanced, with fifty Democratic senators, forty-nine Republican senators, and one independent.

"Here is your chance," I reminded William Weld. Maybe if he sought another ambassadorial nomination, he would have better luck this time. Weld's successor Paul Cellucci was no stranger to the Muslim organization, either. The lieutenant governor had actually visited our hospitality suite in Houston a day before his boss had. I distinctly remember him praising our efforts during an interview conducted in front of an Arab TV channel at the suite.

The good thing for the Muslim community in Massachusetts was that they did not have to start all over to cultivate a relationship with the new Massachusetts governor. Yvonne Boyle was still in office, so the connection and the liaison remained intact. The Massachusetts Muslim community continued to have meetings with Governor Cellucci and his cabinet members, to discuss matters of importance to the Muslim community.

In the political world, one needs to cultivate relationships. These contacts have to be maintained in an effort to convert them into political assets. Our organization's smooth transition from one governor to the next was an example of successful and ongoing networking.

This contact relationship maintenance motivated me to attend Cellucci's State of the State address. It may have been a cold night on January 17, 2001, but that did not discourage me — nor did it prevent the people of the Commonwealth of Massachusetts to pack into Mechanics Hall in Worcester. People came from all across the state to listen to Governor Cellucci deliver his third State of the State address.

Among the invited guests were Parwez Wahid, former secretary of the American Muslim Alliance of Massachusetts and myself. "I got the invitation by mail," Mr. Wahid told me, "and decided to attend, and I am glad I did. The view from the balcony was very clear. I felt the Governor delivered a fine speech. I believe most of the crowd enjoyed it, too; you could tell from the resounding applause he got from the audience. The message got out pretty well; maybe one of the reasons was the speech time was just right," observed Mr. Wahid, "not more than 25 minutes."

After the speech, a reception followed at which Mr. Wahid and I met with the governor and his cabinet members. House Speaker Thomas Finneran was a delight to talk to. He appeared to be in jolly moods that day. We also met with Congressman Jim McGovern, whose district this was. I reminded the congressman about the forthcoming meeting with the Muslim community. McGovern was not only well aware of the meeting, but also knew in whose house it was to be held. We were really impressed when McGovern correctly pronounced the host's name: Muttasem Razzaq.

Steve LaBlanc of the Associated Press was interested in getting my comments on the State of the State address. I told Steve that Governor Cellucci was eloquent, articulate and pretty much straightforward. He did live up to what he had been saying all along, improvements in health care, housing and education. While Steve was busy taking all this down, I told him about a speech Cellucci gave at Anthony's Pier Four restaurant during a fund-raiser sponsored by the American Muslim Alliance. This was a bid to increase support for his gubernatorial candidacy. I remember how the acting Governor Cellucci had mentioned the need for downsizing the classroom to improve teacher-student ratios. Steve agreed with me that the governor had fulfilled that pledge. Not only did more teachers get hired, the classroom size was cut, indeed.

As a software engineer I could relate to the Governor's "e-government plan" to improve state government.

"How do you mean?" Steve wanted to know.

I started to explain what "on-line services" meant. I pointed out to him that the governor articulated that well: "on-line services provide easy access, better communication, hence better government." And I agree with Governor Cellucci on this, I told Steve.

On the economy front, the governor was very clear but cautious as he said, "By most indicators, we are seeing the end of the longest economic growth period in our nation's history. I am confident that the state of our state is excellent. By nearly every measure — whether economic or social — the people of Massachusetts are experiencing a remarkable level of prosperity."

Parwez Wahid noted that the governor outlined areas for improvement, "This year, Jane Swift and I have established five areas where investment is required and accountability is expected: education, housing, health care, e-government and government reform."

"I liked his comment about e-government when he said, 'Massachusetts ought to be in the e-government vanguard'...E-government will make state government more immediately responsive to the needs of our citizens." Parwez added as he was leaving for home.

I always had a great deal of respect for Parwez Wahid and his wife. The young couple was among those I cherish immensely. They and others had come to have their blood tested at the bone marrow drive conducted at the Islamic Society of Greater Worcester. They were willing to donate their bone marrow to my son Yaser, who was suffering from leukemia, if the results indicated a match.

As Parwez Wahid started to hurry down the stairs on his way out, he paused for a second, turned around and said, "I think the evening proved to be productive, but do you know Tahir, I feel more Muslims should have participated."

Someday, I said to myself.

CHAPTER 4   *Bush—Gore—Nader—Buchanan*

[All the ships rise with the rising tide: Seeking interaction with Bush, Gore, Nader and Buchanan, and consequences].

The story of interaction with presidential candidates actually started with Bob Dole. Toward the end of his campaign, Dole's campaign office had contacted the Muslim community for their endorsement. The Muslim community in turn asked Dole's campaign to take a public stand on four issues:

First, that America had acquired a Judeo-Christian-Islamic heritage; second, that he supported Muslim civil rights; third, that he called for negotiation with all Muslim countries; and fourth, that he supported an even-handed policy towards the Middle East.

In his letter dated October 16, 1996 to Saeed, Dole did manage to address the four issues outlined by Agha Saeed. Dole made it very clear in his letter, "I truly believe that America draws strength from its churches, synagogues and mosques." The letter went on to say, "Since the end of the Cold War, many American Muslims have been the targets of stereotyping, bias and discrimination. This discrimination has been seen in the workplace, where Muslim workers were denied reasonable religious accommodation, in schools, and in the media, where our Muslim citizens are often unfairly associated with acts of violence." On the issue of airline profiling Bob Dole wrote, "While demanding increased security measures for the traveling public, I would oppose any discriminatory procedures for screening airline passengers based solely on race, sex, economic status, national origin, or political beliefs." On the foreign policy, Dole made the supporting point, "I would also seek to open constructive dialogue with all Muslim countries working for peace, representing as they do, one fifth of humanity. A goal of my Administration would be to support a clear, long-term and even-handed foreign policy that is consistent with our nation's vital interests." This was all very encouraging and refreshing for Saeed and Muslim Americans; but when asked if Bob Dole would be willing to state the same in a nationally televised conference, he declined to do so. Consequently, the AMA and other Muslim groups refused to endorse Bob Dole.

Muslim groups were to learn later that it was Bob Dole's foreign policy advisor Jeane Kirkpatrick who had advised him not to repeat these positions during a television press conference. Political observers have noticed that even though the Dole campaign was asking Muslims for their vote, the Muslims were still handled through the foreign policy (and not domestic policy) adviser – as if they were foreigners and not American citizens. Subsequently Muslims did not endorse Dole. Recalling the breakdown of these negotiations, Dr. Saeed has repeatedly recalled that in a way he felt relieved, because "had Dole agreed to hold a press conference I would be in serious trouble because I would not have been able to deliver him 3 votes." It was now very clear in Saeed's mind, and he realized that he had to help create a mechanism for consensus building in the community. This realization led him to convene a series of meetings with other Muslim leaders and, finally, in a meeting held May 30, 1998 at the Islamic Center of Southern California in Los Angeles, the new umbrella organization was formally named the American Muslim Political Coordination Council (AMPCC). Present at the meeting with Dr. Agha Saeed were: Dr. Shabbir Safdar and Abdul Kunbargi of the American Muslim Alliance (AMA); Omar Ahmad and Nihad Awad of the Council on American Islamic Relations (CAIR); Mujahid Ramadan of the American Muslim Council (AMC); Dr. Maher Hathout, Mr. Salam Al-Marayati and Dr. Aslam Abdullah of the Muslim Public Affairs Council (MPAC); Dr. Yasmeen Khan of the American Muslim Caucus; Nasif Majid of the Coalition for Good Government (CFGG); and Ghazi Khankan of the National Council of Islamic Affairs (NCIA).

The main goals of the Council were to avoid duplication of efforts; work together with a unity of purpose in mind; and – because of the community diversity, treasure of resources and talents – maintain a division of labor. A ten point agenda was thus adopted by the council at the meeting that included:

1) Creating a unified action plan.
2) Getting candidates elected who support the interests of the council.
3) Political education and empowerment.
4) Voter registration.
5) Lobbying.
6) Creating think tanks.
7) Defending civil and human rights of Muslims.
8) Articulation of strategies to counter anti-Muslim propaganda and activities.

9) Coalition building.
10) Strategic action on *Al-Quds* (Jerusalem) and other important Muslim issues

Thinking on the same wavelength was American Muslim Council's founder, and later its executive director, Abdurahman Alamoudi, who towards the end of 1997 in his letter to the community wrote that, "the time has come to establish a Coordinating Council of American Islamic Organizations." In this letter, he acknowledged the achievements of the existing political organizations. He wrote, "It is clear that the spark lit by the establishment and development of the American Muslim Council and other national and regional U.S. Muslim organizations since 1990 has created a wave of interest in political advocacy work in the American Muslim community. Today there is not a major U.S. city that does not have at least a few prominent Muslim activists or Muslim organizations. This is in addition to the existence of several major Islamic organizations on the national scene." Alamoudi noted that diversity in the Muslim community is an asset. He added, "We can use that diversity to our benefit rather than consider it a major obstacle or challenge…. In fact, within our community we have both ultra-liberals and ultra-conservatives. Between these two poles, however, there is a broad swath of American Muslims who share similar goals and priorities." Alamoudi was looking ahead into the future and hoped the community would heed his call for unity and resolve in forming a council of leaders for consensus building. He pointed out the urgency of the matter and wrote, "We must begin the process of establishing such a council quickly if we are at least to establish our presence at local levels in this 1998 election year and prepare to make an impact in the national elections of 2000."

The AMPCC, as formed assumed a political identity only, and not a religious identity in the sense that the council consisted of the existing four national political organizations. None of the existing national religious organizations at that time, ISNA or ICNA to name a few, either decided not to join on their own or the AMPCC's charter did not align with their religious mission. Thus, AMPCC was formed and its members consisted of AMA, AMC, MPAC and CAIR – Agha Saeed was at its helm.

In a meeting held January 23 in Washington DC, four areas of coordination and cooperation were identified: 1) The future of

Jerusalem. 2) Civil and human rights. 3) Arab and Muslim participation in the electoral process. 4) Access and inclusion in political structures.

Of the four possible U.S presidential choices the American Muslim predominantly decided to vote—in unison and in large numbers—for George W. Bush. But why did the Muslim community choose Governor George Bush over Ralph Nader, Pat Buchanan and Vice President Al Gore? Was Bush really the first choice?

It was through a process of consultation, and the results of a survey that helped in the decision-making. All three candidates were evaluated. Their voting habits and records were studied on issues that were extremely important to Muslims, such as stand on foreign policy(ies) affecting the Muslim world: Bosnia, Kosova, Palestine, Kashmir and Afghanistan. But these were not enough. American Muslims had to rely also on opinion letters as a reassuring mechanism, and as a tool of influence.

Richard Curtiss, former U.S. Ambassador, was among the few who realized early on that the time had come for American Muslims to emerge and assert themselves. I had the pleasure of meeting Mr. Curtiss in the year 2000 at the 4th Annual National AMA Convention in New York. He spoke slowly but precisely and made one point very clear to me and to others in the group, "the Muslims have to flex their political muscle power."

Mr. Curtiss could not attend the following year's convention in Irvine, California, but he asked his daughter Dalinda Hanley to deliver a message on his behalf. The AMA posted that message on its Web site for all Muslims to read and act on accordingly: http://www.amaweb.org/strategicnews/muslim_and_arab_bloc_vote.htm

Here are Dalinda's words from that meeting:
"I would like to read a speech my father Richard Curtiss wanted to give himself, here today. As you know, the Muslim- and Arab-American bloc vote has been his greatest goal in recent years. I promised him that I would give you his speech and his heartfelt greetings and good wishes.

Muslim-Americans and Christian Arab-Americans have an unprecedented opportunity to put themselves on the U.S. political map this year, and also to begin turning around American policy in Palestine, Kashmir and other areas where

Muslims are suffering. But it involves a lot of hard work in the next month to organize a bloc vote in the presidential election. If the opportunity is lost, obviously it won't return in less than four years. But in fact it may not return again in the lifetimes of anyone in this room, because there may never again be such clear differences between the Republican and Democratic candidates on Middle East policy.

The Israel lobby has been using bloc votes on the national level

First let's examine how the Israel lobby has been using bloc votes on the national level for years. Then let's look at how Muslim-Americans have been using bloc votes on the local level in recent elections. Then we'll talk about some of the problems encountered to date in trying to organize U.S. Muslims to do the same thing nationally. And finally we'll discuss how Al Gore and George Bush differ on the Palestine problem, and how their differences will also affect other areas of Muslim interest like Kashmir, Bosnia and Chechnya.

What is the "Israel lobby"? What can we learn from it?

Today there are, at most, 5.5 million Jews in the United States. That's just two percent of the 275 million residents of the United States. The definition I'm using is the same one used by Jewish organizational leaders and the weekly newspapers that tie together members of the Jewish community in the United States. In reaching this arbitrary figure, Jewish leaders simply include those who consider themselves Jews, whether or not they are members of a synagogue, and whether or not both parents were Jewish. National Jewish leaders recognized early that these diverse people of many different ethnic backgrounds and differing religious views ranging from totally secular to totally orthodox could be molded into a single community first by their horror over the Holocaust, the murder of half of the Jews of Europe during World War II, and later by their support for Israel.

How American Jews vote

That's only part of the story, however. Most American Jews vote for Democratic over Republican candidates. But how members of the Jewish community vote at the presidential level is largely determined by the candidate's stand on Israel.

According to exit polls, Democrat Jimmy Carter got little more than 60 percent of Jewish votes when he ran for reelection in 1980 because American Jewish voters opposed his pressure on Israel to sign a peace treaty with the Palestinians similar to the Israeli-Egyptian peace treaty that Carter brokered.

In 1992 Bill Clinton got the support of 85 percent of Jewish voters because they were angry at the pressure George Bush and his no-nonsense Secretary of State James Baker were putting on Israel to reach a land-for-peace agreement with the Palestinians. In 1996 Bill Clinton got 88 percent of the Jewish vote against Bob Dole because the Israeli press had labeled Clinton the most pro-Israel president in U.S. history, and because of the extraordinary number of Jewish appointments made by the Clinton administration, which by now include both Clinton appointments to the Supreme Court and to more than half of the top foreign-policy-making jobs in the Clinton Administration.

For the tiny American Jewish community, bloc voting and coordinated, heavy political donations have paid off handsomely.

Now let's look at the Muslim lobby and the Arab lobby.

There are between 6 and 8 million Muslims in the United States, using the broad definition that a Muslim-American is an American who considers himself part of the Islamic community. He may go to the mosque every Friday and pray five times a day. Or he may do neither, but nevertheless consider himself Muslim and support Muslim causes. Using the same broad definition, there may be as many as two million Christian Arab Americans, whose opinions on the Palestine problem, and the necessity of keeping Jerusalem open to all members of the Abrahamic religions are the same as their Muslim brethren.

Eight million Muslims and an additional two million Christian Arab-Americans are 10 million people, more than 3.6 percent of the population, and growing. That's almost double America's Jewish population, which is static, and may even be diminishing. Yet what impact have the Muslims, or Muslim- and Arab-Americans combined, had on U.S. foreign policy — or domestic policy, for that matter? There are no Muslim members of Congress, no Muslims on the Supreme

Court and, most shocking, no Muslims in any foreign-policy-making position in the State Department, the White House or anywhere else in the bureaucracy, so far as I know.

Let's look at Muslim effectiveness at the local level

Muslims, however, have been effective at the local level. In 1996 Muslims endorsed Richard Zimmer, a Republican candidate for an open Senate seat in New Jersey. Zimmer, afraid of Jewish criticism, announced publicly that he had not sought the endorsement. So New Jersey Muslims, in a miracle of organization, announced they were withdrawing their endorsement of Zimmer and endorsing his Democratic opponent, Robert Torricelli. Torricelli won narrowly and has said publicly on many occasions that he owed his election victory to the Muslim vote.

That was a bloc vote, and it worked. And, on matters involving the Middle East, Torricelli sounds very different from other senators from the northeastern states. He weighs carefully what stands he can take without offending New Jersey Muslims. The same is true of other elected officials in New Jersey, notably Governor Christine Todd Whitman, who has become a regular guest at Muslim events in New Jersey.

There are hardly any Pakistani-Americans in North Dakota, and perhaps that's why a former North Dakota senator, Larry Pressler, attached his name to a piece of legislation that effectively cut off U.S. aid to Pakistan because Pakistan was working on a nuclear weapons program. When Pressler came up for reelection, Pakistani Americans collected campaign donations for his rival, Tim Johnson. The donations bought a lot of radio and television advertising and Johnson won a closely contested race.

Thus there are two members of the Senate who owe their seats to Muslim bloc voting and coordinated donations by Pakistani-Americans. There are many other Muslim success stories at the local level.

I have personally attended meet-the-candidate events in which Muslims representing all of the mosques in the area invited all candidates for elective office to an event where they heard a brief introduction to Islamic concerns, and then introduced themselves to the Muslim audience, sometimes expressing their own willingness to address those concerns. I have attended a variation on this theme, where individual candidates were invited to fast-breaking meals at local mosques during Ramadan.

These activities in all of those cities resulted in preparation of a list of recommended candidates. Where there were no clear distinctions in terms of Islamic issues between rival candidates for the same office, the recommendation went to the candidate who showed he or she took the local Muslim community seriously by showing up. The lists were made available in every mosque or Islamic center in those cities, and Muslim voters were invited to take the list into the voting booth with them in order to reduce the chances that Muslim voters were canceling each other out. In the cities where such meetings have been held in the past, in each election cycle a higher percentage of local candidates shows up.

This year there already have been many such meet-the-candidate meetings sponsored by the Arab American Institute (AAI), the American Muslim Alliance (AMA) and the Council for American-Islamic Relations (CAIR), with recommendations emerging from local cosponsoring organizations for candidates for local office in last spring's primary elections.

What are the pros and cons for a Muslim bloc vote?

For several years the Council of Presidents of National Arab American Organizations and the Coordinating Council of Muslim Political Organizations have held joint meetings. This year the member groups are working together to register everyone in the two overlapping communities to vote. They are organizing get-out-the-vote drives, making sure that all of the registered voters remember to vote on election day, are provided transportation when necessary, and that they carry with them into the voting booth lists of recommended candidates.

This already has been done at the local level in 1996 and 1998, and it seems certain that it will be done in many more communities this year. But, although there was an attempt to organize such coordinated action at the national level in 1996, it failed.

So the result was that, instead of forming a bloc of all or nearly all of the registered voters from a combined community of some 10 million people, Muslim- and Arab-Americans simply went to polls, voted their individual preferences and, for all intents and purposes, canceled each other out — in the same election in which 88 percent of Jewish voters were reelecting Bill Clinton to a second term.

How have Arab- and Muslim-Americans traditionally voted?

This could easily happen again. No one knows for sure, but it appears that a majority of Arab-Americans tend to support Democratic candidates, a majority of African-American or indigenous Muslims also support Democrats, and a majority of socially conservative immigrant Muslims and their descendants support Republicans. There are historical reasons for all of this. With some Arab- and Muslim-Americans, individual party loyalties already have replaced community loyalties. With most others, however, the tie to the Arab-American or Muslim-American communities is much stronger than the party preference.

And now the ultimate question — can they unite?

Is it possible to unite all of these diverse individuals into a single voting bloc? And if so, on what issues will they judge the candidates? And who makes the final decision on behalf of the communities? Total unity is impossible, as the Jewish community demonstrates: in 1996, while 88 percent of American Jews voted for the Democratic presidential candidate, 12 percent were voting for the Republican candidate.

So it should be understood that some Arab-Americans and Muslim-Americans have to become party activists before anything else. That's fine. Leaders of the Muslim community should listen to their arguments on behalf of the candidates of their party. But then the Islamic leaders not affiliated with any political party should make up their own minds, hopefully in a coordinated way.

There are two other hazards, but they can be negotiated if they are properly understood. In 1996, when leaders of national Muslim political organizations sought to encourage a bloc vote, they were given a warmer reception by the Dole campaign than by the Clinton campaign, which was afraid of alienating essential Jewish donors and the highly disciplined Jewish bloc vote.

Nevertheless, when it came time to make an endorsement, the Muslim political leaders held back. It later became apparent that several leaders felt that they had a special "in" with the Clinton administration. So, to gain a competitive advantage over other Muslim groups in terms of members and donations, they broke with the rest of the Islamic political organizations.

So there was no Muslim bloc vote in 1996. And, although the Muslim leaders did not endorse Dole, the Clinton administration has treated them like losers. In my opinion, those who can't demonstrate that they can turn out their communities to vote, as a bloc, will be treated like losers no matter which candidate wins. An opportunity was lost in 1996. What's important now, however, is that it doesn't happen again.

What Is the Unifying Issue?

There are those who say the Muslim vote should not be based on foreign policy. But what domestic policies can Muslims unite around? Are all Muslims able to agree on a single health care or schools program, or whether budget surpluses should be used primarily to pay down the national debt or grant tax relief? I don't think so. The wealthy Pakistani-American physician, the Arab-American entrepreneur, and the inner city African-American struggling to protect his neighborhood from drug dealers may all agree that they want their children to have an Islamic education and be protected from Hollywood sex and violence. But they may differ as widely as do the candidates on how all this is best achieved.

Agreeing on Jerusalem

On the other hand, Muslims from all ethnic backgrounds and from all social classes can agree on Jerusalem. And, until the Palestinian problem is solved, it is going to be increasingly difficult to be a Muslim in the United States.

What difference does a bloc vote make?

By chance or divine providence, according to your viewpoint, most American Muslims and a very high percentage of Christian Arab-Americans, are concentrated in major metropolitan centers of a very few states in the United States. They are the tri-state area around New York City, Ohio, Michigan, Illinois and California. In a very close election, as it appears this one will be, if most of the Muslim votes are cast as a bloc in those states, the Muslim vote probably will determine which candidate wins in those states. And under the "winner-take-all" U.S. system, whoever gets the majority of popular votes in a state like California gets all of that state's electoral votes. Neither candidate can win unless he gets the votes of most of those "swing states." Other states where the Muslim vote can be very influential are Texas, Florida, Virginia and — because of the high concentration of Muslims in the suburbs of Washington, D.C. — Maryland as well.

If Muslim voters demonstrate the discipline this year, in such a close election, to turn out their communities to vote, and vote as a bloc, and publicize their vote, the United States will never again be the same. Its Middle East policy will become even-handed for the first time since the creation of Israel. U.S. South Asia policy may also be liberated from the current influence of the Israel-Indian alliance. And there will be a weapon to use against the pernicious culture of drugs, sex and violence emanating from Hollywood, and actually driving many Muslims to send their children back to their original homelands to protect them during their formative years.

My father Richard Curtiss has always deeply felt that what Muslims want is what's good for America. Eventually the American public will come to understand this, as the Israel lobby's grip on the mainstream media is weakened. Most Americans are unhappy with the direction the United States is taking at home and abroad. If U.S. Muslims unite to make their influence felt in the world's only remaining superpower, it will be a present to the entire world. It would be the greatest gift Muslims could make to their fellow Americans. And it would also be a great joy to my father. I have watched him work so hard for many years to help inspire Muslim- and Arab-Americans to work together for a bloc vote. He wanted to tell you himself to use the bloc vote this year to get a real voice in our country. Now I'd like to ask you to help me out. Because I'll be in big trouble when I get home if I can't tell him, "There will be a bloc vote in the year 2000."

The debate among the Muslim community and the task for its

leadership was picking the right moment for deciding which presidential candidate to endorse. The choice had to be made between Bush and Gore; Nader and Buchanan had to be taken out of the equation. Simple logic suggested that, if the intent was to get Muslims recognized as a political entity in the United States, then to vote for a candidate destined to lose was not a wise move.

This was not an easy decision for many Muslims. There were alternate suggestions — vote for Nader in those states where the candidate of our choice would surely lose due to the lack of his party's support historically. In a way, such a strategy did make sense. If Bush were our choice, then it would be safe to vote for Nader in Massachusetts. In a winner-take-all system, voting for Bush in Democratic states like Massachusetts meant throwing away your vote, yet the same votes cast in favor of Ralph Nader would be beneficial for the Green Party. If that party got five percent of the nation's votes, it would become eligible to receive Federal election funds the next time around. It sounded good, but whatever strategy was to be adopted had to convey, loudly and clearly, the message that Muslims did vote in large numbers, did vote for the same candidate and did vote as a bloc. Hence, the term *bloc vote* could at last apply to the Muslim vote.

Information on all of the candidates was readily available on Web sites. Of the three candidates, Ralph Nader of the "Green party" seemed to be the least popular among Americans, although he was a favorite among American Muslims. The information circulating was that Mr. Nader's ancestors came from Lebanon. A few Americans that I talked to; the Green party was the "most well known and dynamic alternative party in the United States."

Ralph Nader's campaign trail brought him to Boston on October 2, 2000. He was scheduled to speak at the Fleet Center in Boston, which was almost at full capacity. I managed to get backstage, where I met former daytime TV talk show host Phil Donohue. After introducing myself, I wasted no time in telling him about the resolve of Muslim-Americans to vote as a bloc. I showed him *The MetroWest Daily News,* the paper that had the headline "Muslims Organize Voting Bloc," and requested Phil to ask Ralph Nader, on behalf of the AMA, why 7 million American Muslims should vote for him? Phil said, "I'll do better. Ralph will want to see this [newspaper]. I will introduce you to him, and you can ask that of him."

Phil Donahue lived up to his word; he did introduce me to Ralph

Nader. After delivering his speech, Mr. Nader was escorted under heavy security to his private office in the center. No one was allowed in this office except his immediate family members, campaign advisors and close friends. The only news media allowed was CNN. Phil told Ralph that he needed to listen to me, at the same time turning towards me and saying, "Show Ralph the paper." Mr. Nader studied the headline and the article with great interest. I realized that this was as good a time as any to talk about the goals and mission of the AMA, and inform Mr. Nader about Muslims organizing to form a bloc vote.

Ralph Nader and I talked at great length, with CNN recording our conversation. I paused to change the subject, and asked Mr. Nader if he would care to respond to the question, "Why should the American Muslim vote for him?" I assured him that his response would be relayed to American Muslims. Mr. Nader spoke in a soft voice, and said, "because I am for Democracy, ethnicity and nurturing a society where noncommercial values matter more."

Ralph appeared very interested in the newspaper and asked if he could keep it. He promised me that his office would contact Dr. Agha Saeed, with whose name he was apparently familiar with.

Later, I accompanied Mr. Nader to a fund-raising event being held for him in a restaurant in the Fleet Center. I estimate that close to a hundred people attended. The faces in the crowd with whom I was familiar at the time were those of Dr. Karim Khudairi and Dr. Reda; both were very supportive and spoke highly of the AMA's recent fund-raisers featuring Former First Lady Hillary Rodham Clinton and Congressman David Bonior.

Dr. Khudairi, voicing an opinion not uncommon among Arab-Americans, wondered if the AMA would be sponsoring a fund-raiser for Ralph Nader. The Arab-Americans' rationale was very simple: I recall Dr. Khudairi once saying. "Do you know Tahir, Ralph Nader is of Arab descent? The Muslims should all vote for him. The AMA should sponsor a fund-raiser for him."

"Why don't you [Khudairi] and Dr. Reda spearhead that effort?" others suggested. Without any hesitance I agreed to delegate that authority on behalf of the AMA, because our emphasis was more on voter registration drive, and that to me was top priority.

Ralph Nader differed from Governor Bush and Vice President Al Gore on many issues: health care, national defense, stewardship of the environment and — an area of particular interest to Muslims —

campaign finances. He was clear on this point: "...no corporate soft money contributions." Like most communities new to the United States, this was acceptable because money is a scarce commodity among immigrant Muslims.

In the same context, Mr. Nader was vocal about refusing to accept any Political Action Committee (PAC) contributions, and he supported full public financing of public elections. He went so far as to ask the Fleet Center audience that night if they wanted a "Green party watchdog."' If so, they would have to *build* the Green party in an effort to "end legalized bribery" — a term the Green Party used to make their point that "big business invests in politicians and political parties by giving them millions of dollars, and, in return, those businesses get corporate welfare and tax breaks worth billions of dollars." Ralph Nader wanted to "shift this power" back to the people.

It was no coincidence that Ralph Nader was in Boston a day before the first scheduled debate between Gore and Bush was to be held in that city. His Green party had failed to convince the authorities in the debate commission to include Mr. Nader in the debate, but he was not going to simply go away quietly.

I worked very hard to get a ticket to attend that first presidential debate. I called the Republican state and national party offices, then decided to call Congressman David Bonior in Michigan. The congressman tried very hard for me; I learned later that his office even called Congressman Joe Moakley to see if he could help. Joe turned around and asked if David could get *him* a ticket! David had even requested President Bill Clinton to get me a ticket. Evidently, admission to the debate was a very hot commodity.

In the interim, Congressman Bonior's office informed me that there would be two tickets waiting for me at the Boston Park Plaza Hotel, where Al Gore was scheduled to go after the debate. Presence at the Park Plaza was by invitation only, restricted to an inner circle. Since it would be like a private setting (perhaps with selected representatives of the media), I decided to avail myself of this opportunity, for the simple reason that it would give me a chance to talk about Muslim vote bloc and strategy with Al Gore and/or his campaign manager(s).

On October 3, 2001, the day when U.S. presidential hopefuls Al Gore and George Bush were engaged in a battle of wits, the activist Muslims of Massachusetts were engaged in displaying a unity of purpose and division of labor.

Shereda Hosein, the AMA's vice chair of Republican affairs, decided to join her friend Tara J. Sullivan to go the Massachusetts Republican party's event at the Copley Plaza Hotel. Attendees would
include Congressman J.C. Watts, Governor Cellucci, Lieutenant
Governor Swift and members of the Bush family. Ms. Hosein decided the Bush rally event would be a good place from which to
watch the meeting of the two candidates. Governor Bush did stop at
the rally after the debate.

Anwar Kazmi, chapter vice chair (Democratic affairs) and Abdul
Wahab Koshafa, the AMA's media and public affairs director, along
with over 700 Muslim friends, decided to spend time outside the
presidential debate site at UMass Boston, in a rally protesting the
gruesome current events in the Gaza strip, where scores of Palestinian lives had been lost to Israeli gunfire.

My 21-year-old daughter Uzma, and her two friends, Maria
Ansari and Samira Khan, decided to join me as well. We stopped at
the Park Plaza first to pick up four tickets. But I also got two press
passes. Press passes can be far more useful than tickets: they give
you an opportunity to interview the candidates.

It took us almost an hour to get from the hotel to UMass, because
most of the streets were blocked. When we finally got to the college,
the doors were closed and no one was being admitted in — even those
who had tickets. They assured everyone that it was a standard security measure. "This is as close as we get," we conceded, and retreated.

"That's when we saw Ralph Nader in the midst of police officers
and reporters. The police were not letting him attend the debate even
when he had a ticket," reported Uzma.

"We felt sorry for him," added Maria Ansari. Samira Khan, who
later became an intern at Congressman McGovern's office. Both
young women agreed with their friends and other onlookers: "Ralph
Nader was treated unfairly. After all, he is a presidential candidate;
he should not even have had to be required to have a ticket in the
first place, to be admitted."

This indeed left a very negative impression in the minds of many
who saw the humiliating episode on television. This is what the Green
party had been complaining about, the two-party monopoly.

While at the Bush rally, Shereda Hosein was busy with fellow
Republicans. She noted, "There was big support for Governor George
Bush. We spoke to several chairpersons of the Republican city com-

mittee — discussion remained mostly at a local, grass roots level."

Syrian born Yousef Abou Allaban, former president of the Islamic Society of Greater Worcester and a psychiatrist by profession, attended the "Rally for Palestine," and was convinced that officials were very impressed by the rally, calling it "well organized and well disciplined." Everyone was chanting "Justice for Palestine." Abdul Wahab Koshafa thought that the response from the community at such a short notice was very encouraging. "We offered our evening prayer *Maghrib*, and walked to UMass with small children leading the group, wearing fake-blood-spattered white shirts." This *was* a busy day for reporters inside UMass, where the presidential debate was in progress and outside on Morrisey Avenue where the protesters had assembled.

CNN (www.cnn.com/2000/ALLPOLITICS/stories/10/03/ debate.protests.01/) reported: "Also — on Morrisey Avenue, further away from the debate site, a long line of protesters, many of whom claimed to be Palestinian immigrants, marched toward the debate site chanting "Justice for Palestine."

The Islamic Society of Boston (ISB) in Cambridge was instrumental in organizing the rally. The following day the Harvard newspaper, the *Crimson,* quoted Samer Abu-Ghazaleh of ISB: "We are a group of Muslims, Christians, Americans from different backgrounds, who are here to send a message to policymakers in the United States that tax dollars shouldn't go to support inhumane acts of the state of Israel."

Anwar Kazmi was happy with the turnout at such a short notice. But he was more content with the rally's peaceful outcome. He said, "We had, to my estimate, about seven to eight hundred people. At such a short notice, this is a good turnout. The rally was very disciplined, very dignified. Foreign media took interest, also. We were approached by the Italian and Japanese news reporters."

Supporters of the Green party had rallied alongside as well. That rally, though, turned out to be anything *but* peaceful. The Green party supporters were protesting the exclusion of Ralph Nader from the presidential debates. They were hoping that their voice and protests would be heard, and Mr. Nader would be allowed to take part in the forthcoming debates, one on the 11th and the last of the three on the 17th.

The next day local media covered our rally, but remained focused on the Green party rally that got out of hand. The Green party never got their wish granted. Ralph Nader had to rely on media to get his campaign to the masses.

The responsibility for dissemination of pertinent information on candidates to our community fell on the shoulders of Muslim leadership. Of the four presidential candidates, Ralph Nader, though the least likely to be elected, was still the favorite among the Muslim community. Apart from the news in the local papers, information on the Green party and Ralph Nader were also readily available to the Muslim populace from the party's Web sites.

The Muslim community as a whole was leaning more toward George Walker Bush as their first choice because of a few important factors. First, the Muslims found Governor Bush more accessible than Al Gore. Gore's choice of Senator Joseph Lieberman as his running mate naturally may have influenced some to strike Al Gore from their list altogether. Although the thought did initially cross my mind that a Jew holding such a high place could be disadvantageous for Muslims, that was not the deciding factor for me, nor was it for many others. Many of us also looked at the brighter side — that this move gave hope and paved the way for other minorities and ethnic groups to aspire to high office.

The second presidential debate on October 11ᵗʰ proved to be another deciding factor. Many of us recorded it, because videotape made it easier to review the debate, gather excerpts for further analysis and take the time to "read between the lines."

I took the liberty of electronically sending these excerpts, with my comments added wherever necessary, to my huge e-mail list. The instructions were very clear: read and then forward to as many as possible, like a chain letter. I received my own e-mail with some frequency, forwarded back to me from other sources. Apparently, the mail got forwarded many times, reaching the Muslim community all across the States.

Reactions to the following debate exchanges are representative of what the Muslim community may have taken away from the candidates' encounter.

ON MIDDLE EAST DIPLOMACY
LEHRER: What do you think the United States should do right now to resolve that conflict over there?
GORE: The first priority has to be on ending the violence, dampening down the tensions that have arisen there.... I think

that we also have to keep a weather eye toward Saddam Hussein, ...

BUSH: Well, I think during the campaign, particularly now during this difficult period, we ought to be speaking with one voice. ...I think credibility is going to be very important in the future in the Middle East.

LEHRER: So you don't believe, Vice President Gore, that we should take sides and resolve this right now? There a lot of people pushing, "Hey, the United States should declare itself and not be so neutral in this particular situation."

GORE: Well, we stand with Israel, but we have maintained the ability to serve as an honest broker...And if we throw away that ability to serve as an honest broker, then we have thrown—we will have thrown away a strategic asset that's important not only to us but also to Israel.

LEHRER: Do you agree with that, Governor?

BUSH: I do. I do think this, though. I think that when it comes to timetables, it can't be the United States timetable as to how discussions take place. It's got to be a timetable that all parties can agree to, other than—like the Palestinians and the Israelis.

Secondly, any lasting peace is going to have to be a peace that's good for both sides, and, therefore, the term *honest broker* makes sense.

(Reaction — What most Muslims got out of this exchange was that, though both candidates showed strong support for Israel, Bush made sense when he said, "any lasting peace is going to have to be a peace that's good for both sides.")

ON SECRET EVIDENCE

LEHRER: First, a couple of follow-ups from the vice presidential debate last week.

Vice President Gore, would you support or sign as president a federal law banning racial profiling by police and other authorities at all levels of government?

GORE: Yes, I would. The only thing an executive order can accomplish is to ban it in federal law enforcement agencies...

BUSH: Yes. I can't imagine what it would be like to be singled out because of race, and stopped and harassed. That's just flat wrong, and that's not what America's all about. And so we ought to do everything we can to end racial profiling.

And secondly, there are other forms of racial profiling that go on in America. **Arab-Americans are racially profiled in what's called "secret evidence."** People are stopped, and we got to do something about that. My friend, Senator Spencer Abraham of Michigan, **is pushing a law to make sure that, you know, Arab-Americans are treated with respect.**

(Reaction — Bush cast the spotlight on Arab-American profiling based on secret evidence, and that remark showed American Muslims his opinion while also giving them hope that such targeting would not be on the increase during a Bush presidency.)

ON GAY MARRIAGE

BUSH: I'm not for gay marriage. I think marriage is a sacred institution between a man and a woman.
GORE: I agree with that.

(Reaction — Muslims found George Bush to be more forceful on the issue and thought he was saying the right thing, "marriage is a sacred institution between a man and a woman.")

At the American Muslim Alliance (AMA) "all hands meeting" held October 22, 2000 at the Islamic center in Wayland, Massachusetts, this message was relayed: that on the following day (October 23), there would be a press conference in Washington, D.C., attended by major national Muslim organizations, including AMA, CAIR, AMC and others. The objective was to endorse George Bush for president. After talking to attendees via conference call, that is just what happened. [The dominating question: Why Bush? was adressed].   Based on the second presidential debate, it was quite clear that, whereas Al Gore is 100 percent for Israel, Bush still managed to say, "any lasting peace is going to have to be a peace that's good for both sides, and, therefore, the term *honest broker* makes sense."

Gore got over $125,000 and Lieberman over $250,000.00

from Jewish PAC, whereas Bush got less than $6,000.00 and Cheney nothing. A founding member of "Sound Vision," Abdul Malik Mujahid, elaborated:

"At this moment, the Jewish community, the media and the money are all on the side of the Gore-Lieberman ticket. The pro-Israeli political action committee (PAC) year 2000 contribution to the Democrats' presidential candidate Al Gore is $151,890; to the Democrats' vice presidential candidate Joseph Lieberman, $226,508. In contrast, Republican presidential candidate George W. Bush has only received $5,200 and Republican vice-presidential candidate Dick Cheney, nothing."

On racial profiling, Bush said, "And secondly, there are other forms of racial profiling that go on in America. Arab-Americans are racially profiled in what's called 'secret evidence.' "

Bush, in the second debate, also indicated that somehow Third World countries' debt should be forgiven. Dr. Agha Saeed (AMPCC-PAC head) on the "why Bush" question, made the following comment, "Governor Bush took the initiative to meet with local and national representatives of the Muslim community. He also promised to address Muslim concerns on domestic and foreign policy issues."

The American Muslim Political Coordinating Council (AMPCC-PAC) sent out a statement that read:

American Muslim PAC endorses George W. Bush for president

Islamic political leaders cite Texas governor's outreach to their community

(WASHINGTON, D.C., 10/23/2000) — The American Muslim Political Coordinating Council Political Action Committee (AMPCC-PAC) today announced its endorsement of George W. Bush for president, citing his outreach to the Muslim community and his stand on the issue of secret evidence. "AMPCC-PAC is an affiliated PAC of the American Muslim Political Coordinating Council. AMPCC members include the American Muslim Alliance, American Muslim Council, Council on American-Islamic Relations and Muslim Public Affairs Council."

There are an estimated six million Muslims in the United

States. Muslims constitute a potential swing-voting bloc in states such as California, New York, New Jersey, Illinois, Michigan and Ohio. In several surveys of Muslim voters, the majority said they would vote for Bush. "Governor Bush took the initiative to meet with local and national representatives of the Muslim community. He also promised to address Muslim concerns on domestic and foreign policy issues," said AMPCC-PAC head Agha Saeed.

The Muslim leaders also noted that Bush challenged the use of secret evidence at the second presidential debate. American Muslims and civil libertarians believe secret evidence, as it is currently used in Immigration and Naturalization Service (INS) deportation hearings, is unconstitutional.

They believe that it is used disproportionately against Muslims in America.

A number of Muslim detainees have been held for up to four years based on evidence that is not revealed to them or their attorneys. The "secret evidence repeal act" HR2121 currently awaits passage in the House and Senate.

The statement carried names of:

American Muslim Alliance - Agha Saeed

American Muslim Council - Aly Abuzaakouk

Council on American-Islamic Relations - Nihad Awad

Muslim Public Affairs Council - Hassan Ibrahim

An equally important written argument came from my vice chairman, Anwar Kazmi. I did not have a hard time convincing him, a Democrat who had never voted for a Republican candidate, of the need for a Muslim voting bloc. He understood the necessity for unity of purpose. We discussed the rationale, and he put it on paper, nicely articulated. We distributed the essay in the community, under the heading:

"Why Muslims must vote as a block in 2000"

SUMMARY

The closest presidential election in recent history provides the American Muslim community with a unique opportunity to make some rapid strides on the road toward its political empower-

ment. With the final outcome of the election hinging on the results in a few battleground states, each having significant Muslim votes, American Muslims could play a pivotal role in determining who will serve as the president of the United States for the next four years. All eyes are, therefore, trained on how we vote.

All American Muslim political leaders have unanimously decided that Muslims in America will vote as a bloc for Governor George W. Bush. The bloc voting strategy makes the most sense because it fully capitalizes on our most important political asset: our voting strength. After the unanimous decision, it is even more imperative that all Muslims should set aside their personal preferences and vote en bloc for Governor Bush. This is also in conformity with the teachings of our scholars.

If we do so, political observers (through their analyses of exit poll data) will perceive us as a strong, united, disciplined and highly motivated community, willing and able to fight for its concerns within the constitutional framework. As such, no future political aspirant will risk ignoring us even if Bush does not win the election. If, on the contrary, we ignore the recommendation and vote for Gore or Nader based on other considerations, we will be perceived as a weak, splintered, undisciplined and leaderless community which political leaders can safely continue to ignore.

INTRODUCTION

Several weeks ago, a BBC report on the upcoming U.S. presidential elections concluded that American Muslims might play a crucial role in determining who is the occupant of that office for the next four years. With less than a week to go before election, the race between the two major party candidates a statistical dead-heat, and the final outcome apparently hinging on the results in a few battleground states, each having a significant number of Muslim voters, the BBC report may yet prove to be quite prophetic. From the standpoint of Arab and Muslim-Americans, a number of positive developments have occurred during the current election cycle. At least partly due to the advent of Muslim advocacy groups, who have launched well-publicized voter registration campaigns, political observers have suddenly begun to notice the size of the Muslim vote.

For the first time in U.S. history, many of the country's major newspapers and newsmagazines have carried prominently displayed articles about Muslim voters—their numbers and geographic distribution, their major concerns and their voting patterns. Prompted, in part, by the tightness of the race, the two major presidential contenders have made overtures to the Muslim community, somewhat tentatively and guardedly in one case and a little bit more enthusiastically in the other. This is in sharp contrast to the treatment Muslim voters have received in the past. As late as 1996, candidates invariably turned down requests to meet with Muslim leaders, declined endorsements by Muslim organizations, and, in many cases, even returned campaign contributions from Muslim individuals. All the attention being given to Muslim voters has prompted Muslim leaders to chart a much more active course of participation in the current campaign. Again, for the first time in history, all politically involved Muslim organizations have decided to endorse a single candidate (Governor George Bush) and are urging all Muslims to vote for him *en bloc.*

Even the all-powerful Israeli lobby in Washington has begun to feel the power of the American Muslim voter. In an op-ed article entitled "The Arab lobby mounts a challenge," published in the leading Israeli newspaper *Haaretz* on November 1, 2000, Eliahu Salpeter writes:

For the first time in the history of its political struggle for the State of Israel, U.S. Jewry finds itself in a head-on confrontation with the Arab-American public…American Jews now feel — perhaps for the first time — that the force challenging them is no longer based only in the oil industry, but also in millions of Arab-American voters in a position to influence U.S. politics.

While noting that the Israeli lobby is currently far ahead of the Muslim-Arab lobby in terms of the influence it wields in Washington, Salpeter further observes that, while the influence of Israel on U.S. Jewry is dwindling, and Jewish support for Israel is of a routine and institutional nature, Muslim and Arab support for Palestinians is still at the stage of "youthful passion," and is on the increase.

In another article entitled "Would W's Israel policy be as bad as his father's?" recently published in the pro-Israel magazine *The New Republic*, the authors grimly contemplate the fallout for Israel from the presidency of George W. Bush, elected with the conspicuous support of Arab- and Muslim-Americans, and the equally conspicuous lack of support of American Jewry.

The above-mentioned developments, as well as the opportunity to exercise a decisive influence on the election for "the most powerful office in the world," to use an old cliché, may give many Muslims an exaggerated sense of power in the American electoral landscape. Elsewhere I have argued that several factors besides voting strength determine the level of a community's political empowerment ("Factors Affecting a Community's Political Empowerment," October 2000). Among these are the campaign support resources the community can muster (campaign managers and volunteers), financial support (primarily campaign contributions), media support (newspaper endorsements, op-ed articles, radio and TV commentators, etc.), intellectual support (respected academicians, business, former military and government officials lending credibility to the candidate's positions) and celebrity support (endorsements from famous Hollywood personalities, sports heroes, etc.). With the exception of voter strength, Muslims are far behind other established communities in each of these areas of influence.

It should be obvious from the quotations cited above that, despite the significant edge which American Jewry enjoys over Muslims in all areas of political influence, they view the rising Muslim voter strength as a potential threat to their virtual monopoly over U.S. Middle East policy, and will create obstacles in the path of our political empowerment. The recent Hillary Clinton campaign contribution controversy in response to a McCarthyite campaign orchestrated by pro-Israeli groups, and the growing number of hate-filled op-ed articles appearing in leading newspapers from coast to coast, should serve as a reminder that the effort to impede our progress is already well under way. It is against this backdrop that we, as American Muslims, should examine the opportunities afforded us by the current presidential election, the closest race in recent history. The spotlight has been trained on us due to the pivotal role we might play in determining the final outcome.

The most important thing is that, at the end of the day, political observers perceive us as a highly disciplined community willing and able to fight for its concerns. If the candidate we support is successful, and his victory is perceived in some measure to be due to our support, we will have taken some rapid strides in our long and arduous journey towards political empowerment. Even if the candidate we support does not win, no future political aspirant will be able to ignore a sizeable, disciplined and highly motivated bloc of voters.

BEST STRATEGY: BLOC VOTING

In devising any successful strategy, we must define our objectives and appraise the resources available to pursue the objectives. It is also imperative that the objectives be grounded in reality.

Unrealistic objectives can only lead to wasted effort and frustration. For most Muslims, the objective of participating in the political arena may be summarized in terms of the Quranic injunction of "enjoining good and forbidding evil." This broad objective should be the guiding principle for positions Muslims adopt on various domestic and foreign policy issues. The latter set of issues have a special urgency for American Muslims because of the ties that bind us to the rest of the Ummah, and because of the hostile nature of U.S. policy towards Muslims in so many parts of the world, even as it claims to be their friend.

In reality though, one can only enjoin the good and forbid the evil when others are willing to listen. As noted earlier, not many among those who formulate and execute policy in this country, be it domestic or foreign, are prepared to listen to Muslims. Even in this election, it is doubtful if the candidates would make any effort to reach out to Muslim voters were the race not as close as it is.

To use a common metaphor, American Muslims currently do not have a seat at the table where major policy issues are debated. In fact, we are not even inside the chamber where the debate occurs. Continuing with our metaphor, a short-run strategy would be to remain outside the chamber and voice our concerns to the policymakers if we can catch them going in and out of the chamber. A long-run strategy would be to focus our energies on obtaining our own seat at the table inside the debating chamber. Once seated, we can voice our concerns and have a better chance that people will listen. I believe we have a much better chance of achieving our objectives if we adopt the long-run strategy.

Looking at the other side of the ledger, our most important asset for pursuing our objective is the voting strength of the American Muslim community. How can we utilize this asset to derive maximum advantage for our community? In physics we learn that to be most effective a force must be focused and targeted. By analogy, our voting strength would be best utilized if we vote as a bloc for the candidate who would provide the most benefits for Muslims in the long run If Muslims vote in overwhelmingly large numbers for the same candidate, political observers will see us as a highly motivated and disciplined bloc of voters to be taken seriously in future political contests. On the other hand, if we split our vote several ways, especially after our leadership has unanimously decided to vote for a specific candidate, they will draw the opposite conclusion. We will remain consigned to our familiar place outside the policy-making arena, where we can shout our concerns till we become blue in the face.

NOW THAT A DECISION HAS BEEN MADE LET US CLOSE RANKS

The bloc voting strategy, by itself, does not determine which candidate should receive the Muslim vote. That decision should be based on other criteria, namely, the candidates' positions on domestic issues (such as social security, health care, education policy, tax policy, supreme court nominations, immigration, etc.) and foreign policy issues (such as Palestine, Iraq, Kashmir, Chechnya, etc.).

Initially, there were three meaningful choices: Bush, Gore or Nader. Now that all the leading Muslim political organizations have unanimously decided to endorse Governor George Bush, the other two choices are no longer available within the framework of a bloc voting strategy. As Muslims, we should close ranks behind the unanimous decision and vote for Governor Bush. This is in conformity with the teachings of our scholars.

It is no secret that many American Muslims prefer to vote for Democratic party candidates. There are also many Muslims who have no faith in either Democrats or Republicans. They would either vote for Nader or not vote at all. Many of these Muslims feel uncomfortable with the decision to support George Bush. The remainder of this essay briefly addresses their concerns in the hope that they will be persuaded to vote with the rest of the Muslim community.

APPEAL TO MUSLIMS WHO TRADITIONALLY VOTE DEMOCRATIC

To those who may prefer to vote for Al Gore (and this includes many of our African-American brothers and sisters, who traditionally vote Democratic), let us acknowledge that you have valid concerns on issues such as the economy, education, gun control, more liberal immigration, cleaner environment, and many others. But please balance these concerns with the foreign policy that Al Gore is likely to pursue. Now that some of the details have begun to emerge about the so-called "peace process" which the Clinton administration has pursued in the Middle East for the last eight years (even some leading rabbis who were initially great supporters of the peace process, have called it a "cruel hoax" for the Palestinians), we know how bad Clinton has been for Muslims and Arabs in the Middle East. It is reasonable to expect that Al Gore will be a lot worse. Under four (and possibly eight) more years of a Gore-Leiberman administration, completely beholden as it will be to the Israeli lobby, the Israelis will completely change the character of the West Bank to complete their ethnic cleansing.

APPEAL TO MUSLIMS WHO
MAY WISH TO VOTE FOR NADER

Many Muslims might prefer to vote for Nader in the hope of helping him reach the threshold of five percent of the votes cast, thereby making his party eligible for federal matching funds in future campaigns. It is not clear what would be accomplished even if Nader qualifies for matching funds. The history of third parties in this country is not very encouraging. The hijacking of Ross Perot's Reform party by Pat Buchanan is only the most recent case in point.

Many Muslims also find Nader's radical and idealistic positions very appealing. As an example, he calls for a complete cut-off of aid to Israel. However, it can be argued that Nader can afford to be so idealistic and radical precisely because he has no chance of winning the election. If it were a close three-way race, Nader would probably sound a lot more like Al Gore or George Bush.

Recently, Ralph Nader has begun appealing to liberal voters to vote for him in states where Gore is far ahead of Bush. He argues that this could help him attain five percent of the votes without jeopardizing Gore's chances of winning the election. Some Muslims believe that they should follow a similar strategy as well. Thus, for example, in Massachusetts where Bush has no chance of winning, they are inclined to vote for Nader. Unfortunately, this seriously undermines the objective of presenting the Muslims as a disciplined voting bloc. Please stay away from this temptation.

Finally, let us acknowledge that the unanimous decision to vote for George Bush does not mean that he is the ideal candidate from the standpoint of American Muslims. The only things we can say for sure are that he actively sought the endorsement of Muslims, that he seemed sympathetic to their concerns and was even willing to articulate some of these concerns in the nationally televised debates. How this will translate into actual policy if he is elected cannot be ascertained at this stage. It is even impossible to say what changes, if any, will come about in US Middle East policy if Bush is elected. What we do know, however, (and so does Gov. Bush, for sure) is that the American Jewish Community twice voted overwhelmingly in favor of his father's opponents (Michael Dukakis in 1988 and Bill Clinton in 1992), and will again vote overwhelmingly in favor of his opponent. If elected, therefore, he should feel no obligation to the Israeli lobby, and may prove to be open-minded towards Muslim concerns.

CONCLUSION

In the final analysis, the best hope for changes in U.S. policy so that it deals fairly with issues of concern to Muslims, both domestically and overseas, is a strong community of American Muslims, perceived as disciplined, willing and able to fight within the constitutional framework for its concerns. God willing, the bloc vote strategy proposed by the American Muslim leadership will help us achieve that status. The leadership has done their part. It is now up to us to follow their lead. May God help us all.

The paper was also posted on the business Web site of "Sound Vision," managed by Abdul Malik Mujahid. Motivated and concerned Muslims even dug into American history to highlight the fact that by just one vote history was made, and to expand on the statement "what a difference *one vote* can make."

In 1776 - one vote made English the official language of America instead of German.

In 1845 - one vote brought Mexican Texas into the American Union.

In 1868 - one vote prevented Andrew Johnson from being impeached.

In 1876 - one vote elected Rutherford Hayes as U.S. president.

In 1876 - one vote changed France from a monarchy to a republic, and

In 1923 - one vote gave Adolf Hitler the leadership of the Nazi party.

In order to be fair, pertinent information on Ralph Nader was also being circulated to Muslims. The data was mostly extracted from sites such as:

Nader Declares Candidacy http://www.nader2k.com

Nader, Ralph - The Nader Page http://www.nader.org/

Ralph Nader is a consumer advocate, lawyer, and author. He was born in Winsted, Connecticut on February 27, 1934.

In 1955 Ralph Nader received an AB magna cum laude from Princeton University, and in 1958 he received a LLB with distinction from Harvard University.

He began his career as a lawyer in Hartford, Connecticut, in 1959, and from 1961 to 63 lectured on history and government at the University of Hartford. In 1965-66 he received the Nieman Fellows award and was named one of 1967's ten Outstanding Young Men of the Year by the U.S. Junior Chamber of Commerce. Between 1967 and 68 he returned to Princeton as a lecturer and he continues to speak at colleges and universities across the United States.

In his career as consumer advocate, Mr. Nader founded many organizations, including the Center for Study of Responsive Law, the Public Interest Research Group (PIRG), the Center for Auto Safety, Public Citizen, Clean Water Action Project, the Disability Rights Center, the Pension Rights Center, the Project for Corporate Responsibility and *The Multinational Monitor* (a monthly magazine).

Ralph Nader has been called one of America's most effective social critics. He also has been called everything from muckraker to consumer crusader to public defender. His documented criticism of government and industry has had widespread effects on public awareness and bureaucratic power. He is the "U.S.'s toughest customer" as *Time* magazine noted. His inspiration and example have galvanized a whole population of consumer advocates, citizen activists and public interest lawyers, who in turn have established their own organizations throughout the country.

The crusading attorney first made headlines in 1965 with his book *Unsafe at Any Speed*, a scathing indictment that lambasted the auto industry for producing unsafe vehicles. The book led to congressional hearings, and a series of automobile safety laws passed in 1966.

CHAPTER 5   *Phil the Barber*

[Reality check and how Muslim Americans are being perceived by other minorities].

A good source of information and a different viewpoint, I am told, can be readily obtained by chatting with a bartender. Another, equally good source is the town barber. Both offer friendly conversation to every customer they serve, and both hear a lot of information about town goings-on. In my home town, that responsibility falls on the shoulders of Philip J. Evangelous, the town barber.

Every town has an icon, and in ours Phil is just that. Unlike his namesake in Punxsutawney Pennsylvania, Westborough's Phil is often right on target. Born in 1942 to Bessie and John, both of Greek heritage, in Marlborough, Massachusetts, Phil moved to Westborough in 1987 and has been here ever since.

Phil is known for the breadth of his knowledge and his skill at conversation. You could talk to him about current affairs, sports, politics, Red Sox—even the New York Yankees, but that would leave him in a bad mood. I normally talk politics with him. How did he vote? How did the Greeks vote? Was there a Greek bloc vote? Other times I would relax, wait my turn and just listen to Phil talking to other customers.

My thirst for information—and the need for a haircut—brought me to Phil's place once again. And, like everyone else in the barbershop, I was anxiously awaiting my turn. Phil had owned the place for quite some time. "I have been here for 35 years," Phil once told me. "I am tired." He added jokingly, "I used to cut hair in the army." Phil served in the Army at Fort Dix, New York, from 1960 to 1962.

One of his clients agreed, "Uh huh. I can see why you are pretty handy with the shears." And that he was.

Phil's barbershop, located right in the center of town, looked out on the town rotary. The shop, sandwiched between a shoe repair shop and pizza parlor, shared a weathered blue awning with the shoe repair shop.

On any given day, most of the customers were youngsters. There were a few very good reasons for this customer base: Phil was good with kids and, besides cutting hair, he also sold baseball cards. Sometimes he would even give them away, "just for the satisfaction of making a kid happy."

"I told a 7 year old, take the cards—they are free," Phil revealed. "The kid gave me a suspicious look and said, 'if it's free it must be junk.' Coming from a 7 year old, that was refreshing not offensive."

Phil Evangelous, a proud Greek-American in his mid-fifties who stood a little over 5 feet, seemed to have a way with kids. He had his own bag of tricks. A black plastic spider tied to a string, a live ferret and a few Nintendo games the kids loved to play as they happily waited their—as they hoped for while playing—belated turn for a haircut.

"Sit down kiddo." Phil gestured to one of his young customers. "How do you want your hair cut?"

"Like my brother." Came the confident, knee jerk reply.

"You wanna look like your brother. You sure? You wanna look weird?" Phil paused for a second and continued on to say, "You don't wanna look like me?" Phil went on: "What's your name?"

"Sam."

"I like your name, Sam. My name is Phil. You like my name?"

"Yes."

"Smart answer, since I have the shears in my hand." Phil seemed to be a natural, enjoying every minute of the conversation. "The last kid who said no, I cut off his ear." Phil said as he reached under the chair, and brought up a jar filled with some kind of clear liquid, and a rubber ear floating in it. "See?"

I finally got into the chair.

"Your son was here last week for a haircut. He is a smart kid."

"He is in the *Who's Who among American High School Students*," I bragged to Phil. What father wouldn't?

"Wow."

"Two years in a row, and that's not easy to get."

"You got every right to be proud of him. He is going to UMass Amherst, I think that's what he said when he was here the last couple of times."

As Phil started to get his clippers ready, he wanted to know how I wanted my hair cut.

"Short. But leave enough on the top to hide the bald spot."

"You got a lotta gray showing."

"Yeh. Can you just cut the gray?"

Phil joined me in laughter as he started shearing the side of my head.

"I just saw you on TV, just the other day," Phil told me one day.

I was not surprised, because after 9/11 I *had* been on the news a lot. So I asked Phil to tell me what it was about. "I turned the television off the minute I saw you," Phil replied with a chuckle, "You were being interviewed for a convention."

It had been almost a month and a half, back in October when I was in San Jose attending the AMA's sixth annual national convention. It was during that time when I had conducted the press conference to which Phil was referring.

Phil shared his anger with me—the same rage as that of many Americans in describing the 9/11 attack. "Most absurd. This was an unprovoked attack on innocent people." I reminded Phil that the American Muslims, Islamic centers and Muslims all over the world have repeatedly condemned these attacks on strongest terms. They unequivocally called the attack "vicious and cowardly, an attack not only against human law but the divine law as well." Sadly, it's easier to get a person to listen to reason when they actually know you, a member of a minority group that isn't their own.

Phil the barber made use of every inch of his wall. There was not one spot on the wall that wasn't covered with either pictures or an old framed poster hung on a nail. You could hardly miss the sign from 1919 that hung on the wall. It announced the cost of a haircut as 25 cents, shampoo 25 cents and shave 15 cents. The sign bore authentication in the form of a statement inscribed on it: "Adopted by Local No. 389 J.B.I.U of A., Oct. 25, 1916."

One side of the wall is full of signatures and names of his customers. He calls that side his "wall of fame." The signatures and graffiti alike appear to be inscribed with great care, pride and respect. The wall on the opposite side is mostly covered with photos of his young customers. Some of the photos on the wall were crossed out with an X, which meant "the kid no longer comes here—he is Xed out." And believe me, you don't want to be Xed out of Phil's place. Other kids will make fun of you. "Ah ha, you've been Xed out. You know how kids are," Phil said with a gleam in his eye.

I started to look closely at the pictures hoping to find one of my son Yaser. At the same time, I wasn't quite sure how would I react if it was Xed out. There was no photo of Yaser to be found.

I remember a day about eight years ago, when I accompanied my son Amir to Phil's for a haircut. Phil had noticed that Yaser had stopped coming with me or with my wife Labiba.

"Is your other son angry at me?" Phil asked. "He hasn't been here in a while for a haircut."

I could not find the words to answer Phil, but said to myself, "you won't have to worry about him anymore for a haircut." What Phil did not know at the time was that Yaser had been diagnosed with leukemia, and one of the side effects of the chemotherapy was a complete loss of hair.

The regimen was so strong that it would leave Yaser's legs almost lifeless. I would have to carry him up the stairs to his bedroom. Then after a day or two, when the treatment's dire effect would wear off, he would go outside and play like a normal eight year old, completely unaware of the fatal consequences of the disease he had.

"How much time?" I managed to ask one day of our family doctor Ramesh Mundra, at UMass Memorial Medical Center in Worcester.

"Six to eight…," came the reply.

"Years?"

"Months."

CHAPTER 6   *Don't Miss the Bus*

*[Muslim experiences in Europe, intersecting of Muslim identity struggle
with Muslim identity struggle in the U.S., and how larger issues like
Kashmir began to insert themselves them into identity forming pro-
cesses].*

"You're planning on leaving tomorrow morning, *at nine?*" asked my
father, in apparent disbelief as everyone else in my family joined in
the laughter. All except my mother; whose dementia, a form of dis-
orientation similar to Alzheimer's disease, had depleted her mind of
its sense of timing.

"That will be a first," my younger brother joined in, laughingly.

If it were to actually happen, then it would be a first. I do not
recall ever leaving my parents' place in Montreal that early to return
back home to Massachusetts. Normally, we would spend the weekend or more, staying with my parents in the city, where the French
language was favored over English. Close to a hundred visits to
Montreal to date, and we would still find every excuse to extend our
stay a little longer. If we failed at that, we still were able to justify
waiting until just before dark to leave.

The following morning, we left Montreal shortly after ten instead
of nine; nevertheless, it was still uncharacteristically early. Normally,
we would still be sound asleep at this time. Of course, there was no
way that we could be back in time for the rally we wanted to attend.
It's roughly 330 miles between our point of origin to our destination—that is, if we were going to Westborough. We were headed
another 20 miles from there, to be in front of the City Hall in Worcester. The rally was scheduled to be over around 3:00 p.m. This was a
peace rally in support of the people of Kashmir. Lord Nazir Ahmed,
a native of Kashmir who was appointed to England's House of Lords
by the queen in 1998, the first Asian Muslim to become a member of
the House of Lords, was the main attraction and the keynote speaker.
"It's good that this happened on Sunday and the news will be out on
Monday. There would hardly be any coverage had this taken place
on Tuesday. The newspaper will be preoccupied with the coverage
of Tim McVeigh's death by lethal injection. Oklahoma will not be

the same after that," noted Anwar Kazmi, my predecessor in chairing the Massachusetts of the American Muslim Alliance.

By the time we got back, the rally attendees had already dispersed. I had missed the proverbial bus, even though I was really driving fast. "I bet you could not have turned those corners at this speed, if you were driving the van instead of the 190E," my son Amir Ali said with pride. He was instrumental in getting the Mercedes and he knew that.

Then what we were all worried about happened. A state trooper was just pulling up the side of the highway. I managed to hit the brakes long enough to bring the speed 20 miles an hour slower to approximately 70. "You are going to get a ticket," Labiba was quick to point out. Somehow, the minute you spot a state trooper on the highway, you get that sinking feeling. I had only gone a few yards further and out of sight when my son advised me to take the exit, "He will not be able to find us." This was not a good time to set a further bad example, so I declined his advice and told him that one must face the consequences for one's actions, not run away from them. Luck was with me: the trooper never followed.

Before we left for Montreal on June 11, 2001, I did get a chance to interview Lord Nazir Ahmed in the Westborough studio. Nazir was scheduled to stay in Massachusetts only for the weekend, and his time here was carefully scheduled. Right from the airport on Friday evening, he was driven to *WCAT* TV studio so that I could interview him before I left for Montreal.

Nazir Ahmed told the viewers that his mission to the United States was a multipurpose one. "I want to launch the 'Peace Bus' here in the United States. The bus has been traveling all across Europe, promoting the message of self-determination for Kashmir." Roger Talanian, Pakistan consulate aide, assured Nazir Ahmed that the bus will ride from Boston to Worcester, visiting Islamic centers on the way, and stop in front of "Historic Worcester City Hall," where the rally for support of the Kashmiri's was to take place on Sunday.

During our interview, I pointed out to Nazir Ahmed how the Muslim bloc vote in United States played a pivoting role in electing George Bush, and followed that with a question as to what part the Muslims of England played in the recent landslide victory for Tony Blair. Lord Ahmed admitted there was no bloc vote, and that their voting is different from the United States. "Why? You do not recount votes there?" I said laughingly. "And we do not have judges decide who the winner is, either," Lord Ahmed was quick to add.

Shahid Ahmed Khan, an activist and an executive member of the "Pakistan Congress" had been instrumental in arranging this visit. At the end of the interview recording, he joined us in the studio and congratulated us for a fine interview, especially well done since we had no prior preparation. Lord Nazir took a copy of the tape with my permission, to show it in England and Pakistan.

Saturday afternoon, Nazir Ahmed met with students from MIT, Harvard and Tufts, and gave a lecture on "The Human Rights Crisis in Kashmir and Prospects of Peace," at Harvard University. The same evening he spoke at a fund-raising dinner in the Islamic center in Sharon. Dr. Muzammil Siddiqi, president of ISNA, spoke at the fund-raiser, as well.

Most of Nazir's day on Sunday was spent riding the 'Peace Bus,' traveling from Boston to various Islamic centers in Massachusetts, to the rally that I missed right in front of Worcester City Hall.
Lord Ahmed took an early Monday morning flight out of Logan back to England. He thanked the Muslim community for their ardent support and great hospitality. I may have missed the bus, but did get a chance to talk to the reporter who had covered the rally. I have included some excerpts from the leading newspaper in central Massachusetts, the Worcester *Telegram & Gazette*, now owned by *The New York Times:* (http://www.telegram.com/news/east/ kashmir.html)

At the rally, Lord Ahmed had called on the U.S. to help realize a 1949 U.N. resolution for Kashmir to hold a plebiscite (a vote by which the people of a country express an opinion on an issue) to choose its form of government.

"Peace between the two countries can only happen when the Kashmiri people have the right of self-determination," he said. "There are 700,000 Indian soldiers involved in a war against the Kashmiri people. Our message has come to Worcester. The U.S. is the most influential country in the world. Let us not spend money for nuclear weapons, but for peace.

Lord Ahmed called for Amnesty International and the United States to investigate what he termed human rights abuses in his homeland, such as the killing of Kashmiris who speak out against Indian occupation. He expressed his wish that efforts such as the Peace Bus would continue across the United States, Europe and Asia, and urged citizens to contact their elected officials and the president in an effort to get the United States to help.

"After the British elections we decided to bring the Peace Bus here," he said. "There's a continuation of abuse that is not reported. We're asking the American people. If democracy is good enough for America and Europe it is good enough for Kashmir...Our message is that the Kashmiri people should be involved in the talks. Surely the Kashmiri people have a right to their own future."

Anwar Kazmi, chairman of the American Muslim Alliance of Massachusetts, said the bus should now be in Kashmir instead of on another continent. "This is a reflection on the sad state of affairs that the route has to be so convoluted," he said. "We hope and pray that one of these days the bus will arrive in Srinagar (the Kashmir capital)...in peace, and that people of all faiths can meet in peace."

Ghulam Nabi Fai, director of the Kashmiri-American Council in Washington, D.C., said that despite being the most populous democracy in the world, India has 700,000 military and paramilitary forces occupying Kashmir against the wishes of the Kashmiri people.

The article ended quoting me: "It's about time that the suffering of the people of Kashmir be put to an end. The solution must be demilitarization of Kashmir through the withdrawal of all outside forces, followed immediately by a plebiscite under U.N. auspices to determine the future status of Kashmir."

Nazir also said that the recent landslide re-election of British Prime Minister Tony Blair, a member of Lord Ahmed's Labor party, could aid efforts aimed at a plebiscite. I told the reporter that Nazir could play a pivotal role with Tony Blair's help, and where others have failed, perhaps Lord Ahmed could succeed with Mr. Blair's help.

CHAPTER 7   *White House Briefing*

[Mainstreaming of Muslim Americans and how some get threatened by this mainstreaming and seek to deny access to them].

The American Muslim Council (AMC) sent out a communiqué on June 18, 2001, indicating that Vice President Dick Cheney and Senior Policy Advisor Karl Rove would address the American Muslim Council's 10th Annual National Convention. This was supposed to be the first time in the history of the AMC Conventions that a U.S. vice president was to personally address an exclusively Muslim audience at the White House. The briefing was to highlight domestic and foreign policies of the Bush administration that were of interest to the American Muslim community.

It was part of the four-day AMC Annual Convention titled "American Muslims in Politics: From Dream to Mainstream," which reflected the increased involvement of American Muslims in U.S. politics at all levels.

I boarded the train at the Metro Park station in New Jersey in the wee hours of the morning. It was a bright day on Friday, the 22nd of June, 2001. This was a fast train; it got me into Washington, D.C, just after nine that morning.

"Do you think you can get me to the Old Executive Office Building before 10:00 a.m.?" I nervously asked the cab driver at the train station. "It is on 17th and Pennsylvania Avenue."

"Plenty of time," the cab driver replied as he cautiously pulled out of the cab line-up into the heavy traffic. I noticed his name, John E. Quansah, next to his picture on the taxi license that hung on the visor. He was dark skinned and spoke with a foreign accent. He told me later that he came to America eight years ago, from Ghana.

"John, how do you think the president is doing?"

"He is trying. Bush is a good man, but he is too conservative. But I think he will be okay," John was eager to add.

"You think so, in view of his party losing Senate majority?" I asked, in an effort to keep the conversation alive.

"Big change; he can't get his policies. It will be a big difference. Republican leaders did not handle Jeffords properly, that's why he defected. Who knows what the actual reasons are? He knows, nobody else knows." John opened up, "Now during Clinton's time, every person felt good about himself, you didn't think of losing your job."

"What about the affairs he had?" I sort of wanted to know how the cab driver would react to that comment.

"The gals were after him. And he sure made them happy," John rushed in to Clinton's defense. "Almost every body is doing it in Congress. A 24-year-old intern has been missing since two days from D.C. Her boyfriend is a congressman, and he's gotta wife."

After a few more blocks of driving through the streets of D.C., the taxi finally came to a halt in front of the Old Executive Office Building (known in the capital as the "OEOB").

"That will be six dollars."

I handed him seven and thanked him for getting me there on time. I was told by a confidential source who wishes to remain anonymous that the vice president was very particular about time. "He gets very angry if you arrive late to his meeting."

As it got close to 10:00 a.m., many of the officials—notably Aly Abuzaakouk and Yahya Basha of the American Muslim Council—appeared to be missing, and the people waiting in the meeting room appeared restless. It didn't take a genius to figure out that something was wrong. Anxiety and restlessness grew stronger as the minutes went beyond the hour, and no Dick Cheney. It's these moments that Jay Leno's jokes about Dick Cheney's weak heart really start to sink in and make sense.

Last time, when we were scheduled to meet the president for the *EID* [A Muslim holy day] dinner, it was the Monday when, not only was the East Coast brought to a standstill due to the snowstorm, but it was also one of the times Dick Cheney had to be rushed to a hospital on account of his heart. That *EID* dinner meeting never took place. Reportedly, it is now expected to take place sometime in July—of course, that remains to be seen.

"The vice president regrets not being able to make it..." Tim started to say, as he introduced his replacement speaker, a "*Shiate* Muslim," as she said when she introducing herself. Someone in the audience rightly pointed out, "You should not refer yourself as a '*Shiate* Muslim,' but a Muslim, lest this become a tool for divisiveness."

"You are right." She agreed.

She talked about the education bill, parental choice and how can non-profit schools benefit from the education plan.

Karl Rove entered the room briskly and stood at the podium. He paused for a moment, then started with his opening remarks, "Welcome to the 450 [the OEOB]. This is the largest meeting room." Karl talked briefly about the history of the building. "The OEOB was originally designed for three departments, the State, War and Navy. One by one, the three departments for which it was built outgrew the OEOB." I couldn't figure out what the letters OEOB stood for, until later it dawned on me when I noticed the same letters on our badges. The OEOB was designed by the supervising architect of the Treasury, Alfred Bult Mullett (1834-1890). He was never paid architectural fees, because the design of the building was not part of his job at the Treasury. Mullett ended up suing the government, lost his case and committed suicide in the same year *(source: Columbia Historical Society)*.

"It's a fantastic place to work in, the White House," Karl told the audience. "I have known the president for 24 hours. He is thoughtful, smart, funny and a good human being."

He went on to add, "when you go to meet him, better go prepared, because he knows his stuff."

Karl Rove had a lot of good things to say about his boss. "When he came into office with a 640-vote mandate from Florida, he laid out a thoughtful agenda for the future of America. The first piece of legislation on the Hill on Monday after he was sworn in was education."

" 'Time will be our ally,' the president told us as he put an emphasis behind his agenda. He was absolutely right about his instinct on time. The first week in office he introduced the 'Education Bill.' The second week, faith-based charity. The third week, tax cut. The fourth week, missile defense. The fifth week, social security modernization, and the sixth week, the medical reforms."

Karl Rove began to explain each of the items. "We are working on the education bill and desperately need your help to pass it." He asked us to get our representatives and senators to vote in favor of the bill. "President is for a strong accountability system in education." Rove illustrated his point: "If in Texas you have a failing school, the third week the principal is gone."

As he stressed the need for social security modernization, Karl, reflecting on the return of investment in the current social security plan, said, "You can put money in a mattress and get a better return."

Mr. Rove had time to take a few questions. Aly Abuzaakouk decided to read questions that had been provided to him.

My own questions were direct, "The Senate is vicariously balanced, hence election 2002 is crucial. As some people have commented, the outcome of the election will decide if Mr. Bush will be a one-term president or two-term president. In view of that we are wondering: what is your strategy for outreach and inclusion of minorities. And the second part of the question is regarding the Muslim bloc vote that went in favor of George Bush, and that played a pivotal role in his election. This has been well documented." At this point, I read aloud the headline from *The Metro West Daily News*: "Poll: Bush won support from first-time Muslim voters." "But so far not many Muslims have been appointed in the Bush administration. What is the reason for that?"

"We have a Muslim working for Dick Cheney," Karl replied, and he continued to identify by name a few more Muslims sitting in the audience who worked in the Public Liaison office and other areas of the government.

After attending the White House briefing, I headed toward the Cannon House Office Building to another appointment, with Congressman James McGovern. On the way the cab driver pointed out that the Senate was in session but not the House.

"You see the American flag on the top of the Hill, that means the Senate is in session. See that building over where there is no flag in the flagpole? That means the Congress is not in session. The cab driver, a Caucasian named John Crump, appeared to be quite astute politically, so I asked what he thought about Bush and his foreign policy.

"I don't think he knows what he is doing," John replied rather bluntly.

"You mean about the foreign affairs."

"No. Both domestic and foreign. He is not too swift," John said turning his head away from the road, toward me, before adding. "He's an alcoholic."

"No he's not; he dried out a long time back." It was my turn to defend the president.

"I wish Clinton would become the president for the third time," John said with a deep sigh.

"You really think things were fine when the Clintons were in the

White House?" I wanted to know.

"Yes, I do," came the emphatic reply as he stopped his cab in front of the Cannon house office.

As I paid the fare, he stretched out his hand to shake mine. "You a reporter? Now don't get me in trouble because I said all those things about the president of the United States," John said, slightly worried.

"Don't worry about it." I reassured him and started to walk toward the building as a lady passenger got in John's cab and he drove off, not knowing that I was among those who convinced the American Muslims to vote en-bloc for George W. Bush. "Come on Bush, you are killing me. You are killing me," I muttered silently as I started to scale the steps leading to the Cannon House Office Building.

I would have gotten inside the building much earlier, if it were not for talking to an anchor woman/reporter from *Fox News*. She was very anxious to find out what had transpired at the White House briefing. I had to respectfully decline from making any comments except that we were disappointed that the vice president did not show up, but we understood. These last-minute changes come with the territory when you are dealing with such high-profile politicians. She asked why I was not willing to go on camera.

"It's because they asked us not to. We were told that these briefings are of a private nature and not for media. I would consider it unethical to disregard the wishes of our White House hosts."

She kind of gave me the look that there was more to it than met the eye. Maybe I was camera shy.

" Believe me, that's the only reason—although I don't think there was much said that seemed confidential. I have been on Fox News before. Eric Shawn interviewed me last year during the Clinton-Lazio Senate race, the race that got ugly over the fund-raiser in Boston."

"I remember that."

"Guess who was the chairman of the American Muslim Alliance in Massachusetts at that time."

"You!"

"Bingo. Tell Eric I said hello."

Representative James McGovern was very cordial and happy to see a constituent. I briefly mentioned the reason for my visit to D.C., the White House briefing, and then discussed several issues at length with him. I was wondering what the congressman's stand or willingness was to have a large "tent" policy where there was room for all of us, regardless of our ethnic or economic background.

"I am a strong supporter of the large tent policy," came the reply. "My obligation as a representative is not to some people, but all people, even outside my constituency. I may not agree with every committee member, but I have an obligation to listen to them." The congressman paused for a second and then continued, "When I met with you and others in Worcester a few months back [January, 2001], 80 percent of what we discussed we agreed upon, 10 percent of what we discussed we disagreed on and on the other 10 percent I am still forming an opinion.

"Another thing, I tell you: I don't care what your ethnic background is. It is important to be engaged [in action]...I have a big district, this is a big country. This is a big world...It is important for me to seek out information and also for you to bring out the information to me."

I started to explain the Hillary Clinton-Lazio Senate race and how it got out of hand over the controversy of the Boston fund-raiser. And how she rushed to judgment, without first verifying the accusations made against the AMA leader. She panicked. But Lazio played the race card and had sunk even deeper.

I told McGovern that it was difficult for Muslims to understand what the New York race had to do with Israel, or why anybody — or a political group that opposes Israel — is forced out of the political arena. I wanted to know if it was right that political disagreement be used as a reason for disqualifying people in politics and/or public debate.

"Absolutely not. I disagree with a lot of people I like, and also agree with a lot of people I dislike. But I am entitled to listen to them. It's an important part of democracy."

The Congressman then admitted, "The problem that faces the Muslims in the United States, is that so much misinformation is put out into the mainstream media. Lack of understanding of issues...There is a greater discrimination against Muslims just because they are Muslim — and that's wrong. Their civil rights must be protected."

"Congressman, let me ask you the questions that were posed to Karl Rove at the White House briefing this morning. The Senate is vicariously balanced. As some people have commented, the outcome of election 2002 will decide if President Bush will be a one-term president or two-term president. Given that, what should be the strategy for outreach and inclusion of minorities? Of course, Congressman, I did remind them of the bloc vote in favor of Bush."

"Here I disagree with the American Muslims, in the bloc vote."

"Well, the idea was not to vote for A or B, the idea was to show that American Muslims can unite together and vote *en bloc.* A unity of purpose. Why Bush? Because he talked of undoing the secret evidence law. And…"

"They are not dedicated to protecting civil rights." McGovern interrupted. "Does the President or Dick Cheney know about the bloc vote?"

"Yes, it is known at the presidential level, and by his cabinet members. But not much at the Republican party level."

"They talk the talk, but they do not want to walk the walk." McGovern was quick to add.

"We missed you last week, when Lord Nazir Ahmed of Rotherham was in Worcester on his Peace Bus ride. I was hoping to connect with you. But I am wondering: would you be able to take a ride on the Peace Bus in England, just for a weekend?"

"Not until end of July — my wife is expecting, and I am not budging anywhere."

Daniel Holt, the representative's scheduler, entered the office and told the congressman that his flight was delayed due to the storm.

"There is a storm in Boston?" I wondered aloud.

"I am headed out to Cuba tonight." The congressman said.

I thanked the congressman. And, as I started to leave, I heard him say, "We can do more of this in our district."

It was at the AMA meeting in January 2001, where I formally met Congressman McGovern for the first time, in our own district, in Worcester, Massachusetts. His comment meant that we could take time to discuss matters more fully when we were back at home.

That January meeting was a fulfillment of the AMA's resolve to initiate a series of meetings with local and national politicians. As its chairman I had welcomed the congressman on behalf of the American Muslim Alliance. That was the first time we told James McGovern the important work the AMA has been doing, specifically raising the political awareness among American Muslims. "The results speak for themselves; today we see them participate and portrayed as mainstream," Dr. Khaled Abdel Kader, trustee of the Islamic Society of Greater Worcester, pointed out.

Representative James McGovern spent more than two hours with the community that day, and seemed to enjoy the Middle Eastern and Asian cuisine. Muttasem Razzaq, the AMA's Director of Community Development hosted the meeting at his home in Worcester. Although a born citizen of the United States, he felt strongly about the Palestine issue — especially because his parents originally came from Palestine. Muttasem's comments made sense, "But, by far, the most important impression we wanted to leave him with is our dismay with U.S. foreign policy vis-a-vis the Palestine issue. We wanted to show the congressman that we come from varied backgrounds and nationalities, and yet this is something we are unanimous on."

Earlier in that meeting, commenting on the issue of Palestine, McGovern pointed out, "Fifty-three years later, it's still a referee issue."

Responding to the potential election of Ariel Sharon, the community showed discontent, and McGovern was asked to describe what America's position would be, given Ariel Sharon's hard-line policy toward the Palestinians.

McGovern chose his words carefully and said, "He needs to recast himself very differently from what he is projecting himself as."

At the time, Dr. Khalid Sadozai was the president of the Islamic Society of Greater Worcester (ISGW). He was originally from Pakistan and had recently moved to Massachusetts from Seattle, Washington. His roots were in Northern Pakistan, which is quite close to Afghanistan. He spoke the language of the Afghanis, Pushto, very fluently. He brought up the issue of profiling and how it affects those who travel a lot. Dr. Khaled Abdel Kader joined in as he referred to the Secret Evidence Law. The Congressman was certainly prepared for this one, as well. He told the community, "I gave a speech in favor of the 'repeal of the Secret Evidence Law,' referring to 'Bonior-Campbell resolution HR2121.' "

On the military budget and foreign policy, McGovern said, "There still is cold war foreign policy even though the cold war is over. The budget for weapons is great in America, it is much too large in terms of practicality."

Responding to a question about the sanctions against Iraq, McGovern was very quick to add, " I am against them."

Farooq Ansari, former AMA chairman, stressed the need for recognizing Muslim holidays, excusing Muslim students and not marking them tardy or absent. Here again, McGovern came out strong as he showed his willingness to help in this area, and to set up meetings with the school superintendent. Congressman McGovern really took the community by surprise when he offered his help to set up similar meetings with other representatives.

Someone warned the congressman and his District Director, Gladys Rodriguez Parker at the dinner table, "Watch out, the food could be spicy." "That's how I like it." Evidently this was not his first experience with hot and spicy food.

As McGovern was leaving that night, I told him of the Muslim bloc vote for Bush. Sensing a discomfort in him, Dr. Mohammed Mushtaque pointed out that Al Gore ignored us completely.

"We will have to pay more attention to the American Muslim next time." James McGovern said reassuringly as he stepped out.

I knew that our community enjoyed this meeting. He left us still talking about it after he was long gone. We came out of the meeting much reassured and found the congressman very accommodating. It was quite evident that James McGovern enjoyed this meeting, as well. In fact, it was he who suggested that we should meet on a regular basis.

Isa Mujahid, the AMA's secretary, indicated that the congressman really was at ease, because he not only talked about our issues, but also spoke at length about some of the things that were on his mind, like improvements in Worcester Airport, Union Rail Station, his concern about the transportation of nuclear waste through his city, and things like that.

We decided to meet with the congressman on a quarterly basis. Our goal was clear: to get at least one Muslim intern appointed in each of the ten congressional districts. We thought that McGovern could be instrumental in making this happen, more so because he only had good words about Samira Khan, a graduate in political science and an intern in his office.

We took notice then that McGovern had plans to run for the Senate seat that John Kerry will vacate. The senator reportedly had aspirations of his own. He had his eyes set on the White House.

One of the congressmen James McGovern had talked very highly of at the meeting was Joe Moakley of South Boston. It was because of this admiration for Moakley that James McGovern was now flying out to Cuba. He wanted to hand deliver to Fidel Castro a letter that was written by the late Moakley.

I told McGovern that some of the Muslim community members,

myself among them, attended Representative Joe Moakley's funeral service. It was exactly three weeks ago and still very vivid.

Representative Joe Moakley

The keel of the bagpipes on a sunny 67-degree day in South Boston would have you almost believing that you were in Ireland or Scotland. Several hundred watched as men in uniform carried the remains of Representative Joe Moakley into St. Brigid's Church on Broadway Street.

Friends, family and politicians were already seated in the church, When — almost silently, amidst the hustling and shuffling, and men in black talking into their sleeves — President George W. Bush emerged. He cautiously walked down the aisle, greeted by Acting Massachusetts Governor Jane Swift. He reached over to shake hands with Senator Edward M. Kennedy, then quietly sat next to Jane. He acknowledged with a wave and a nod those sharing the front pew with him — Victoria Kennedy, Former Vice President Al Gore, Representative David Bonior, Former President William Clinton and House Minority Leader Richard Gephardt.

Former President Clinton said of Joseph J. Moakley, "He brought a certain nobility and meaning to public life." Clinton rightly pointed out, "They are all here because of him."

Farooq Mirza and I were among the many at the funeral. "I am glad that we are here; lots of people are here to pay their last respects to the congressman. The TV Channel 56 anchorwoman talking to Tahir appeared in a somber mood as she and the camera crew moved nervously closer to the church to get a better shot," observed Farooq Mirza, an executive member of the Massachusetts of American Muslim Alliance.

Anwar Kazmi, chairman of the Massachusetts AMA, had already paid a visit a day before to the State house where Moakley's casket rested, wrapped in Old Glory. "Quite a few people attended the wake. I signed the register, however, I plan to send a letter of condolence to Moakley's family, on behalf of the Alliance," Kazmi stated.

Representative Joe Moakley of the 9th district in South Boston was known to his constituents as a kind man who always had time to listen. He elevated politics and the lives of many. Moakley succumbed to leukemia at the age of 74, on Memorial Day. William Bulger, president of the University of Massachusetts, offered a befitting eulogy to the "champion of the people," as Thomas Menino, the mayor of Boston remembered Joe Moakley.

I reminded Congressman James P. McGovern, sitting on the pew behind the president, that he called Moakley as his "mentor" in one of our meetings. James McGovern remembered saying that, and then some. "I did not follow the funeral procession to Castle Island or the cemetery in Braintree," Farooq Mirza told me. Nor did I, because that way we were able to get to the Islamic center in Wayland in time to offer our Friday prayer behind Talal Eid, the *Imam* or clergy from the Islamic center of New England.

"This is public relations, it is important. You went there as a good gesture," Talal Eid assured Farooq Mirza after the Friday prayer.

"I think Moakley was an excellent person to represent all citizens of Massachusetts. We hope that other politicians follow his example," said Dr. Karim Khudairi a biology professor at Northeastern University. " I think to have a Muslim representative at the funeral and the wake is an excellent thing to do."

"This is proactivism at its best. Keep it up," urged Dr. Abdul Cader Asmal after learning that the AMA participated. Dr. Asmal informed us that he himself had represented the Islamic Council of New England (ICNE) at the vigil the previous day, as well.

Dr. Mian Ashraf, who has been recognized numerous times for his community service, could not have agreed more, "I wish my health would allow me to continue what you are doing."

Dr. Syed Asif Razvi, president of the Wayland Islamic center and professor of Vascular Surgery at Tufts University remarked, "When we want to remain politically active we need to show up and, more importantly, make our presence known."

Our Muslim presence was indeed known. The Worcester *Telegram & Gazette* and *The Metro West Daily News* interviewed us. The *Boston Globe* quoted my message clearly: "A few months back when I met Congressman McGovern, I remember he was speaking highly of Joe Moakley. I had never met that congressman, but I attended his funeral. After talking to many, I realized he really was the people's congressman. McGovern was right. Trust and loyalty was what he was all about. He truly represented all regardless of their religion or ethnic background." The message ended with: "American Muslim Alliance, Westborough."

{http://www.boston.com/news/daily/29/moakley_board/ messages7.shtml}

The Moakley funeral motorcade had made its way to Blue Hill Cemetery in Braintree, where John Joseph Moakley was laid to rest next to his wife, Evelyn, who had also died of cancer, in 1966. A mourner was overheard saying, "He will be missed, but not forgotten," a sentiment quite obviously shared by many.

CHAPTER 8   *Gideon's Way*

[Today Muslim voters are the brand new political constituency in American politics].

It was by chance that I met Rabbi Gideon M. Goldenholz in Toronto, in the summer of 2001, at the Regal Constellation Hotel near Toronto International Airport. It was a nice day, July 14th. My family and I were there to attend a relative's wedding and the rabbi was one of the speakers at the Convention for the International Federation of Jewish Men, also known as "the Men's Club," which was being held in the next room.

I recall having a conversation earlier that day with Mannan Qureshi, a professional engineer at the Department of Public Works in Fairfax County, Virginia, who was also a guest at the wedding.

"Did you know that the Jews have the inclination to live near their synagogues more than the Muslims desire to live near their mosques?" Mannan asked rhetorically. I was not quite sure where he was coming from, so I allowed him to elaborate on the remark he had made. "If the Muslim community lived close to each other, then we could be even more effective when it comes to getting a message across quickly. A more effective implementation of a resolve. Like the bloc vote, for example."

I could not disagree.

"Can the Muslim leaders and community in general claim for sure that the bloc vote message was received by over 95 percent of the American Muslim voters?" he asked.

I was curious to see if he really knew why the Jewish community might live in the proximity of their synagogues. "Because they are required to walk to their synagogues. And for the same reason, the Israeli airlines do not fly on Saturdays," came the abrupt but confident reply.

Rabbi Gideon and other members of the Jewish community attending their convention appeared fascinated by the wedding celebration going on just a few steps away. On the way to their hotel rooms or to the garage, most of the convention guests could not help noticing the ladies at the wedding, who were all dressed up in traditional flashy, sparkling lace-detailed dresses. Some passersby even took a moment to peek in from the hall entrance. I could not help overhearing one Jewish couple praising the jewelry on some of the ladies, especially the bride.

"Is it traditional for everyone to wear those fancy dresses and the fine jewelry, at Muslim weddings?"

"This is a joyous occasion. This is a Pakistani wedding. This is normal in such weddings," one of the guests at the wedding explained.

"The bride is beautiful." I heard her saying, when I noticed a gentleman looking in with interest. I approached him and joined in appraising the situation, taking the role of host and trying to help him feel more comfortable. He introduced himself as Rabbi Gideon and he seemed quite relaxed. As we talked, I found him an interesting conversationalist, so I asked if he would like to join us, and assured him he would love the food. I reminded him that, this being a Muslim wedding, the food was *halal,* which he could consider kosher.

When I wondered which part of Canada he was from, he replied, "I am originally from Milwaukee."

I told him that I was from Boston. Dr. Gideon M. Goldenholz informed me that he was a rabbi at the Beth El Synagogue in Mequon, Wisconsin. He was very much into interfaith activities and was president of an interfaith clergy association. I found out later that he was held in very high regard as a scholar and an authority among his own colleagues. He was also president of the Wisconsin Council of Rabbis.

When I felt at a loss figuring out what he meant in reference to Sacred Heart Seminary and being an adjunct professor there, he told me, "It's a Catholic seminary for priests."

The rabbi also explained to me that the equivalent of the "Men's Club" is the "National Sisterhood." "Spouses are allowed to come, but most don't. For the ones who do, we arrange alternate programs, like visiting shopping malls, theatres, etc."

I found Dr. Gideon Goldenholz to be a very cordial and pleasant man. He's not what I thought your traditional rabbi would be. He was clean shaven, dressed in a simple but elegant manner, average in height, about 5'10", and if it weren't for the *kippa* covering the back of his head, he would not be taken as a Jew. Now was as good time as any to confirm the observations Mannan Qureshi had made earlier, I figured. I asked the Rabbi if it was all right if I plied him with questions, for use in my writings. The rabbi was more than w lling.

We had hardly sat down at a table inside the hall when a few men from the convention came looking for Gideon. "Rabbi. They need you inside for a group photo."

As Gideon walked out with them, he turned toward me and said, " ̄ will be back."

Scarcely ten minutes had elapsed, when he returned. This time we decided to sit at a table in the hallway outside the wedding room's hall. I started telling Rabbi Gideon about my earlier conversation: that Muslims, unfortunately, did not live near their houses of worship as much as the Jewish community seemed to.

"The traditional Jew tries to live within a close proximity of the synagogue; they need to be within walking distance," he told me. "First, to fulfill the requirement for the Sabbath, we are not allowed to drive to Sabbath services. Second of all, when everybody lives closer to the synagogue, a very close community bond is created, where people can relate to each other and reinforce faith, and help to maintain the uniqueness and identity of their Jewish faith. And also to maintain cultural ties and social contacts."

"Not everyone can live near the synagogue," I interjected.

"The next level is the conservative-moderate level; some of the people live nearby and some drive," Gideon added. "Liberals have no concern at all in building a community and neighborhood. Liberal Jews absolutely don't care."

"Are you sure you want me to write this? You won't get into any trouble?" I asked the rabbi sincerely.

"I won't," he assured me, before explaining more. "Ten percent are very traditional. About thirty to forty percent are conservative-moderate observers [of the traditional Jewish rules]. The rest, fifty to sixty percent, are usually called reformed, and many of this percentage are secular. In other words, they don't have any [Jewish] religious values, and no contact with our faith."

At this point I was asking myself whether or not this distribution of faith among the Jewish community is in complete alignment with the Muslim community. I wanted the rabbi to elaborate more, sort of enlighten me as to how he had arrived at those numbers. Was there a poll conducted? Was there a pattern?

"There is a pattern if you look at the country of origin," Gideon started to explain.

"Israel?" I thought aloud.

"No. It can be any country in East Europe or Russia," the rabbi corrected me. "First generations that have come over tend to be traditional. Second and third generations start to become less. And people…"

Before Gideon could finish his sentence, some of the conventioneers who were returning to their rooms or leaving the hotel stopped by our table and started congratulating him for a well-delivered speech.

"Rabbi, thanks for the views you have expressed. I was really glad that you pointed out some lessons," one of them said, shaking the rabbi's hand vigorously.

In the midst of those high compliments and praise, I hastened to write down what had transpired between Dr. Gideon and me. "Just in case," I told myself, "he loses his train of thought when we resume our talk."

He began again, "Sorry about that. As I was saying, people who came from North African countries: Morocco, Libya, Syria, Persian Iran, Iraq and Turkey have a tendency to be more religious. They are the first generation."

I told him the same probably is true for Muslims who are coming to America for the first time from any of the Muslim countries. But clearly there are varying degrees of practice among Muslims. Not all are practicing Muslims; and for some religion is a habit, rather than the way of life. I was learning that the people of the Torah were no different when it comes to actually practicing their religion. A practicing Muslim ought to pray five times a day, fast during the month of Ramadan, and perform a pilgrimage to Mecca if he or she is financially and physically able to do so. I did not feel the need to go on. Rabbi Gideon was well aware of the five pillars of Islam.

"We also have a resurgence of tradition. It's a new phenomenon. This is the fourth generation that has rediscovered their tradition. There's another phenomenon too: fourth or fifth go back to moderate."

"No fundamentalism?" I asked of him.

"There is a growing fundamentalism, a kind of super tradition. But people who are the fifth generation or so in America, who have become very assimilated and then become ultra-traditional." Gideon was giving fundamentalism an alias: ultra-tradition.

"It's not a Jewish phenomenon only. I think it's global." He paused for a while, then changed the subject to materialism. "It's a kind of a cyclic thing. There is a drift away from spirituality and an increase in materialism."

People who stopped at our table and talked to the Rabbi probably thought I was a reporter of some sort. I had my notebook and was busy writing, though I did not look the part, with a dark colored suit on. The rabbi wore a black suit. Neither of us had a beard; neither of us was in our respective religious attire.

"I see something else happening and it is very sad — people who have left the tradition and have become secular. Then they start looking for spirituality, but then they may find it elsewhere. They find new gods, the god of success. They find Christianity. They find Eastern religions like Hinduism, Buddhism."

I noticed the rabbi left out Islam.

"You find a Jewish boy who is assimilated and meets a Christian girl who is assimilated. What happens to their children?" Gideon asked with a sigh.

"Do you discuss politics in these conventions?" I asked him. "No." was the quick reply. "The traditional ten percent mostly have nothing to do with U.S. politics, but the media loves to hear their opinions — and uses them. But the liberal is always making a lot of noise in the Jewish community. …Moderate Jews, nobody hears about them."

These are the forty percent-ers, I remembered aloud.

"Good. You recall correctly." Gideon was apparently pleased. "The liberals in reality do not represent the Jewish point of view. They use the mainstream political structure as if it's some kind of religious awareness, which it is not."

Once again I asked if he was sure he wanted me to print that. The rabbi was sure. He knew he was not making any of this up. "What does the media like to do? They like to exacerbate whatever tensions may exist." Rabbi Gideon remained calm and in complete control of his emotions as he shared his observations, "I see that people of faith can get along." He had a point there. One of the reasons could be simply because they agree to disagree.

Using the term "political football," he elaborated: "A person becomes politically charged and politically motivated. This can become a highly charged and potentially explosive situation." Turning his attention to the Middle East crisis, Gideon remarked, "Terribly sad. Good people on both sides that want to live in peace. But there are a few that live by the gun, pushing their extreme views."

"On both sides?" I wanted to know.

"Absolutely."

I asked if he was aware of the Muslim bloc vote in this U.S. presidential election.

"That's the way America should be run. It's a healthy thing to do," was Gideon's response and, as he waved to the passing conventioneers in acknowledgement, he added, "If you look at every interest group, when you have a voting bloc, that's what acts as a check and balance."

I was curious and asked the rabbi if he knew how his community voted in the U.S. presidential election.

"All over the place." His response was almost immediate.

I pointed out to him that Senator Joseph Lieberman's candidacy, must have had some effect.

"No effect." He remarked assuredly, "There were many in the Jewish community who believed that Bush is the answer to economic and global issues. There used to be a Jewish bloc vote. Not any more."

We discussed at length how the Muslim community has become a target for bigotry since we have managed to get ourselves on the political map. Special attention was given to us, both bad and good during the New York Senate race between Hillary Clinton and Rick Lazio. I thanked the rabbi indirectly after telling him that it was most of the American Jews like himself that came to our rescue and spoke up in our behalf.

"Catholics were treated this way. American Jews faced the same..." Gideon thought for a second and stared at the ceiling before adding, "Every group trying to assert itself opens itself to criticism. You are the "new kid on the block" and will be attacked, be you Jews, Irish, Italians, Polish, etc....Unless you become part of the scenery, and then no one pays attention anymore. Then there will be another group just like yours, and it will have to go through what you all are going through now," he concluded.

That's correct, I thought: we are the new kid on the block. So fasten your seatbelts, we are in for a long bumpy ride.

CHAPTER 9   *Civil Liberties*

[How the issue of civil rights has had a long-lasting impact on the political identity of Muslim Americans].

The topic of civil rights is one that resonates deeply with the American public. We are very proud and very protective of our civil liberties, and we constantly discuss and debate their various aspects. Here, I will mention two recent talks on the topic of civil rights. One was given by Congressman David Bonior, and the other by me. These talks are interconnected and relate to the theme of this book.

At the time I had no idea that I would be writing this book.

The Muslim community in Massachusetts had the pleasure of participating in a fund-raiser for Congressman David Bonior of Michigan. The AMA-Net message read "Massachusetts Chapter Organizes Second Successful Fund-raiser in Two Months."

The other fund-raiser the message referred to was one for Hillary Rodham Clinton, the First Lady.

We asked Farooq Ansari to be the master of ceremonies, and to have Dr. Kimet Gul Khattak, former chairman of the AMA of Massachusetts, introduce the congressman. It was through Dr. Khattak's efforts that David Bonior had agreed to come to this event.

The dinner held July 16, 2000 at the Wyndham Hotel in Westborough was well attended. Members from neighboring states Connecticut, New Hampshire and Rhode Island had also turned out.

Dr. Mohammed Reda and Anwar Kazmi gave the community address. As the chapter's chairman, I talked about the AMA and its charter.

Congressman David Bonior had a small beard, with some gray showing. To most people, he came across as a soft-spoken but strong individual who would look straight into their eyes. He started by thanking us for hosting the event. Before reading from his prepared speech, he shared a story with the audience.

"There was this stonecutter who was hammering a huge rock in order to break it. He was hammering away, blow after blow, sweating all over and counting each blow loudly. His young son was watching his father toil away at the task ahead of him. Then, finally, at the 200th blow the rock cracked. The son asked, 'Father, why didn't you hit the 200th blow the first time?' The stonecutter smiled and replied, "It was not the 200th blow that cracked the rock, it was the 199 that came before that.' "

We all enjoyed that story. The American Muslims in the audience realized that, while they were far from reaching their 200th blow in the political arena, they were most certainly well past their first. But just how far were they?

As it happened, they didn't have to wait long for the answer to that question. The fund-raiser that we had just held a month back for Hillary Clinton gave rise to an unfortunate series of events beyond anything we could have imagined. We were in for a rude awakening, but at least we found out just how far away we were from that 200th blow.

David Bonior was relaxed at the podium; this was not the first time he had addressed a Muslim audience. It was, however, his first time in Massachusetts and the first time for most of us to hear him speak. He opened his prepared remarks with the Islamic greetings "*Assalaam-O-Alaikum,*" and continued from there.

"Before anything, there's something I want to say to all of you, and that's thank you for your support and for your activism. You're helping to give your community the voice it needs and deserves. That voice has never been heard more clearly than it is right now."

The audience could not help applauding enthusiastically. Bonior acknowledged the applause, and spoke again as soon as the sound of clapping died out. He had spearheaded the fight at the Capitol Hill against secret evidence and went on to talk about the Secret Evidence Law.

"A few weeks ago we won one of the clearest victories ever, when Congress voted overwhelmingly to pass an amendment against secret evidence." The congressman turned to face the TV camera, then added, "I spoke with a reporter from CNN who asked how I would assess the political influence of Muslims. I told her how Islam is the fastest growing religion in America...about the impact Muslims are having in Michigan and California, and here in New England...how we're even seeing Ramadan and other holidays finally being acknowledged by people no less important than the President himself."

Bonior continued, "Muslims may still have a ways to go to make sure your voices are heard. They ought to be; today you are light years ahead of where you began."

The audience and I were greatly encouraged. We had helped leg-islators understand what it means to be Muslims in America.

David Bonior talked about profiling, screening at airports and how Islam is misunderstood in the West. The American population are shown degrading images on TV, in movies and schoolbooks. "Though Islam is the faith of more than one billion people, in U.S., it's regarded as a criminal conspiracy waiting to happen." David added, " They learned about Mazen Al-Najjar, not as some political abstraction, but as a human being, a loving husband, a wonderful father, a good man trapped in a living hell."

He went on to say, "And it made a difference. One member of the Congress who came to vote against our amendment, not only did he vote with us, he spoke in favor of the amendment. And, you should know, that member is Jewish. But our victory on secret evi-dence isn't one to rest on. It's one to build on."

One of the happy coincidences about David Bonior for Muslims was that he was quite familiar with our religion. David Bonior intro-duced Resolution 174 in the House of Representatives to promote "religious tolerance and understanding of Muslims in America."

"The Prophet Mohammed taught: 'God does not judge according to your bodies and appearances, but He scans your hearts and looks into your deeds.' Sadly, many Americans too often fail to judge each other as God would judge us. I introduced the "religious tolerance resolution." I am going to keep fighting to get it passed." The con-gressman had clearly demonstrated an understanding for the issues confronting the Muslims in America. But he was not oblivious to the Muslims suffering the world over, either. "Our mission isn't only to win justice for Muslims here in America; it's to help make America a force for justice for Muslims around the world.

"The Qu'ran teaches: 'If they seek peace, then you seek peace. And trust in God for He is the one that heareth and knoweth all things.' "

Bonior's belief is that America must be a force for peace and should maintain its commitment to winning a comprehensive peace in the Middle East. He realizes, as many members of that audience did, that the embargo against Iraq has cost over half a million inno-cent lives, many of them children. "It's up to us to wipe the blood from America's hands and lift the embargo now!" the congressman stated firmly. The audience jumped on their feet in ovation.

Similarly, on the issue of Kashmir, he believed that the dispute over Kashmir had put two nuclear powers on a collision course. "America must be a force for peace, not a spectator to war."Bonior, a frequent visitor to Pakistan, said, "In April, I visited Pakistan, and Kashmir itself. I had the opportunity to meet with General Musharraf in Pakistan, as well as Kashmiri leaders. They share a deep commitment to peaceful settlement. By turning down a modest autonomy plan for Kashmir, India is accelerating the drift toward war."

In his concluding remarks, the Congressman struck home. "Through your activism, more Americans can better appreciate the beauty of Islam and Arab culture. They can learn that Islam promotes the equality of women not their subjugation, that Islam teaches respect for their faiths not their destruction, that while some leaders talk about family values, your community honors those values every single day."

Those remarks prompted a well-deserved standing ovation. The ladies in the audience were obviously very much in agreement with the congressman. Bonior once again allowed the members of the audience to settle down, before quoting from the Qu'ran. "The Qu'ran teaches: 'O mankind! We created you from a single soul, male and female, and made you peoples and tribes, so that you may come to know one another. Truly, the most honored of you in God's sight is the greatest of you in piety. God is all-knowing, all-aware."

Someone shouted *"Takbir,"* and the audience responded with *"Allah-O-Akbar."*

David Bonior continued on to say, "America was intended to be a nation of many peoples and many tribes. A pious nation where our differences are regarded not as a weakness, but understood to be the true source of our strength. A unique nation, which leaves no one on the outside looking in, and where everyone has a seat at the table. We are struggling to become that nation. But, with your help, we can be.

"Once we are, once men like Mazen Al-Najjar are freed from their imprisonment, only then will all of us be able to look our children in the eyes and say to them that America truly is one country, indivisible, with liberty and justice for all."

The congressman paused for a moment, then added, "That's the America I want my children to live in. With your help, I know we can build it…"

When the speech ended, the congressman received a standing ovation. On behalf of the American Muslim community I presented a plaque to him, acknowledging his stand for Muslims, continued support and for sponsorship of the H.Con. Res.174 and the H.R. 2121. I was kind of curious to know what the congressman himself had thought of the event, so later that day I asked Edward Welch, finance director for Congressman David Bonior, and he replied, "The congressman had a wonderful time, he was very appreciative of the generosity of everybody there."

The second time I had the pleasure of meeting up with David Bonior was at the Islamic Society of North America (ISNA) Convention 2000. Both of us were there to speak at different sessions. David Bonior was to speak during the prime time on Sunday. Other speakers joining him in this session were Dr. Agha Saeed, Congressman Campbell of California and Omar Ahmad, chairman of CAIR. It was in this session that Agha Saeed and the rest of the AMPCC leadership, along with ISNA's leadership Sayyid Syeed and Dr. Muzammil Siddiqi resolved to unite for a unity of purpose; acknowledging that if the American Muslims can make a difference in the U.S. election, it will have to be at the level of the presidential race and any other contest expected to be a close race. The leadership took a covenant from the audience. The audience jumped out of their seats clapping their hands vigorously, in apparent approval.

Next day, I delivered a talk on the hot topic of the "Secret Evidence Act." The fact that someone could be imprisoned on evidence that is kept secret not only from them but from their lawyers as well was a revolting thought for most Americans, but most disturbing to American Muslims, especially the immigrants. I was actually a surrogate speaker standing in for Abdurahman Alamoudi, who was equally as happy as I that I had agreed to fulfill his commitment to ISNA. "Brother Tahir, I will be rightly honored if you can represent me. I cannot think of anyone more fitting for that role than you."

So, come Monday morning, I headed toward the room where the session on "Muslims and Civil Rights" was to be held. Yahya Mossa Basha of Michigan, president of the American Muslim Council, moderated the session. I had not realized at the time that our paths would cross again in the days to follow. Nihad Awad of CAIR was the first speaker, who had to leave right after speaking to catch a plane. I noticed that the audience was growing. By the time it was my turn to speak, the room was surprisingly full for a Monday morning.

"Our next speaker, Tahir Ali, is the chairman of the American Muslim Alliance in Massachusetts. He is a former National Republican Delegate. Ali has represented the Governor of Massachusetts..."

I was a bit nervous as I stepped up to the podium, but relaxed a bit when I looked across the room and saw a few familiar faces in the crowd. The rest came out naturally, as I started in the name of Allah, the most beneficent and merciful...

> *Assalaam-O-Alaikum,*
> Brothers and Sisters,

I would like to thank Yahya Mossa Basha for the kind introduction. Let me confess that, while I have had the honor of twice representing William Weld when he was the governor of Massachusetts, today I feel even more honored for I am representing a true Muslim leader, Abdurahman Alamoudi. The notable difference between Abdulrahman Alamoudi and me is that he is slightly taller. [Alamoudi is almost a foot taller than I am.]

For a Monday morning, this is a pretty large crowd; it is the large size of this grand ballroom that diminishes the effective quality of this large turnout. Let's hear it for the audience!

The topic under discussion, "Muslims and Civil Rights," really needs our utmost attention. These matters are of great concern, as has been indicated by ISNA and the respected speakers on this panel. Quite a bit has been said on it already by Nihad Awad, Dr. Sami Al-Arian and Faisal Kutty, therefore I shall be brief and avoid redundancy.

I am going to divide my talk into three parts:

> 1.The Muslim role in the American civil rights movement
> 2.An analysis and a review of the current situation
> 3.What to do about it

Muslims have played a very prominent and major role in the American civil rights struggle. Allow me to name a few.

One of the two champions in the civil right movement of the 20th century, in the United States was AL-Haaj Malik Shabaz, formerly known as Malcolm X. (The other was Dr. Martin Luther King.)

Mohammad Tufail Mehdi repeatedly spoke against unreasonable "search and seizure," intimidation and harassment, by state agencies and other groups. Mehdi's office was vandalized and he was badly beaten up. Those of you who knew Mehdi will recall that it was he who helped Malcolm X get a visa to go to Saudi Arabia to perform *Hajj* [pilgrimage].

Iqbal Ahmed, if you remember, was arrested along with the Berrigan brothers on charges of plotting to kidnap Henry Kissinger. His case was thrown out of the court. But Iqbal's real contribution was made during the anti-Vietnam-war era, in his tireless campaigns writing and speaking on support of Palestine. It is in recognition of these contributions that the prominent Palestine intellectual Edward Said dedicated his book *Culture and Imperialism* to Iqbal Ahmed.

Imam Jamil Al-Amin, formerly known as Hubert Rap Brown, was a leader of SNCC (Student Nonviolent Coordinating Committee). Later on, SNCC merged with the Black Panthers, and the *Imam* was designated their minister of justice.

Recently he has been incarcerated on the charge of killing a law officer. For 40 years Imam Jamil has been fighting for civil rights. He and others whom I mentioned have all paid a high price for civil rights.

Let's look at the current situation of our Muslim brothers who have been held on secret evidence without even being told what they were accused of. Just to name a few, they are Dr. Mazen Al-Najjar, Anwar Haddam, Dr. Ali Karim, Nasser Ahmed, and Hany Khairedeen. (NOTE: Some have been released since this writing.)

Many Muslim organizations have been working on behalf of Muslim-Americans. I remember calling Brother Alamoudi a couple of years back to see what AMC could do for some of the brothers who were informed by the state government offices that their phone conversations were taped. Brother Alamoudi went right to work on it. The AMC has taken the leading role in this effort; CAIR and AMA have given a helping hand, as well.

I am now going to quote a few excerpts from the submitted testimony of a hearing that the House Judiciary Committee held on May 23, 2000. The hearing focused on H.R. 2121, the Secret Evidence Repeal Act of 1999. AMC attended the hearing, and I quote Aly Abuzaakouk, executive director of AMC, who is present here in the audience. With your permission, I quote: "The fact of the matter is that no person, regardless of ethnicity, race or nationality, should be subjected to secret evidence. No person should be forced to spend time in jail without being charged with any crimes and without knowing the nature of the allegations against them."

Congressman Jerrold Nadler said, and I quote, "How can one defend oneself when he doesn't know the charges against him?"

Congressman David Bonior, who spoke at yesterday's session, and Congressman Campbell called secret evidence a "national embarrassment."

Next I want you to listen to some of the excerpts from the touching testimony given by Dr. Mazen Al-Najjar's sister, the wife of our learned speaker on this panel, Dr. Sami Al-Arian. With his permission, I shall begin to read, and I quote:

> My name is Nahla Al-Arian and I'm a proud American citizen of Palestinian descent. I'm also a mother of five and the proud sister of Dr. Mazen Al-Najjar, who has been deprived of his freedom for 1100 days today, because of the use of secret evidence. This past Friday, my brother entered his 4th year of incarceration without knowing why.
>
> On May 19, 1997, Mazen was handcuffed in front of his three young daughters and taken to a detention facility for, supposedly, a visa violation.
>
> When my parents learned of my brother's incarceration, they were deeply affected. My mother's health has suffered since. She frequently breaks into tears when she remembers the horrible situation my brother and his family are in. My parents always had high hopes that Mazen, their eldest son, will be there to support them in their old age. Unfortunately, they are now faced with taking care of their son and supporting his family.
>
> Everyone who knows Mazen knows that he is a very peaceful man, who has never been charged with anything, not even a traffic violation.

Now I want you all pay close attention to the last part of Dr. Mazen's sister's testimony, and I want all of you to imagine what Dr. Mazen is going through. I am quoting her now:

> "Nonetheless, Mazen's most rewarding achievement was in raising his three beautiful American-born daughters: 11-year-old Yara, 9-year-old Sara, and Safa, who is only 5 years old. Mazen's unfair detention was devastating to these young girls psychologically, emotionally, and academically. They have been traumatized by this horrible experience. During the 1100 days of Mazen's unjust

incarceration, they were only allowed to hug him four times! This, my brother told me, was the hardest thing in this ordeal—the fact that "his daughters have to live almost like orphans." When he was taken away, his youngest daughter, Safa, who was barely 2 years old at the time, refused to eat dinner for many days without her father's presence. She told her mom she was waiting for her dad to come home. The middle child, Sara, had nightmares for weeks, while the oldest, Yara, had withdrawal symptoms that affected her personality and behavior."

Now imagine that it was you in place of Dr. Mazen.

So what do we do about this?

In the absence of a clear strategy, all efforts made or resources spent will be wasted. There needs to be a civil rights strategy. I believe there are four main components to the civil rights strategy, (1) the political component, (2) the media and public relation component, (3) the legal component, and (4) the economical component.

Economical component

Boycotting of a product or buying only a certain product in the name of the cause, affects the economical component. Uplifting of a community, providing funds are effective measures. What is needed is the mobilization of resources to build institution and community structure.

Legal Component

Fighting in the courts, serving lawsuits. A good example is the NAACP (National Association for the Advancement of Colored People). NAACP alone filed close to 2,000 lawsuits to challenge and dismantle various racist and discriminatory laws and practices.

Media Component

We all know the power of media and timely dissemination of information, what effects it has. Bringing the information to the attention of the Muslim community not only educates the community of the real issues, but also creates an avenue for support and awareness.

Media definitely plays a pivotal role. CAIR has taken the leading role in this field. Not only are their media alerts timely, the alert also deals with the issue at hand, with enough substance. Another public domain is conferences, like this one, that also provide a similar effect.

I would like to commend ISNA for including this topic in the year 2000 convention, which has a record number of participants, reportedly over 35,000. Let's give them a big hand.

Political component.

Fourth and not the least, the political component. Actually, in my mind, the most important component. The first speaker you all just listened to, whose name is synonymous with CAIR, Nihad Awad, had earlier stressed this as well. We need the political power. There are organizations that are working very hard on this (AMA, AMC and CAIR). The American Muslim Alliance is taking the lead role in this effort, empowering Muslims nationwide. All three organizations talked about the importance of voter registration. Dr. Agha Saeed, in yesterday's session, indicated that Muslims could make a difference in the upcoming U.S. presidential race.

It is also imperative that we continue supporting candidates who have supported the Muslim cause. We had a successful fund-raiser for Michigan's Congressman David Bonior and raised double the amount we promised. The checks are still coming in. This was done under the AMA Massachusetts chapter. It was my pleasure presenting him with a plaque. This was our way of saying thank you and recognition for his forceful advocacy on behalf of the American Muslims, specifically introducing HR2121, repeal of the Secret Evidence Law.

In the event the congressman and the Muslim community were wondering why we in Massachusetts were supporting his candidacy in Michigan? "It is because of the simple fact that it really doesn't matter what state you run in or what political party you belong to, as long as you have the Muslim interests at heart, we are all with you."

This is the year when we should organize a Million Muslim Walk to D.C., and vote as a bloc in the upcoming U.S. presidential election. This year the Muslim vote can make a difference. When we have the voting power, when we use this power wisely, collectively, only then people like Mazen Al-Najjar can walk free. The Islamic viewpoint is missing in U.S. mainstream politics; let's put it there."

The questions and answer session that followed was quite lively, but revealing as well. I had not realized until then just how many lives the infamous secret evidence was affecting.

The session finally ended. Dr. Muzammil Siddiqi and Sayyid Syeed, ISNA's president and secretary, respectively, were apparently delighted with the outcome. Dr. Siddiqi embraced each one of us. That was his way of showing gratitude and his way of saying thank you.

CHAPTER 10   *Hillary Rodham Clinton*

[The political multiplier. Even today, Most people don't recognize the implicit connection between the Muslim bloc vote and the electoral controversy in Hillary Clinton's election in New York].

Should we raise $50,000 for Hillary Clinton? That was the question being discussed at Shahid Ahmed Khan's home in April of 2000. Present were Dr. Kimet Gul Khattak, then chairman of the Massachusetts Chapter of the American Muslim Alliance; former chairman of the chapter Dr. Mohammed Saeed; former president of the Pakistan Association of Greater Boston; Dr. Siddiq Abdullah, a professor at Pine Manor College; Tahir Choudhary, who a year later was to become the president of the Islamic center in Wayland; and an officer in the Pakistan Navy, who wanted to remain nameless for security reasons.

Although we knew that $50,000.00 was a lot of money, some of us agreed that a high-profile fund-raiser would give the American Muslim Alliance the boost it needed to surface into the mainstream. But Dr. Mohammed Saeed, who was still smarting from the bitter experience with Senator John Kerry's fund-raiser, was in no hurry to be humiliated again and refused to allow the AMA to become involved. It really was Dr. Khattak's call, but he also seemed to be in agreement with the former Massachusetts AMA chairman. I normally did not like the idea of winning over a candidate or an incumbent by way of a fund-raiser. But I also understood this *was* the American way.

Consequently, Shahid and the Pakistani Navy officer had really no choice when they decided to take on the task anyway, without the blessing of the AMA. June 13 was set for the date and the Boston Plaza Hotel was chosen for the location. Invitations went out.

But the response to the fund-raiser was less enthusiastic than expected, as I found out a few weeks later when I met Mohammad Khusro, founding chairman of AMPAM, at Friday prayers in Lowell.

"The American Muslim Alliance should help Shahid," he told me. "He is having a hard time getting community support and raising the money for the first lady's fund-raiser." He reminded me that since I was now the Massachusetts AMA chairman, it was my obligation to undertake the endeavor. This was no easy task, since time was not on my side. There were less than two weeks remaining until the event and raising another $30, 000 at such a short notice was a big challenge.

But first things first. I called Agha Saeed in California to get his opinion on whether or not the AMA should sponsor the fund-raiser. One of his main concerns and questions was who was really behind this event and donation? "Otherwise, you will just end up promoting *him*. He will get favors from the Clintons, and you all will be out fifty thousand," warned Saeed. In a way I agreed with Dr. Saeed, because contributions without political negotiations is an exercise in throwing good money away.

Shahid Ahmed Khan understanding my concern found a way to resolve the dilemma I was facing. Shahid connected me with David Rosen, who was one of the financial officers on the Hillary Clinton campaign team. This was a three-way call. Shahid introduced me to David as the chairman of the AMA. I asked David to reveal to me who really was behind this fund-raiser. David's response was very specific, "In no way shape or form is Mansoor involved with this fund-raiser." That was enough to convince me, and later when I discussed the conversation I had with David Rosen with a few concerned community members they gave me the "thumbs up."

There was less than a week before the event, and the funds were far from being collected. After making several phone calls, we were successful in mobilizing the community and winning its support. At a meeting that took place at the Islamic center in Wayland a day before the event, we discussed the agenda to be adopted at the fund-raiser. I passed around the plaque that I proposed to present to Mrs. Clinton. This was a pleasant surprise: I had made the decision to make this presentation on my own, and, when I bounced the idea off Agha Saeed, he thought it was a great idea. The members present at the meeting agreed. The plaque was considered not only to be a good idea and a nice gesture, but also the right thing to do. The plaque read: Presented to
   THE FIRST LADY
   HILLARY RODHAM CLINTON
   In Honor & With Sincere Appreciation
   For Your Stand on Human Rights
    AMERICAN MUSLIM ALLIANCE
    MASSACHUSETTS JUNE 13, 2000

Dr. Amin Rathore, Dr. Malik Masood Khan and several AMA members approached me and said that they were glad that the AMA was taking charge of the event. Before they left, they placed their checks for the fund-raiser in my hand.

The event was a resounding success, and though part of the credit for which rightfully goes to Shahid Ahmed Khan and his friend, it was really the the American Muslim community that was coming of age through events like this fund-raiser. Hillary's presence at the event was a clear indication that astute poiticians were beginning to recognize the emergence of the American Muslim as a new political constituent. They were able to count us both in terms of money and votes way before we were able to do so. This was the first time such a high-profile political figure ever attended a Muslim event in a public forum. She *was* the first lady of the United States of America, and even one day could be the president. The reception took many forms of appreciation: "The reception for Mrs. Clinton on June 13, 2000 at the Park Plaza Hotel in Boston, hosted by the American Muslim Alliance, may be summed up as: very successful, largely attended, high visibility, quality program, superbly executed, the audience enchanted."

Barry Hoffman, Pakistan consul general in Boston, attended the event and called the program successful and a big plus for the AMA. "Mrs. Clinton really appeared to be enjoying it. I think she was really pleased with the way the program was executed. Very professionally done. My congratulations to Shahid and the AMA. The event may not have been possible if you all had not put your heads together." This was a very crucial and a bold step that the Muslim community in Boston had taken. The general belief among the participants at the time was that this event might even prove to be an important step in the journey into mainstream politics.

Shahid Ahmed Khan was content with his task of introducing each guest to Mrs. Clinton. The deal included a "photo-op" with the first lady. After the photography session was over, Mrs. Clinton joined the Muslim community gathered in the adjacent room. Farooq Ansari, the master of ceremonies, welcomed Hillary Clinton on behalf of the American Muslim Alliance. After Mrs. Clinton gave her talk, Mr. Ansari introduced me as the Massachusetts chairman of the AMA, and mentioned that my name is engraved on the wall honoring President Ronald Reagan. Due to the brief time we had available with Mrs. Clinton, he could not fully read from the certificate itself:

The undersigned officers of the
REPUBLICAN PRESIDENTIAL TASK FORCE
do hereby authorize that the name of
Mr. Tahir Ali
be engraved on the Founders Wall at the Ronald Reagan
Republican Center honoring President Ronald Reagan and
those Task Force members who are leading the way this
year to elect a Republican president worthy of the office
and the legacy.

Signed and authorized this 8th day of May, 2000.
PRESIDENT RONALD REAGAN, Founder
Signed by: Senator Larry Craig, Chairman."

I thanked Mr. Ansari for the flattering introduction, then added jokingly that my name was probably being scraped off as I spoke. Presenting Hillary Clinton with the plaque for her stand on human rights, I also thanked her on behalf of the Muslims present in the audience for her forceful advocacy on behalf of the Muslims in Kosova. I read aloud the message on the plaque. Mrs. Clinton gently pulled me toward her to pose for her photographer. My friend Malik Khan was quick enough to capture that pose on his camera as well. It was this photograph that was used in our report. We were unaware that the photograph would be widely distributed across the nation finding, its way to CNN and other media offices.

National AMA carried the "Hillary Clinton" report for an extended period on its official Web site. *Pakistan Link,* a L.A. based Muslim newspaper, printed the same report in its June-July edition that year:

AMA Massachusetts Holds Fund-Raiser for First Lady Hillary Clinton
The Massachusetts of the American Muslim Alliance (AMA) held a successful fund-raiser for First Lady Hillary Rodham Clinton at Boston's Park Plaza Hotel on June 13. Nearly 100 American Muslim leaders and activists attended the reception. After an informal introduction and photo shoot with Mrs. Clinton, com-

munity members had the opportunity to meet on a one-to-one basis with the senatorial candidate.

Master of ceremonies for the event was Farooq Ansari, a co-founder and former president of the AMA Massachusetts chapter. He welcomed Mrs. Clinton on behalf of AMA and the Muslim community, highlighting her achievements as First Lady.

Mrs. Clinton opened her remarks by explaining to the Muslim audience why they should support a candidate for the U.S. Senate from New York. "The U.S. Senate deals with policy issues that affect a great many people who are living abroad and who live in other states," she noted.

Crediting the president's leadership for the strong U.S. economy and the prosperity of the American people, she went on to stress the importance of continuing with the current political structure and leaders to ensure continued economic prosperity.

On domestic issues, the first lady vowed to pursue fairness and justice in the issue of secret evidence and the Anti-Terrorism Act.

When asked about the plight of children of Iraq, Mrs. Clinton, while admitting that the sanctions on Iraq are not working, stated that they were the only alternative to going to war. AMA Massachusetts presented Mrs. Clinton with a plaque commending her for her stand on human rights.

A month later we organized another fund-raiser, this time for Michigan's Congressman David Bonior. By this time, both AMA membership and confidence in us had grown. The Muslim community put together a diverse executive team for me to lead. This time the task ahead of us needed the entire community's attention and its full support. The next step in the process was to encourage Muslims to register to vote. The Muslim voter registration became a national campaign.

Words of encouragement came from many corners. Hasan Ahmed, a Stanford graduate, came to Canada when he was two years old. He told me, "Of course we need to encourage the Muslims to be politically involved, but I believe it will be even more advantageous for the government to encourage Muslims to get involved in politics." Hassan, who started out as a contractor in a network company, is a CEO of a network company: *Sonus Networks*, Inc. was named, "Best Entrepreneur in Massachusetts Tech," Hasan's father Nighat Ahmed, originally from Pakistan, is a Physicist by profession.

Former AMA executive committee member, Lebanese born Ziad Ramadan, received his master's degree in civil engineering from Massachusetts Institute of Technology (MIT).

"I lived for some time on the streets of Boston, literally a bum. I took refuge in shelter for the homeless", Ziad recalled one day as we worked together at the Islamic contruction site on the East Mountain Street. Now he is the CEO of a software company in Massachusetts.

Ziad and his wife Imane have six children – a son Mazen, 21 year old and five daughters – 20 years old Duniya, 19 years old Yasmeen, 15 year old Jehan, 12 year old Saousan and 6 years old Ryanne.

Zahid "Iqbal" Ali, originally from India, also had a background in engineering. When he came to America in late 1989 he started out his career as a film editor working at the Community Access Television station channel 66, in Hudson, Massachusetts, but was unable to make ends meet. So he decided to try his luck in real-estate in 1993. He is now a proud owner of several real-estate companies.

"I started out with an investment of only $5000.00. That's all I could afford at the time." Zahid Ali confessed.

Zahid is usually on the construction site very early in the morning, and in the evening he spends what he refers to as "family time" with his wife Mohib "Bilquees" Ali and three daughters - 14-year old Afra, 10-year old Sajda and 6-year old Nigha.

I pointed out to Hassan how I have seen his wife, Aliya Ahmed, is involved in community social events, I asked if she is the person behind his continued success, to which he replied, "She is. You have to have a supportive family. It is key to any success. I am sure it is same for you." Hassan continued. "All this success in political activity and immense contribution to community involvement and putting us on the political map, cannot be possible without the family's support."

Hassan and Aliya got married in 1982. They are proud parents of 3 sons and a daughter: 17-year old Osman, 16-year old daughter Ayesha, 12-year old Qaasim and 7-year old Ameer.

"My children keep me busy enough all day," Aliya told me that

Hassan works long hours at work, "and you would expect him to be a grouch when he gets home, on the contrary he is calm, and spends quality time with the children, playing ball with them, helping them with their homework", Aliya excused herself for a while to attend to her 7-year old son. She continued "Hassan has so much energy. I keep asking him jokingly whether he was on steroids"

Aliya has a college degree in nutrition. When I asked her whether she was the key ingredient in Hassan's success? A modest Aliya replied "Hassan is".

Hassan Ahmed, Ziad Ramadan and Iqbal Ali, besides providing words of encouragement also make substantial monetary contributions to Muslim run events that include, but not limited to, political incumbents or candidates running for office.

All three have lived the American dream. Their success stories serve as inspiration for others.

I headed toward the Islamic center in Cambridge (ISB). This was the first time I had visited the center. According to a study conducted by CAIR, there were approximately 2,500 mosques (a/k/a Islamic centers) in the United States I believe the number is on the rise. But not many were built like a traditional mosque. In some cases, older buildings including abandoned churches were bought in "as is" condition. These were then renovated and eventually converted into Islamic centers.

The Islamic center that I am a member of, the Islamic Society of Greater Worcester (ISGW), is a good example. In early 1980 a handful of Muslims living in the greater Worcester area collected enough funds to buy an abandoned church at 57 Laurel Street in Worcester. That Islamic center still stands as strong as ever and to date remains active. Jane Lampman of the *Christian Science Monitor* visited our center and ISB in 2001 and wrote a good article outlining various activities in both centers.

I arrived at Prospect Street and was pleasantly surprised to discover the Islamic center in Cambridge was indeed built like a mosque. I parked my car in the parking lot and was escorted into the mosque. I was a guest speaker with a monumental task at hand. I had to convince the audience to do what most were completely indifferent about: first, to talk about the importance of the vote in this country, and then convincing them to participate in the forthcoming U.S. election. Finally, I wanted to motivate those who had not previously registered to vote to get out and register this year. It was reminiscent of "Star Trek." I was about to "boldly go where no man has gone before."

Abdul Wahab Khoshafa, an ISB member warned me, "This is a tough crowd. Most of them are of Arab origin, and you know as well as I do that historically most American Arabs have ignored voting, but you will find our *Imam* (cleric) Basuni Nahela supportive."

Abdul Wahab, named after the town of Khoshafa in Yemen, was well respected for his hard work and relentless community service.

I assured Abdul Wahab that I would try my best, and instructed him to get out the voter registration forms and have them filled out right in the mosque once I give the signal to do so.

The process of successful Muslim voter registration was well on its way across the United States.

It was sometime in the month of September, 2000, at the home of my neighbors Mirajuddin Ahmed and Dr. Shamim Ahmed that their son Sirajuddin Ahmed told me a reporter from the *Daily News* in New York had called him a few weeks back. Sirajuddin was in his early twenties, a law student at Wisconsin Law School, a newlywed and the reason for the party. The reporter, Sirajuddin admitted, was very polite as he started asking apparently harmless questions in reference to the Hillary Clinton fund-raising event that newlyweds Sirajuddin Ahmed and Sana Junaid had attended. This was sort of a wedding gift from their parents, who had purchased two tickets at $500.00 each.

"The caller indicated that he was simply gathering information in order to write an article about the fund-raiser," Sirajuddin said. "…[he] asked me various questions regarding the location of the event, how well it was organized, how many people attended, etc. I told him the AMA fund-raiser was well organized, and my wife and I had the opportunity to meet Hillary Clinton and have our photos taken alongside her." I thanked Sirajuddin for the compliment about the organization.

"The questions appeared simple enough at first," Sirajuddin continued, but he confessed that he was really disturbed by some of the queries that followed. "He asked me how much money my father had contributed to the fund-raiser. I informed him that my father had purchased two tickets, and so the total contribution amounted to $1,000." Sirajuddin paused for a moment, then added, "Finally, the reporter mentioned at one point that he already had in his possession a list of the contributors, along with the dollar amount each individual had contributed."

I was just about to ask Sirajuddin if he knew where the reporter was leading him with this line of questioning, but his next comment satisfied me. "This struck me as odd, especially in light of the fact that this reporter had earlier claimed that he did not know how much we contributed, and that he needed me to give him an exact number. My immediate reaction was that of suspicion. *You know.* You read a lot in the papers about misuse of political campaign funds, both raised or spent on the campaign trail. My angry response to him was if he *knew* how much my parents donated; why was he asking? I wasn't quite sure why he wanted to know this after two months. So I asked the reporter why he wanted to know?"

Sirajuddin was right to think that way. Why all the belated interest in an event that took place a few months back? Nobody was asking any questions in June or July. The reports were available on the AMA Web site as well reported in one of the New York based paper *The Minaret,* and Los Angeles based paper *The Pakistan Link.* There were many fund-raisers being held all over the States by Muslims and non-Muslims alike, so what was so unique about the Hillary Clinton fund-raiser event?

"What else?" I interjected as I saw Sirajuddin hesitating a bit. I was curious also, now that he had my undivided attention.

He managed to maintain his composure as he continued on to say, "Then he wanted to know who sponsored the fund-raiser? That's when I realized there was more to this that meets the eye. I told the reporter what I knew at the time, and politely instructed him to talk to the AMA chairman." Sirajuddin hesitated nervously and asked with a worried look on his face, "I did the right thing, right? Has he called you?"

I replied in the affirmative and in the negative to his questions, in the order he asked them. I may have taken the New York's reporter query more seriously if there were no other pressing things on my mind. But I was trying to make good on what I had said in my talk at ISNA on Labor Day of that year, "This is the year when we should organize a Million Muslim Walk to D.C. and vote as a bloc in the upcoming U.S. presidential election."

On behalf of the AMA, I had been stressing that point with the leaders of ISNA and AMC as well. On the Labor Day weekend, at the ISNA convention, I discussed the logistics in organizing a Muslim walk with Abdul Malik Mujahid of *Sound Vision* in Chicago. He advised me that this would take a lot of commitment and hard work, but the major Muslim organizations — both national and local — should participate heavily in the program.

Mr. Mujahid, who was the chairman of the Bosnia Task Force, was instrumental in organizing the Bosnia rally in Washington, D.C., on May 15, 1993, was speaking from experience. I had earlier discussed the plan at length with AMC's Abdurahman Alamoudi, founding member of AMC, who was in full agreement with me and admitted this is as good a time as any to implement such a plan, where Muslims could get together on one platform. The time was just right. The 37th annual ISNA convention was just a few weeks away. Most of the major Muslim organizations were to be represented at the ISNA convention in that year, 2000. And that became the motivational force in deciding to attend the ISNA convention.

Mr. Alamoudi told me that he was not planning to go to the convention that year, even though he was an invited speaker. I found that rather disturbing and, in an effort to convince him that he should attend and uphold his commitment to talk at the ISNA convention, somehow I ended up agreeing to surrogate for him. "Ali, I cannot think of any one else other than yourself to represent me. I'll be honored." Alamoudi was very generous in his remarks, for it was I who really felt honored.

There were two tasks that the Muslims were now ready to undertake: one, extensive voter registration drives; the other, participating in a rally of some sort. We had our job cut out for us, trying to help coordinate with ISNA, AMC and other national organizations to arrange a rally similar to the Bosnia rally in 1993. I was very up front about this when I told Nicole Simmons of *The MetroWest Daily News* on September 18, 2000.

> "It is our task to educate and make sure the Muslim viewpoint is put into the politicians' hands," Ali said.
>
> To get their voices heard — and as a sort of litmus test to see which candidate responds — Ali said the AMA may sponsor a walk to Washington, D.C., before the election, where the candidates will be invited to speak.
>
> The reaction to the potential invitation may be enough to indicate the candidate's attitude toward American Muslims, Ali said.

By this time the preparations for holding a national rally were well under way. The major Muslim organizations were in synch with each other. AMC's president Yahya Basha and AMC's secretary Aly Abuzaakouk took a leading role in this effort, in a similar manner to that of AMC's secretary Alamoudi, who had provided leadership in the Bosnia rally in 1993, organized by Abdul Malik Mujahid of Chicago.

"My name is Larry Cohler-Esses. I am with the New York *Daily News.*" When Larry indicated to me that the reason for his call was his interest in doing a story on the Boston Hillary Clinton fund-raiser, the conversation I had had with Siraj Ahmed a few days before came back to me. I have to admit Larry was very polite and was asking what seemed at the time relevant questions.

In order to save time, I simply directed him to the AMA national Web site, and told him he would find the AMA's report on the fund-raising event for Mrs. Clinton well documented. The report carried a photograph of Mrs. Clinton holding the plaque, with Farooq Ansari at the podium and me between them.

I believe Larry sensed that I did not seem too thrilled and excited — as one often is when interviewed by a popular newspaper. *"Daily News* is a big newspaper," Larry assured me. He was right to do so — as he may have surmised, I had no idea how reputable the New York *Daily News* really was at the time. I realized later that it is considered by many to be in the same league as *The New York Times.*

I had to cut short the interview, for I still had quite a few phone calls to make and e-mails to send regarding the D.C. rally planned for October 28, 2001. Then there was the matter of arranging private buses to be available for those who would rather go by bus than drive all the way to D.C. I told Larry he could call me later. There was nothing in the interview that made a lasting impression on my mind or seemed like a reason for worry. I expected Larry to follow up, because he knew as well as I that the story, if there was any worth reporting, was not complete.

"Tahir, could you be in D.C. on October 23rd? The time has come to announce our endorsement. I want you to arrange a press conference," said a determined Agha Saeed. Those who have had the pleasure of meeting Agha Saeed, usually feel that they want to see him or hear from him again. His perspicacity and the manner in which he discusses any issue dear to his heart would convince most people to agree with him wholeheartedly.

The statement he made to me indicated the American Muslim Political Coordination Council (AMPCC) endorsement of George W. Bush for president was well on its way to newsrooms all over the States.

We could have used a few more Muslims in the audience to fill up the hotel room on Monday, October 23rd, but were content with the turnout we had. The reason we chose a weekday over a Saturday or Sunday was simply to guarantee the media showing up. Interfacing with many reporters and news editors, one thing I learned quickly from them is that they have only a skeleton staff working on weekends, so providing coverage to a lot of events is not always possible.

About 20 members of the press did show up, although not as many as we had hoped. It was not considered a "breaking story." Apparently, there was nothing unique about endorsing a president. Among the major newspapers like *The New York Times* and *The Los Angeles Times* that did not show up, we knew they could pick up the news from the wire: "U.S. Muslim Coalition Endorses Bush," by Paul Shepard of the Associated Press (AP) on October 23, 2000. The *Boston Globe*'s headline "Muslims eye role at U.S. polls," reported by Michael Paulson appeared on the same date, but this report talked more or less about the plan for endorsing Bush, not the press conference.

Michael Paulson, however, built up good coverage as he included interviews from Muslim scholars like researcher Ihsan A. Bagby of Shaw University in North Carolina and researcher Zahid H. Bukhari of Georgetown University, whom I had had the pleasure of meeting at the last two ISNA annual conventions. Dr. Agha Saeed introduced me to Dr. Bukhari in a meeting in a hotel room overlooking the Rosemont Center, home of ISNA convention. Dr. Bukhari was a speaker at the same ISNA conventions that Dr. Saeed and I were speaking at.

Addressing the reporters at our press conference were Dr. Agha Saeed and Mr. Eric Vickers of AMA; Dr. Yahya Mossa Basha and Mr. Aly Abuzaakouk of AMC; Mr. Omar Ahmad, Mr. Nihad Awad and Mr. Ibrahim Hooper of CAIR; Mr. Salam Al-Marayati of the Muslim Public Affairs Council (MPAC).

The representatives of ISNA and the Islamic Circle of North

America (ICNA) were there, but elected not to address the conference. Still, their presence as observers was support for the endorsement.

Dr. Agha Saeed, who was also the chairman of AMPCC announced the endorsement; others joined in to expilicate and reinforce. Aly Abuzaakouk pointed out that the criteria for the committee [AMPCC] decision on which candidate to endorse was not party based, but rather issue oriented, "The endorsement was not intended as a declaration of the American Muslim community's partisanship toward one party over another, but rather as an illustration that American Muslims will vote for specific candidates, depending on their record and relationship with the community and on how that candidate addresses issues of concern to American-Muslims." However, Ibrahim Hooper outlined various factors that *were* considered: "the main factor [in choosing Bush] was the governor's accessibility to Muslim leaders." Mr. Hooper's views were in complete alignment what the American Muslims felt at the time. The same was even noted then by youth Ruheena Razvi of Weston, daughter of Dr. Syed Asif Razvi, President of the Wayland Islamic center and professor of Vascular Surgery at Tufts University, "He [Bush] has definitely made an effort to communicate with Muslims, Al Gore just dismissed us from the beginning."

One of the underlying determinants was the fact that Bush challenged the use of secret evidence. American Muslims and civil libertarians alike felt secret evidence used by the INS in deportation hearings was unconstitutional — a violation of individuals' civil liberties and the right to defend oneself. It appeared that the Secret Evidence Act was designed with Muslims in mind, as it was used disproportionately against Muslim-Americans.

AMC's president Yahya M. Basha was evidently very upset with the Secret Evidence Law. He characterized the law as being "not the American way," and noted, "We've got to do something about that."

Agha Saeed elaborated further on this point in his address. "In the nineties, Muslim civil rights were significantly curtailed due to an executive order of 1994, the secret evidence clause of the Anti-Terrorism and Effective Death Penalty Act of 1995, and the ADC versus Janet Reno decision of the U.S. Supreme Court, of April 1999." Dr. Saeed asked the reporters and the audience to take note of the facts that he just pointed out. He wanted their full attention on what he had to say next. "Our collective efforts are aimed at rectifying these setbacks. It is extremely important for Muslims to vote for a civil rights agenda this year."

For such an important step taken by American Muslims the coverage was mediocre at best. But this was going to change in just a few days. Larry Cohler-Esses called again to get the rest of the Boston's Hillary Clinton fund-raiser story. This time around I noticed his line of questioning was different compared to the first time he talked to me. During the elapsed time Larry and his colleagues evidently had been talking to the Hillary Clinton campaign personnel. He appeared confused as to who really sponsored the fund-raiser.

What really was the big deal about a fund-raiser that took place a few months back? New Yorkers were well aware of the reason why the Clintons became residents of the Big Apple. Hillary Rodham Clinton wanted to run for the U.S. Senate seat from New York and she was not hiding the fact, either. According to the Clinton Campaign, the Boston fund-raiser was not sponsored by AMA but by two businessmen, one of them being Shahid Ahmed.

At the time I was speaking with Larry I was very much convinced that it was the AMA which sponsored the event. Still, I managed to point out that, although the AMA got involved at the last minute, the credit definitely belonged to the original planners, Shahid Ahmed Khan and his friend. I did not want to attribute any dishonesty in the first lady's direction, and clearly indicated that she probably did not know who the real sponsors were. The AMA's involvement may not have been very obvious from her one-on-one contact and photo opportunity with the distinguished guests, and perhaps the remarks from the podium failed to tip her off, even though the AMA was specifically identified as the host.

Master of Ceremonies Farooq Ansari had welcomed her on behalf of the AMA, and I had read aloud from the plaque before presenting it to her, stating clearly that this was on behalf of the AMA. Even the America Muslim Alliance's name embossed in a large font size stood out on the plaque. To prove my point I even sent him some of the correspondence that took place prior to and after the event. The interview carried on nicely. I sent Larry the "Bush endorsement" announcement, which had contact phone numbers for AMA, AMC and others.

I must admit that I had a good feeling after the interview. I found Larry to be very professional and courteous. We also talked at length about the Bush endorsement and the Muslim bloc vote for Bush. No matter what has occurred since, I felt then and still do that the first lady's Boston fund-raiser with American Muslims served as a major milestone on the path to political empowerment, and its importance cannot be diminished as it is now a matter of public record. My main reason for talking to Larry was to bring to the surface the news of a Muslim bloc vote and the Bush endorsement. Larry Cohler-Esses's list of contacts expanded to include Dr. Agha Saeed and others also recognized as the architects of the Muslim bloc vote and the Bush endorsement.

Then came the first blow. I was completely at a loss of words and very disturbed when I read the story that the New York *Daily News* printed the following day. During my entire conversation with Larry Cohler-Esses the State of Israel was never mentioned even once, yet the headline said: "ISRAEL FOES GIVE HIL $50G," Muslim group backs Palestinian use of force.

The article carried the same photograph of Hillary Rodham Clinton that was taken by Dr. Malik Khan at the Boston Plaza during the fund-raiser. This photograph was also included in the fund-raiser report that was on the AMA Web site. In this photograph, she is holding the human rights plaque presented to her on June 13, 2000. The article also carried a close-up photograph of the plaque, and the following words were readable: "Presented to the First Lady Hillary Rodham Clinton" from "American Muslim Alliance, Massachusetts; June 13, 2000."

It is a matter of public record that Mrs. Clinton had called for the creation of a Palestinian state, had embraced and kissed Suha Arafat, wife of Yasser Arafat, on the cheek after Suha gave a speech about how the Israelis were poisoning Palestinian children. That event took place in 1999 and was not favored by many in the Jewish community. But in a race in a city where the Jews make up 12 percent of the votes, Hillary could not let that kiss be a kiss of political death.

She was not far behind in her criticism of Palestinian leader Yasser Arafat for the uprising in Palestine that month. The fact that Mrs. Clinton was distancing herself from her pro-Palestinian stance was not disturbing; as I told Larry, I was not regretting having had the fund-raiser. I meant no disrespect to Hillary Clinton when I told Larry that the idea here was for Mrs. Clinton to win the election, and that I understood her "change of tune." So it really did not mean anything. It was just at the spur of the moment that she found she had to say these things, maybe to be politically correct. It was this remark of mine that Michael Tomasky picked up in his book *Hillary's Turn*. Michael referred to my quote in the New York *Daily News* as "saying the following apropos Hillary's newly buffed fealty to Israel." [pg. 266, *Hillary's Turn,* published by The Free Press]

But I did allow the benefit of doubt to go to Mrs. Clinton, as I made it very clear that because AMA got involved just a week before the event, it was quite possible that Mrs. Clinton had no idea who hosted the Boston fund-raiser.

Another photograph showed Abdurahman Alamoudi of American Muslim Council. The New York *Daily News* had an affiliated story about him, but it was not focused on his $1,000 contribution to the Clinton campaign. Instead, its emphasis was more on the claim that Alamoudi had made public statements numerous times supporting Hamas.

What I knew about Hamas at the time was what the U.S. media was projecting it to be. Hamas, a Palestinian militant group who — by their own admission — took responsibility for carrying out many of the suicide attacks on Israeli targets. Subsequently, Hamas was declared a terrorist group by Israel and the United States anyone in either country showing sympathy for Hamas would incur guilt by association. However, at one time Israel was reportedly supporting Hamas against Al Fatah, Yasser Arafat's faction of the Palestine Liberation Front (PLO).

But the most devastating part of the news was made in reference to Agha Saeed. He was accused of supporting Palestinian terrorism against Israel and saying that the Palestinians had the right to take arms against Israel to defend themselves. He was quoted, "First and foremost through peaceful means. But if that fails, the U.N. resolutions say specifically they have the right to resist by armed force."

It was easy to take the quote out of context and use it as an inflammatory weapon. Especially so since the world was watching with keen interest Israeli's gunfire response to quash the rock-throwing Palestinian uprising. The Palestinians had been protesting Israeli illegal settlements in the "occupied territory," but paying a heavy price — their lives.

The following day, October 25th, after the New York *Daily News* broke that story, I hardly found a moment to tear myself free from answering telephone calls. I was obviously perturbed, but at the same time angry at Larry Cohler-Esses for turning the story inside-out in such a demeaning manner.

But nauseating news was just building up. Allegedly, Mrs. Clinton and her campaign officers were taking the news very seriously and were contemplating returning the contributions. This, I felt, was a feeble, hasty act and a crude attempt to keep the damage under control.

The first news about returning funds was on the wire courtesy of the Associated Press, filed at 1:12 on the same afternoon, October 25, 2000. "Mrs. Clinton Returns Contribution" read the headline.

The first casualty of Larry's report was Abdurahman Alamoudi, whose contributions of $1,000.00 each to the Bush presidential campaign and to Hillary Clinton's Senate campaign in May, 2000, were to be returned. The obvious reason was his alleged support for Hamas, a position that he was not disputing.

Abdurahman Alamoudi and other AMC officials were invited to the White House by the Clintons to celebrate *Eid-ul-Fitr*, one of the major Muslim holidays, a joyous occasion similar to Christmas. To make things worse Alamoudi was quoted as saying, "We are the ones who went to the White House and defended what is called Hamas." Rick Lazio characterized the money given to Mrs. Clinton as blood money; that really infuriated the Muslims. Reference was made to money brought in by the Boston fund-raiser, but there was no mention of Hillary Clinton returning that money. Apparently, Lazio's political machine, fueled by blood money, was working on that—as was evident from the report in the New York *Daily News* the next day:

> **RICK HITS HIL ON 50G DONATION**
> **She vows to return contribution by Israel foe**
> New York *Daily News*; New York, N.Y.; Oct 26, 2000; LARRY COHLER-ESSES and EDWARD LEWINE, *DAILY NEWS* STAFF WRITERS With Bob Port, Russ Buettner, Joe Calderone and Joanne Wasserman

I have to admit that I was not sure how to handle the press and the news that was being disseminated. It was quite disheartening to read derogatory remarks made by Former Mayor Ed Koch accusing us of setting up the first lady. Ed Koch and Former City Public Advocate Mark Green [who ran for mayor in New York City but failed in his bid to succeed Rudy Guilliani] were calling the controversy a smear tactic to steer potential Jewish voters away from Mrs. Clinton—

if they could be convinced that she was pro-Ararat and not pro-Israel. There was nothing wrong with trying to win the election and, if the Jewish votes counted heavily in New York, then it would be politically naive to offend the Jewish community.

That part American Muslims understood, but to accuse them of deceit was more than they could bear. Muslims found themselves caught in the crossfire between Hillary and Lazio. This was a fight not of their choice. Muslims realized that Hillary Clinton did not have the stomach to face Lazio. She rushed to judgment when she hastened to accept accusations about the American Muslim Alliance without inquiring about the accuracy of those accusations. It was now up to Muslim leadership to find ways to absorb the shocks and minimize the impact on Muslims.

I called Agha Saeed, who asked me to get a hold of myself. His words were comforting: "You have done nothing wrong, the AMA has done nothing wrong. Anti-Muslim forces are orchestrating all this. We need to stand our ground...While I can understand Hillary Clinton's political predicament, I am profoundly disturbed by her hasty generalization about our organization [AMA]."

"We all are." I assured Agha Saeed. Both of us were in full agreement that an official written response and a press conference were not only in order, but imminent. We discussed at length what issues must be highlighted in such a statement.

The telephone recording machine was full with messages from various reporters — Bob Port of The New York *Daily News;* Dean Murphy of *The New York Times;* Liz Moore of *News Day;* Dave Martin, Catherine Herridge and Eric Shawn of Fox News; Jane Lampman of *The Christian Science Monitor;* New York's Pam Tyghan of ABC TV — but, more importantly, there were messages from a panicky David Rosen, Hillary Clinton's Senate campaign financial director. Dean Murphy of *The New York Times* wanted to interview me. I decided to chat with him, and asked him to call Agha Saeed as well. I found Mr. Murphy a no-nonsense kind of person, a straight shooter. He came on as a true professional with a clear mandate in mind. In making reference to the New York *Daily News* report, he asked, "Did your group sponsor the fund-raiser?"

I told Murphy exactly what I told Larry. But I made one thing very clear: that this was not the AMA's first fund-raiser involving a high official. I pointed out to him that, because of the AMA's bipartisan nature, in Massachusetts alone the AMA had held similar events. A few examples that came to mind at the time were of fund-raising events for Representative Peter Blute (R), Representative David Bonior (D), Representative Peter Johnson (D), Massachusetts Governor Paul Cellucci (R), and U.S. Senator John Kerry (D).

How I did I feel when Mrs. Clinton declared that she was going to return money raised in Boston? "I am returning all $50,000—every single penny." Mine was a mixed reaction. First, there was the dilemma of facing the Muslim community, especially those who had voiced their opinion against holding the fund-raiser in the first place. Second, there was a feeling of remorse, humiliation and insult. But somehow this untimely and negative action, followed by Rick Lazio's anti-Muslim remarks and divisive tactics, brought the Muslim community even closer than I had thought possible.

Instead of showing anger at us, Muslims declared their support and encouragement with responses that mostly said, "We are with you. We are all in it together." Letters of support started to pour into the newsrooms of many papers, including *The New York Times*. I was honest in telling Dean Murphy how I really felt, "hurt" in the same way as if someone returned a gift I had carefully chosen for them. But I was truly feeling sorry for the first lady; she was put in a position where she herself felt it would hurt not just herself but her campaign to keep our gift.

Even though I told Dean Murphy—and he quoted me as such—that I blamed the "Jewish community lobby," that it was they who were "trying to intimidate her," I realized later that I was making the same mistake in rushing to judgment with a broad-brush approach. This was politics. Smear politics at best, and it was *really* her opponent Rick Lazio who was trying to intimidate her. In a Queens, New York, press conference, Hillary was reportedly on the defensive, yet firm and was not holding any punches, either.

Steven Emerson, a free-lance journalist who makes his living by attacking Muslim leaders and Muslim Organizations, made use of this opportunity in propagating his own message. I am not sure how one becomes a "terrorist expert," but Steven Emerson had gained some popularity at the expense of Muslims, when in 1994 his documentary "*Jihad* in America: An investigation of Islamic extremists' activities in the United States," was broadcast across the nation. This total misrepresentation of Islam, based on incorrect information and innuendoes, may have been a crude attempt to ignite anti-Muslim sentiments. Now Emerson was claiming that, in the research material he provided to reporters, it could be seen that the American Muslim Alliance was disseminating "anti-Semitic tracts," an accusation that Dr. Agha Saeed refuted, calling it nothing but a fabrication of "misquotations and statements taken out of context."

Toward the end of the interview I asked Dean Murphy what exactly he meant by "sponsor"?

"Who paid for the food or the hall rental?" Murphy clarified.

When I told him it was not the AMA who paid for that, he wanted to know who did pay for it. I asked Shahid Ahmed Khan the same question, and he confirmed that the "Hillary campaign took care of it."

I called Dean Murphy back with the information and gave him Shahid's telephone number when he asked for it. I should have realized then that it was not about who actually sponsored the event, but who the hosts were — Muslims.

I was glad that Murphy called Dr. Agha Saeed. This gave Dr. Saeed the opportunity to clear up the muddy waters a bit. He indicated that his remarks had been distorted, and, as far as his remark about "armed resistance by the Palestinians" was concerned, that was made in the context of a United Nations resolution, which Agha Saeed promised to provide Murphy with a copy of. Dr. Saeed insisted that he supported the peace process, but at the same time had the right to criticize the Israelis if they killed people.

Dr. Yahya Mossa Basha, AMC's president, was adamant about his organization's position on Hamas — that it was nothing more than an "overseas issue." He was correct in saying that because it should not have been projected as a homeland issue; for Muslim-Americans, the United States is now their homeland.

October 26, 2000, Thursday
Mrs. Clinton Says She Will Return Money Raised by a Muslim Group

By DEAN E. MURPHY (NYT) 1539 words Late Edition Final, Section A, Page 1, Column 5

ABSTRACT — Hillary Rodham Clinton says she will return $50,000 in political contributions received at a fund-raising event sponsored by a Muslim organization based in California; says she is offended by remarks attributed to members of that organization, the American Muslim Alliance, whose president was quoted as defending a United Nations resolution allowing for use of armed force by Palestinians against Israel; other members of the group have been accused of making anti-Semitic remarks; Clinton will also return $1,000 from another group, American Muslim Council; leaders of both organizations say some of their members have extreme views on Israel, but that they are mainstream and oppose terrorism.

Larry Cohler-Esses called me once again on Thursday morning, October 26th, and wondered if I could talk to him some more. I told him quite bluntly that, after what he wrote in the first article, I had to decline talking to him any more on that subject. He realized I was unhappy the way the piece had turned out in print.

"It was coming out to be a pleasant story, but the comments made by some of the other leaders turned the story in a different...," Larry began, almost apologetically — as if it was really not in his hands how the article portrayed Hillary Clinton, my fellow Muslim-Americans or me. Before he could complete his sentence, I praised Dean Murphy and made reference to his report in The New York Times.

"How is that different?" Larry wanted me to comment.

It was a moot point.

David Rosen was a constant caller. He was rightly concerned about the fate of Mrs. Clinton's bid for the Senate seat if the "AMA thing," as it was known in her campaign offices, kept stealing headlines in tabloids in New York state, as well as in national and international media.

The first thing — and the thing that mattered most to me — was to find out if Mrs. Clinton was really going to return the money and, if so, why? Mr. Rosen could not help noticing the anger in my tone as he attempted to put my mind to ease by quoting Mrs. Clinton, " It was an excellent fund-raiser. It really doesn't matter what they [Lazio campaigners] are trying to do after five months. I still respect the Boston area Muslims." I mentioned to him that Pam Tyghan of ABC wanted to interview me, and that Catherine Herridge had been calling to get me on Fox News.

I had been avoiding appearing in the prime time media, but I thought it would be a nice gesture to clarify, if I could, the fundraiser situation — not for my sake, but for the first lady's. For some reason, I felt I owed that to Mrs. Clinton. Mr. Rosen reminded me that the controversy had gone beyond the fact of who really sponsored the event; it was now more negative and smear campaigning, a territory that Muslims should keep away from for some time.

I even suggested holding a joint press conference with Mrs. Clinton if it would help. The first lady may have appreciated our candor, but Rosen wanted us to keep a low profile in the hope that the "AMA thing" would soon fade out.

Then, as an acknowledgment of my truthfulness, I wondered if Hillary Clinton would find it in her heart to send a letter of apology to the Boston Muslim community. I am still waiting.

In the interim, Agha Saeed and I were discussing what to put in the official statement. We both agreed that—since he was attacked, misquoted and had comments taken out of context more than anyone else-a clarification must come from him. I referred to the news items and asked whether he had criticized Israel or not?

"The First Amendment," he responded, "gives everyone the right to criticize any country's injustice without being intimidated in the tabloids and political arena. Don't you agree?" Agha Saeed did not wait for my answer, but continued, "Muslims anywhere cannot be silent when atrocities are carried out against their fellow Muslims."

Agha Saeed then reminded me of a saying of Prophet Muhammad (*pbuh*) which directs Muslims, if they see injustice, to try to stop it by hand, if not by hand then by tongue, or else feel bad about it "in the heart, and that was the weakest of the faith."

There was no argument there; wherever there was injustice, someone had to speak out. But this should be based on the true sense of the word *injustice,* notable to all and not just based on ethnic or religious lines. Terms like *McCarthyism, xenophobia, religious stereotypes,* and *bigotry* came into normal day-to-day usage among the Muslim community, for now they knew in exactly what context these words were used.

Was it so difficult for the candidates or incumbents to openly accept contributions from Muslims and declare that he or she was for inclusion not exclusion?

"And that's why we need to denounce this bigotry," Agha Saeed said.

"In the strongest terms," I interjected.

Muslim resolve was stronger than ever. This was the time to stand up and fight for rights usurped. The statement had to stress this point to pull the community still closer.

Agha Saeed appeared excited as he revealed that he had found the information on the U.N. resolution he was referring to in his interviews.

The statement was now complete and became the AMA's official response to the Hillary-Lazio controversy. It was issued as a press release on October 27, 2000.

The response, captioned "American Muslim Alliance Responds to Return of Donations by Clinton Campaign" was posted on the AMA Web site, with Farooq Ansari as the contact person.

(Fremont, California, 10/27/2000) The American Muslim Alliance (AMA), a civic educational Muslim organization, today responded to the controversy over the return of contributions from Boston-area Muslims by New York Senate candidate Hillary Rodham Clinton.

In the AMA statement, AMA National Chair Dr. Agha Saeed said, "The recent decision by Mrs. Hillary Clinton to return contributions by Boston-area Muslims was a response to a news item in a local tabloid bearing the headline, 'Israel Foes Give Hil 50G: Muslim Group Backs Palestinian Use of Force.'

"I believe that any American has the First Amendment right to criticize Israeli injustice without being marginalized or intimidated in the American media and political arena. While I support a peaceful resolution of the Mid-East conflict and denounce all acts of terrorism, I do not believe that Muslims should feel they must be silent while Israelis kill those whose land and lives they are occupying illegally.

"The peace process is not a license to kill. As long as the Israeli government and Israeli settlers continue to kill Palestinian men, women and children, we will continue to condemn their atrocities and to expose the hideous nature of their neo-colonial occupation.

"Whether individually or as a group, Muslims should not be judged by some litmus test on blind support of Israel and should not be hindered from criticizing unjust Israeli tactics. As Dr. Martin Luther King, Jr. insightfully observed, 'Injustice anywhere is a threat to justice everywhere.'

"The participants in the Boston fund-raiser and the AMA have been greatly appreciative of Mrs. Clinton's willingness to include all Americans in American public life. Therefore, contrary to assertions by Ed Koch and others, AMA has not sought, nor will it seek to undermine the First Lady's campaign, particularly in view of Lazio's xenophobic and divisive approach.

"We are, however, deeply troubled that Mrs. Clinton has accepted accusations about a major mainstream Muslim organization by a New York tabloid without inquiring about the accuracy of those accusations. This lack of inquiry was clearly demonstrated when she said that she was 'offended by remarks *attributed* to the members' of the AMA. While we understand her political predicament, we are profoundly disturbed by her hasty generalization about our organization. Mrs. Clinton has likely been the victim of a vicious smear campaign, orchestrated once again by those who oppose justice and fairness in the Middle East. It is unfortunate that a prominent politician once again succumbs to anti-Muslim McCarthyism. Boston AMA members whose checks are now being returned, as well as many among the estimated one million Muslim- and Arab-Americans living in New York state, have expressed deep disappointment in Mrs. Clinton's recent public statements.

"We believe this attempt at political marginalization is being prompted by groups that have maintained a monopoly over America's Mid-East policy for the last several decades and who perceive a threat in the increased participation by Muslims and Arab-Americans in this country's political process. In this smear campaign, ethnic and religious stereotypes, distorted information, partial citations and complete fabrications are used as tactics of intimidation. Some xenophobes, under the professional disguise of journalism, are calling political candidates and asking outright racist questions, for example, 'We understand you are accepting contributions from Muslims.'

"We denounce this bigotry in the strongest terms and we expect every decent American politician to say, 'Yes I am, because I am seeking to represent all Americans and I will not tolerate the exclusion of any community or its legitimate representatives.'

"Determined to fight the anti-Muslim McCarthyism, AMA

encourages its members and all Muslims to redouble their efforts at participation in this year's election. Muslims are encouraged to register, vote, volunteer for campaigns, contribute to candidates and run for office. As a major mainstream American Muslim organization, AMA will carry out statewide get-out-the-vote campaigns in the swing states of Michigan, Ohio, Illinois, Iowa, Wisconsin and Florida. We also plan to vigorously participate in the senatorial elections in New York and California. The nationwide publicity generated by Mrs. Clinton's recent remarks has only served to increase our resolve and visibility in making a difference in our communities all across America.

"Finally, AMA unequivocally denounces terrorism by both sides: Israeli as well as Palestinian. Some reports imply that I and, by association, AMA, support 'armed struggle' in the Middle East. Nothing could be further from the truth. My reference to a particular U.N. resolution was a reference to the reasonable and peaceful route that the Palestine authorities had adopted through the Oslo Accord, even when the international legal community had afforded them the option to pursue their independence through armed struggle. The existence of this international precedent of allowing armed struggle for the Palestinians also serves as a reminder of the urgent need for a just peace in the Middle East. It is a reminder that there cannot be peace without justice. At the request of various media representatives, I am providing the following excerpt from a U.N. General Assembly resolution from the mid-1970s, which is still on the books, and which recognizes a right to armed struggle for oppressed peoples. U.N. General Assembly Resolution 31/34 of 30 November 1976, [c]ondemning all governments which do not recognize the right to self-determination and independence of all people under colonial and foreign domination and alien subjugation, notably the peoples of Africa and the Palestinian people, '[r]eaffirms the legitimacy of the peoples' struggle for independence, territorial integrity, national unity, and liberation from colonial and foreign domination, and alien subjugation by all available means, including armed struggle...'"

That evening on October 27 I headed out to D.C. to attend the rally and show solidarity for *Al-Aqsa* Mosque and Jerusalem. The rally scheduled for October 28th was expected to draw thousands of Muslims from across the States. I wanted very much to avail myself of this opportunity to talk about the importance of the bloc vote. I realized that my presence that weekend in Boston or New York City was equally important, if not more, especially after the AMA's official response. But I was confident that, with Agha Saeed on the West Coast, Farooq Ansari on the East Coast and me in the U.S. capitol city, between the three of us, we pretty much had our bases covered. Farooq Ansari that day, in an interview with a reporter from *The Los Angeles Times,* managed to give a good account of the Hillary fundraiser event. He answered questions and tried his best to do damage control. He was successful in clearing up some confusions and ambiguities that were on many minds.

Rally participants under a clear, sunny sky were zeroing in on Freedom Plaza, the rendezvous point in D.C. Law enforcers in helicopters hovering above would have a bird's-eye view. I can imagine the scene from up above, with most women wearing a *hijab* over their heads and with men converging from around the block to a central location on the Plaza, like ants swarming onto an anthill or human spokes of a wheel. Participants came to the rally from all across the States. Speakers were busy delivering their message to the people gathered. I had missed my cue, as Mohammad Khusro and others in the Massachusetts delegation told me when I met them in the crowd. One of them could have spoken in my place and represented Massachusetts had the organizers not called me by name.

Nevertheless, I was not about to miss my other speaking engagement at Lafayette Park. Aly Abuzaakouk, executive director of the American Muslim Council, was happy to see me and embraced me. "Where were you? We were looking for you. We were calling your name." This scene brought back to memory a similar encounter. Deja vu?

The first time I met Aly Abuzaakouk was in 1993 at the AMC annual convention where I was a scheduled speaker. I stopped over en route to South Carolina, where I was headed to see how my son was doing. Yaser was being treated for his leukemia at Richland Memorial Hospital in Columbia, South Carolina. Alamoudi told me that he would understand if I canceled my speaking engagement. "A commitment is a commitment," I told him.

At the registration table, when I introduced myself to the lady taking names, a man turned around and shouted with glee, "I found him. I found Mr. Ali." This was Aly Abuzaakouk, who had been anxiously on the lookout for me. I arrived there just minutes before my session was scheduled to start. I could swear that he was wearing the same glasses in D.C. as he did that day, his eyes appearing magnified through the bifocals.

Aly Abuzaakouk and I joined the thousands in the march from Freedom Plaza to Lafayette Park. It was well organized and very peaceful. The protesters were assembled in an orderly fashion in Lafayette Park, directly across from the White House. We took our seats on the large stage with the rest of the speakers. Behind us was a large screen where images and related videos were being projected, along with stage activity.

The Washington Post, in its issue of October 29 reported, "The rally, one of the largest in the United States since the Middle East peace process disintegrated, was organized in less than two weeks, not normally enough time to muster this many people, organizers said. But they came from as far away as Detroit and Boston."

CNN [http://www.cnn.com/2000/US/10/29/dc.protest.01/] had this to report: "Thousands of American Muslims attended a march and rally in front of the White House on Saturday in protest over Israeli attacks on Palestinian civilians and Islamic holy sites in Jerusalem. At its height, organizers estimated there were about 15,000 demonstrators."

This was in reference to the October 28, 2000, rally that drew over 10,000 Muslim-Americans. News agencies covering the event included among others: ABC, NBC, CNN, *Al-Jazeerah* TV, Reuters, the Associated Press (print and TV), Agence France Presse (AFP), *The Washington Post, The Washington Times, The Detroit News* and National Public Radio (NPR). I learned later that the event was televised live in Palestine and other parts of the Arab world.

According to the report filed by AMC:

10,000 Rally in Front of the White House for Al-Aqsa and Free Jerusalem

The "Jerusalem Day" rally organized by the National Task Force for the Crisis in Jerusalem, was addressed by Dr. Muzammil Siddiqi, President of the Islamic Society of North America (ISNA), who also serves as the national coordinator of the Task Force.

Dr. Siddiqi said, "...civilized people everywhere have unanimously condemned the use of excessive force by Israel against the Palestinians and Al- Aqsa Mosque, Islam's third holiest site, and against American strategic support and funding of Israeli atrocities."

The rally was accompanied by 130 marchers, many of whom were children, dressed in black and carrying paper tombstones bearing the names, ages and pictures of Palestinians killed by Israel as of Saturday in the recent aggressions. Carrying American and Palestinian flags, and flourishing signs calling for an end to the aggression and the illegal occupation of Jerusalem, Palestine and Palestinian territories and Jerusalem, they convened in front of the White House where they stood side by side and performed *Zuhr* and *Asr* prayers.

Members of the National Task Force for the Crisis in Jerusalem:

> American Muslim Council (AMC)
> American Arab Anti-Discrimination Committee (ADC)
> American Committee on Jerusalem (ACJ)
> American Muslim Alliance (AMA)
> American Muslims for Jerusalem (AMJ)
> Arab American Institute (AAI)
> Council on American Islamic Relations (CAIR)
> Islamic Association for Palestine (IAP)
> Islamic Circle of North America (ICNA)
> Islamic Institute Foundation (IIF)
> Islamic Society of North America (ISNA)
> Muslim-American Society (MAS)
> Muslim Public Affairs Council (MPAC)
> Muslim Student Association (MSA)

Mahdi Bray of the *Muslim Public Affairs Council* (MPAC) was hoarse at the end of the day. It was a tremendous task for the master of ceremonies, but Mahdi took on the feat and managed to stay *on* his feet the entire day. Aly Abuzaakouk is an effective speaker, and he outlined the purpose of the rally in a broad sense. "This rally signifies the unity of the Muslim-American community in its stance on *Al-Aqsa*, Jerusalem and Palestine. Our administration must show fairness and not favoritism brokering a just peace in accordance with United Nations resolutions and international law. Jerusalem is in the heart of every Muslim."

Executive Director of the Council on American Islamic Relations (CAIR) Nihad Awad, overwhelmed by the huge turnout, commended the crowd for their action and unity.

Muslims were not the only speakers at the rally. The protesters were utterly amazed when Orthodox rabbis also joined in and endorsed the Palestinian protest. That had to be the climax of the day. There were about twelve rabbis who had a joint statement scribed by Rabbi David Weiss, spokesman for Neturei Karta International, an organization of Orthodox Jews opposed to Zionism, according to the statement they handed out. They all stood silently on the stage observing their Sabbath, while Mehdi Bray read their message:

> "We are grateful to the creator for allowing us to participate in Washington today with the National Task Force for Jerusalem's demonstration of solidarity with the suffering of the Palestinian people.
>
> "For 52 years the world has ignored the just claims and rights of the Palestinian people. We condemn the actions [of Israel] in these past weeks. The justice of the current situation lies entirely with the Palestinian people. They have been dispossessed. Political control over the land belongs to them.
>
> "The wrong committed over the past 52 years by Zionists against indigenous people of the Holy Land is a ghastly crime. It is particularly imperative that Jews stand together with our Arab cousins. It is most important, from a moral perspective, that Torah Jews the world over express sincere Jewish regret over the deeds of the state of Israel."

The statement also read, "Jews are a people in exile. We do not desire in any way, shape or form Jewish sovereignty over the Holy Land. With the advent of the Messiah, all mankind will live in harmony and peace and serve G-d in joy."

I was not quite sure why the statement spelled G-d with a blank, and, before I could get a chance to ask them, they had left. (Uness they are not supposed to actually say the name of GOD.)The statement had their street address in Monsey, New York, their phone number and even their e-mail address.

To witness the twelve bearded rabbis in their religious attire standing with the rally's participants was sight for sore eyes. Their statement, I thought, was very strong, and the views they expressed were unexpectedly very sympathetic towards the Palestinians. It must have offended some Israeli supporters. I for myself do not like to use the "Z-word." Maybe there *is* hope. Maybe the "Israeli-Palestinian" differences can be best resolved on religious grounds, after all.

But the message that I wanted to convey at this juncture was directed more toward the American Muslims. I had stuck on the podium an enlarged copy of the front page of *The MetroWest Daily News* showing the headline "Muslims Organize Voting Bloc" in large print. One of my purposes for showing up here was to capitalize on the gathering and urge the Muslims not to lose sight of the bloc vote.

"We keep wondering why the candidates do not listen to us." I told them. "Maybe it is because their political advisers' assessment of us is true: that the Muslims have no one issue they can unite on, they lack a voting strategy and Muslims of Arab heritage ignore the voting process.

Will you allow me to correct them by conveying your resolve today? That all Muslims *are* voting as a bloc; all Muslims are voting for *one* candidate; and we *do unite* on one issue, and that is '*Jerusalem*.'" The jubilant response from the crowd convinced me that my message had gotten through.

I was a little further into the crowd and away from the stage when Abdurahman Alamoudi was introduced as the speaker. He was not too far into his opening remarks when he made reference to his comments in the media with regard to the Hillary-Lazio Senate race.

"I have been labeled by the media in New York to be a supporter of Hamas. Anybody support Hamas here?" I must admit, the crowd did go wild in agreement. After getting approval from the crowd repeatedly, he turned his head towards the White House and continued, "Did you hear that Bill Clinton? We are all supporters of Hamas. I wish they added that I am also a supporter of Hezbollah." Then he added once again, "Does anybody support Hezbollah here?" The crowd gave once again screamed in excitement. *Hezbollah*, meaning the "army of God," had in 1983 claimed responsibility for a bomb explosion that left 239 American Marines dead in their barracks in Beirut.

Toward the end of the rally, when I met Alamoudi in the park, we discussed in some detail the Hillary-Lazio factor. I was curious to find out what his plans were in pursuing the allegations made against him. Alamoudi mentioned one Stanley Cohen to be his counsel. "You just made Cohen's job more difficult by making those remarks about Hamas and then Hezbollah. I am sure it will be used against you," I told Alamoudi. I was quite sure that his remarks would be in the New York papers. I soon found out, when I returned to Boston.

A funny thing happened to me on my way to Boston that time. I took a break in New Jersey. There is a street in Iselin, New Jersey, that is known as "little India." There are stores on both sides of the street where you can get groceries from India and Pakistan. The street is normally full of shoppers who are of Indian or Pakistani decent. Whatever stores I visited there, people would turn around and look at me as if they knew me or recognized me from someplace.

It was my brother Hamid and his wife Azra, whose house we were staying at, who told me that the photo showing Mrs. Clinton and me, with her holding the AMA plaque, had been shown there "round the clock." It had even made national TV.

Alamoudi's remarks, so boldly voiced at Lafayette Park, had indeed made it into the news, and Lazio grabbed this opportunity to further embarrass and attack Mrs. Clinton. The Lazio campaign somehow even got hold of an amateur videotape of Alamoudi making those remarks and added that video clip to their smear campaign against Hillary Clinton. News agencies like CNN were showing the video clip. Actually, this was a boost for the Lazio campaign—a way out—a face-saving opportunity to dig themselves out of the hole they'd been in over the USS Cole fracas.

Governor Pataki was quoted as saying the calls were wrong. Hillary Clinton had better campaign advisers and loyal friends. Former New York Mayor Ed Koch came to her rescue once again, this time using the same tactics as Lazio. He appeared on a TV ad not long before Lazio was airing Alamoudi's footage. Koch with a big smile on his face appeared saying, "Rick, stop with the sleaze, already!" Then, speaking over a picture of Rick Lazio with Yasser Arafat shaking hands and smiling, Koch added, "This means Lazio supports terrorism? Come on!"

I have to hand it to the first lady and her campaign strategists. They used the same tactic as Lazio had, inferring guilt by association in a fitting manner.

After I got back from D.C., the first thing I did was send an e-mail to Muslims in Boston. I owed them that. The news about Hillary Clinton's fund-raiser and the controversy surrounding it was a constant media event, both national and international, as evident from the few examples here.

> **Al-Ahram, Issue No. 507, Cairo, Egypt.** 11/15/00
> "Thus the woman [Mrs. Clinton] who, on a visit to Gaza with her husband a couple of years ago came out strongly in favor of a Palestinian state, earning herself a standing ovation from the Palestinian parliament, recently announced that she was returning $50,000 raised for her campaign by the American Muslim Alliance, because they were supporting "terrorism," i.e., the Intifada. This shocking announcement, obviously designed to boost her credit rating with New York's strong Jewish constituency, reflects badly on democracy in America…"

> **Christian Science Monitor**; "Muslim-Americans work to make their vote heard"
> By: Jane Lampman on 11/02/2000
> "Muslims' efforts to enter the political mainstream can be fraught with difficulty. In the New York Senate race last week, Hillary Rodham Clinton returned campaign contributions from members of the AMA after it was charged that Agha Saeed, a professor of political science and chair of the AMA and AMPCC, was a supporter of armed force against Israel…
> Tahir Ali, a software engineer who chairs the Massachusetts of the American Muslim Alliance (AMA), is active in state Republican circles and was an adviser on a 1996 Republican presidential campaign task force.

> **Australian.** "BUSH v GORE"
> highered.theoz.com.au/flathtml/extra/bushgore/congress9.html
> "…returned $US50,000 ($94,600), collected at a fund-raiser sponsored by the American Muslim Alliance, and insists she did not know of its involvement in the event…"

Reported in *L'Alsace Monde.* **France** 10/26/00

Moslem funds for the countryside of Hillary Clinton

"A group of Moslem Americans supporting the armed struggle of the Palestinians against Israel organized in June a meeting of fund collection in favor of Hillary Clinton during which 50 000 dollars were gathered, the daily newspaper *Daily News* revealed. The spokesman of Mrs. Clinton, Howard Wolfson, confirmed that the meeting was held, but gave assurance that the First Lady had attended it thinking that it was organized by members of the Moslem community of Boston and not by the American Muslim Alliance (AMA)."

By this time, the AMA official response had been sent to me by the AMA national site for wider distribution. On October 30th I did just that, also including my response in *The New York Times:* "But I mostly feel sorry for the first lady."

Tariq Malik at the time was the president of the Pakistan Association of Greater Boston (PAGB), and Shahid Ahmed Khan was a PAGB executive at the time. Apparently, PAGB executives were the ones approached first to host a fund-raiser for Mrs. Clinton. Tariq Malik had insisted that any political activity falls under the charter of AMA. In his e-mail Tariq wrote:

"...I also feel sorry for Hillary Clinton for another reason and a fact. The fact is that Boston fund-raiser organizers were not forthright in their dealings with Mrs. Clinton while arranging a fund-raiser in her honor. Mrs. Clinton and her campaign office had made it clear right from the first meeting [Tariq did not provide a date] at Wayland Mosque that they would not participate in any fund-raiser organized by a Muslim organization, e.g., AMA, AMC, etc. This was a point of great concern, and some members present at the meeting (Dr. Siddiq Abdullah, Mr. Tahir Choudhary and myself) raised this issue with Mr. Mansoor Ijaz (Hillary's liaison for the Boston fund-raiser).

A large number of community members disengaged themselves from this event for lack of purpose and vision of the event. Hillary's campaign office set up a temporary office in Boston (two weeks prior to the event) to handle invitations and logistics of the event. They printed the invitations. There is no mention of AMA as a host. So far, so good.

A couple of days before the event the organizers realized

the lack of funds to support the event. They called AMA and asked for help. Credit goes to AMA Boston chapter for coming forward on such a short notice. Their effort perhaps is even more commendable since they were totally marginalized by not being invited to planning meetings that had been going on for two to three months. I am not sure that AMA Boston chapter was told about Hillary's condition when they asked for help.

Hillary can invite Muslims to celebrate *Eid* at the White House and can even go out on a limb once in a while for Muslims (remember her visit to Middle East and her meeting with Mr. Arafat and his wife). But do not expect her to back you up, when you blatantly ignore the fundamental agreement of a contract and shaft her with a plaque at the last minute. Poor Hillary is right when she says that the Boston event was hosted by a businessman, Mr. Shahid Khan, because that's what the verbal agreement was between the two parties, and that's what the invitation said. But when she was reminded of receiving a plaque, her answer was, "I receive hundred of plaques and I hand them over to my aides." Perhaps Mrs. Clinton would have been better off if she had taken a good hard look at the plaque she received in Boston. But even if she had taken a good look at the plaque, what could she have done? How could she return the plaque, when so many of Boston Muslims were there with good intentions and best wishes for her. Some were even claiming that she will be the next president of the U.S., and Muslims will have a true friend in the White House, and so on. A couple of things have happened here:

1) Boston community in particular and Muslim community in general have been marginalized, even with all the good intentions.

2) New York Muslim community did a fund-raiser for Hillary three weeks prior to Boston fund-raiser. Hillary is not returning their money because whatever the verbal agreement between the two parties was, it was honored.

3) AMA Boston chapter efforts to make this event a success, at least for that evening, are noteworthy.

We could have avoided a lot of confusion if Tariq Malik had made this information available to me before the AMA got involved with the Hillary Clinton fund-raiser, or even a few days after the event was over. It would have better prepared me to talk to reporters, hence avoiding contradictory statements. However, there were two ex-presidents of Massachusetts AMA who were indeed against the fund-raiser, not in principal because of Mrs. Clinton's terms, but because of the reasons indicated earlier in this chapter.

At this point in time American Muslims were at a tremendous disadvantage. They watched in horror as Lazio used deceptive campaign tactics at their expense. This witch-hunt had to stop. Appropriately, on Halloween day, American Muslim organizations condemned this "anti-Muslim bigotry" and released a joint statement which read:

> We condemn Rick Lazio in the strongest possible terms for his deceitful accusations about American Muslim organizations and individuals. In a desperate bid to win November 7 elections, Mr. Lazio is trying to turn Muslims into "the Willy Horton of 2000." He is telling New Yorkers that Muslims are guilty by virtue of being Muslims. This reprehensible tactic is designed to malign the entire Muslim community and to lock its members out of the political process. His scurrilous campaign is an attack on democratic norms and on our constitutional rights.
>
> We also condemn Lazio for his racist logic. It is the same logic that was used to conceptualize and justify the internment of Japanese Americans during the second World War. The Japanese Relocation Order of February 19, 1942, was based on calling into question the loyalty as well as the human dignity of those American citizens who had a different ethnicity and a different religion.
>
> We call on all Americans to "just say no" to Mr. Lazio's anti-Muslim racism and ask that political leaders of all parties take a stand on this issue. Failure to speak out against Mr. Lazio's recent actions and statements will send the message that there is room for racism and bigotry in America.
>
> Signed by:
>
> Dr. Agha Saeed, American Muslim Alliance
> Dr. Sayyid Syeed, Islamic Society of North America

Mr. Omar Ahmad, Council on American-Islamic
Relations
Mr. Aly Abuzaakouk, American Muslim Council
Dr. Ashraf Uzzaman, Islamic Circle of North
America
Dr. Maher Hathout, Muslim Public Affairs Council
Dr. James Zogby, Arab-American Institute
Mr. Khalid Saffouri, American Islamic Institute
Mr. Shafi Refai, United Muslims of America

Catherine Herridge of Fox News had been a constant caller
throughout this exigent and mortifying episode. She always was
sympathetic in her approach. She understood and respected Muslim sentiments, emotions and anger for being tossed around by both
Lazio and Mrs. Clinton. She had been gathering quite a bit of information, using me as a resounding board. I gladly verified some of
the information she had collected: "Have any of the members received the money from Mrs. Clinton?" and, "Who is Stanley Cohen?
Is he Mr. Alamoudi's lawyer?"

She had offered to bring a camera crew right to my house if I
was willing to be interviewed. I agreed to go to their studio in Newton, instead. Eric Shawn of Fox News assured me that Catherine,
Dave Martin and he were all part of the same team. Eric found common grounds with me and told me he used to live in Westborough.
"I lived on the other side of the tracks." The crew was nervously
waiting for me at the studio in Newton and, the minute I showed up
with my family, they got me in a chair in front of the camera.

Eric Shawn discussed the format with me. We talked a little off-
air so that I was comfortable with the format. I could only hear him,
since he was in New York and the interview was being done via
satellite.

Eric's questions were very clear and right to the point. He did
not dance around the issues, nor did he try to trick me into answering any questions that could have proven embarrassing for the Muslim community or me. Except maybe the one he asked me at last,
"Mr. Ali, are you a terrorist?" In answer to which I burst into laughter and he joined me. But even the way he asked the question, it had
sounded almost rhetorical.

Eric was amused when I told him where I got the plaque idea —
my son Amir Ali, who received a plaque for being in *Who's Who in*

American High School Students. At this interview I was again very careful not to say anything that could jeopardize Mrs. Clinton's position further, as I told Eric that what really hurt was the fact that she rushed to judgment.

The interview was on Fox News Live with John Gibson and aired on November 4th at 5:00 p.m., with not enough time for me to get home to watch it. So I called AMA's treasurer Jamila Khan from the studio, and asked her to watch it. "The interview was fine," she told me later, since I missed it. "I enjoyed your comment when you suggested that Lazio and Hillary should put on gloves and go to Madison Square Garden and knock themselves out there." They thought it was funny too, you could hear Eric and John chuckling in the background. In fact, Eric agreed saying "...maybe that's what it will come to, a boxing match in this race."

Jamila, originally from Trinidad, advised me to get a copy of that evening's news, including the interviews with Hillary's and Lazio's campaign officers that followed right after mine.

John Gibson introduced Eric Shawn as a senior Fox News correspondent. John talked about the results of the new polls that showed the undecided votes swinging toward Hillary Clinton. He characterized the Hillary-Lazio Senate race as "*Intifada* [uprising], New York style" over which candidate most firmly supported Israel, which candidate was trying to take contributions from Muslim groups while saying he or she was not..."

Eric agreed, "*intifada* [uprising] is really the right word for this situation here in New York. Mrs. Clinton is under attack from Rick Lazio, his campaign claiming that she has met with people. Hosted them in the White House. Taken money for her campaign from people who support Mid-East terrorists. She says that this type of allegation is absolutely beneath even Rick Lazio. Last night she was really angry about that at a dinner."

Eric paused for a second then added, "We've been following this story...It really centers on a fund-raising event last June in Boston, in which she was given fifty-thousand dollars. She says she's giving that money back because it turned out that some members of that group support armed force against Israel. Turns out that she sent a thank-you letter to that group after having claimed that she didn't know who hosted the event—a thank-you letter on White House stationery. She said last night that she didn't even know about this letter..."

Eric then went on to add that, earlier that afternoon, he talked to me and that I was "outraged and sad." Footage from my interview was shown next, the part where I made the comment about a "rush to judgment" on Mrs. Clinton's part.

Eric pointed out to John that none of the checks had been returned yet. My comments on that had held some hope that the reason for the checks not being in the mail was, perhaps, because her campaign had realized that whatever Lazio was saying was just a manifestation of bigotry and smear politics. Maybe Hillary Clinton and her campaign had done their homework and realized that "this was good money." I told Eric that, but with the hope that it might be true, that if Lazio didn't do his homework, Hillary had done hers.

Eric was kind enough tell his audience something about me, "Mr. Ali wants everyone to know that he is an American, an honest American, and his children are American. And they have been very hurt by all this."

Gibson with his final question hit it right on the head in identifying one of the root causes of this fiasco, "If there hadn't been this uprising in Israel right now, would these candidates have been so embarrassed about taking this money?"

Eric's reply was fair; "It would not have been such a big issue as it is in the campaign now. If it had been quieter in the Mid-East, this issue would have been on the side, because Muslims in New York City have long been active — but it's possibly those other issues that have thrust these to the forefront."

Jamila Khan was correct in her assessment regarding the interviews that followed. She had mentioned that the last portion of the interviews was very important to the issue. Leading executives from Lazio and Hillary campaign offices were Gibson's guests.

John's next guest was Victor Kovner, Hillary Clinton's adviser. Victor indicated that 500,000 calls in reference to the USS Cole were made by Lazio campaign.

I believe this is where Lazio, blinded by bigotry, went overboard — big mistake. Most Republicans, particularly Mayor Guilliani and Governor Pataki, confirmed as much as they were backing out. Lazio had added more fuel to the fire, further inflaming Muslim passions and anger. Saghir Tahir in his e-mail suggested that the AMA should sue Lazio and his campaign. Saghir indicated to me that he was "hanging on" to the newspapers. Eric Vickers of AMA national sent out a press release on November 1st stating that "AMA intends to spearhead a multimillion-dollar suit against Lazio and others for USS Cole bombing being linked to Mrs. Clinton and the AMA, calling this misinformation the cause for "actionable outrage." The statement also indicated that "the legal action was against Rick Lazio, the New York Republican State Committee, the Lazio for Senate Committee, the New York *Daily News* and others, in relation to recent media reports and Republican phone canvassing seeking to link the AMA to terrorist groups in the Mid-East."

The phone campaign seeking to link Mrs. Clinton and the AMA with the groups bombing the USS Cole was indeed outrageous, demeaning, false and malicious. It was "damaging to the reputations of the AMA and the individuals whose contributions were returned, who now appear guilty by association."

John, as usual, asked the direct question: "Is Hillary Clinton embarrassed about having taken Muslim money?"

"The answer is *absolutely not.*" Victor tried to explain the main reason for returning the money was Alamoudi, "she is embarrassed by a particular person and a particular group who had supported violence in the Middle East, and that's why she gave back that money." He pointed out that Governor Bush accepted money from the same person, "Alamoudi is his name, who, by the way, had a job in the Pentagon, originally from President Bush's administration, doing work with our chaplains."

I admire the style of John Gibson's questioning. Regarding the "museum flap" — Hillary's campaign mistakenly calling the American Muslim Council the "American *Museum* Council." "A typo? Or really trying to cover up where that money was coming from?"

I agreed with Victor's response to that query: it had to be a typo because it was too stupid to be considered a deliberate attempt to hide the facts. "Non-issue," Victor tried to explain. "Plainly, it was a typo. All the people's names were listed. Only one particular person who has supported violence, but who played a leading role in this particular group, was the reason that not only was his check returned, Governor Bush also returned his check. And he returned it just a week ago."

Victor dragged in Alamoudi as he continued on the defense, "So that no one should have any question Hillary, announced that all the money raised at that fund-raiser should be returned, and she didn't know which group was supporting that fund-raiser. So that no question would be raised Hillary announced that all the money raised at that fund-raiser would be returned."

By saying that, Victor confirmed what we had always said: that Mrs. Clinton did rush to judgment and return the AMA funds without even first taking the time to investigate the allegations. The correct thing for her to have done, in my opinion, would have been simply to return Alamoudi's money and do her homework regarding the AMA. If she had done so, she would have found that the money raised in Boston was mainly from professionals, like physicians, professors, engineers, and businessmen and women, people who had worked hard for the dollars that were given to Hillary Clinton. Then Lazio made things even worse, calling this hard-earned money by law-abiding, taxpaying citizens "blood money."

John seemed to be done with this issue, because his next question was concerning Bill Clinton.

But Victor was not done yet with Lazio. He respectfully waved off the Bill Clinton question and continued, "It is very troublesome that Republican tactics have demonized the Muslim-American community. There are hundreds of thousands millions of Muslims who are being lumped, as a result of the Lazio campaign, into association with violent conduct, and it is extremely divisive for our society."

John Gibson was not done yet either; he wanted to give Lazio's campaign manager Bill Dal Col an "equal chance." I am not sure why Gibson decided to adopt what appeared to be a "cat and mouse" style interview. If he had all three of us on at the same time, the outcome would have been interesting.

Bill appeared relaxed, as well. He agreed with Gibson that the race was at a "dead heat. It will come down to the wire," and outcome would depend on "voter turnout."

This was true, because it was the Muslim voter turnout that made the difference in the New York Senate race. Lazio lost his bid for the seat for want of almost a million votes. An AMA survey indicated that most of the Muslims and Christian Americans of Arab heritage, more than a million people, voted en bloc against Lazio.

Gibson wasted no time in getting to his next point, "So what is your response to Mr. Kovner's charge that you and Rick Lazio are behind these phone calls that were made linking Mrs. Clinton to the bombing of the U.S.S. Cole?

Bill did not argue that point at all, "We asked that the phone calls stop; they stopped." But he was not about to let that turn totally against Lazio. "The only person talking about it for the last six days is Mrs. Clinton. She's attempting to use it as a political weapon to damage Rick."

I could not help laughing at this. Look who's talking I said to myself. Isn't that what Lazio was doing all along? Now it was Bill's turn to be on the offensive, so he also dragged in an Alamoudi reference to support his argument. "Mrs. Clinton has got to explain what she was doing inviting someone who supported terrorism into the White House and accepting money from them. And, beyond that, your own network broke the story — to date no one has gotten their check back."

Bill defined Mrs. Clinton's actions in his own way: "Watch what she says versus what she does."

I personally thought you could say that about pretty much any candidate or incumbent. I remember what Congressman James McGovern said to me in his office in D.C., on the 22nd of June 2001, "They talk the talk, but they do not want to walk the walk."

Maybe John thought it was time to throw a bone to Bill when he raised the "museum flap" question: "Now what about the typo? Will you at least give them credit — or maybe a demerit — for maybe making a mistake"

Bill was in no hurry to budge. "It's part of a pattern; until they're caught, they don't acknowledge it. For example, they suddenly released a letter — an auto-penned letter — from the White House acknowledging that she had received a plaque and met with the very group that did the fund-raiser for her. It was magnanimous of them to hold the press conference. Why did she do it? Because reporters had already called saying they got the letter. So, with Mrs. Clinton, what you have to watch is when she gets caught, then she comes forward with the information."

Gibson's final question was an acknowledgment of the fact that there were a significant number of Muslim voters in New York. "New York has a quite sizeable number of not only Jewish voters but Muslim voters." The comment was fine, but the question that followed seemed derogatory, "Does Muslim money have a stink on it now so that you can't accept it?"

"No it doesn't not at all." Bill Dal Col's responded, but the rest sounded like a broken record.

Bill mentioned the thank-you letter addressed to me, which was sent by Hillary Clinton. What I found awkward was that Eric did not mention this letter during our interview. It was during a call from a *News Day* reporter from New York that afternoon that I learned such a letter existed. Elizabeth Moore brought my attention to the thank-you letter from Hillary Clinton addressed to my attention.

"You must have been getting a lot of calls," Liz was saying, in reference to the letter, and I responded in the affirmative based on the accuracy of her typical comment. When she started to mention the letter, I had no idea what she was talking about. On my request, she read the letter to me and was surprised that it was the first time I had heard about it.

There was always the possibility that the letter had gotten lost in the mail. Then it occurred to me, and I asked Liz what the mailing address was. The mystery was solved: the letter addressed to me had the mailing address of the National AMA in California. The interview with Liz went on for a while, and I continued to support Mrs. Clinton, which Liz mentioned in her news report the next day.

After I finished talking to Liz, I called Agha Saeed to find out why the letter was kept a secret from me. The correct thing for AMA to do, I thought, would have been to redirect a copy to me. Dr. Saeed calling it an "oversight" and indicated that the letter dated August 8, 2000 was printed in the AMA's 5th annual convention brochure. The convention was held on September 30, 2000, in Irvine, California. I was scheduled to attend, but elected to bow out at the last minute, due to a more pressing matter needed my attention. Dr. Saeed believed that Steven Emerson who was at the AMA convention might have kept the copy of that letter.

This letter may very well have been Lazio's ace up his sleeve. But before he could play it, Hillary's campaign people were one step ahead of him. Late Friday on November 3rd at the Plaza Hotel in Manhattan, where she was scheduled to speak at the annual conference of the Anti-Defamation League (ADL), Howard Wolfson handed out copies of the thank-you letter to reporters present there. It was a bold — but a good — move. Somehow Hillary's campaign must have learned that it had been leaked to a few reporters already.

Unfortunately for her, this missive written on the White House stationery was addressed to me via the American Muslim Alliance, dated August 8, and bore her signature at the end. In this letter, she was clearly acknowledging receipt from the AMA of the plaque presented to her during the fund-raiser in held in June. The letter posed yet another threat to her credibility; she had been asserting herself as being unaware of AMA's involvement in the Boston fund-raiser.

"It was a pleasure to be a part of the Massachusetts chapter meeting of the American Muslim Alliance," the letter read. "The plaque is a wonderful reminder of my visit. Please extend my appreciation and thanks to the entire membership."

The note, by her own admission, was a "typical thank-you letter" and her "auto-penned" signature, a computer simulation. "Gifts and plaques, and things that you pick up along the road are turned over to the White House gift unit," Mrs. Clinton told reporters that day. "I often don't even see the gifts that are given to me."

That got me wondering: how would all those who received auto-penned letters feel when they heard or read Mrs. Clinton's remarks and learned that the gift receiver does not even retain any knowledge about it, and shrugs off the gesture as a matter of routine. But what she was saying made me realize now, even more, the importance of the letter that Former Governor William Weld had sent me. I noticed that part of my name "Tahir" was handwritten in the opening address, "Dear Tahir Ali…"

"The governor did that to let you know that he read it and it was not auto-penned," the secretary who had typed the letter revealed, when I inquired out of curiosity.

I remember that, during my conversation with Eric Shawn, I had made reference to remarks of Mrs. Clinton's quoted in *The New York Times* of October 26, 2000: "We have 13 days left in this election; fasten your seat belts. This is just the beginning. You have no idea what is going to be thrown at me. It is going to be everything, including the kitchen sink."

"*You* are the kitchen sink." Shawn had replied.

Support and criticism came in many forms. It came from people we knew and from others we had never met in our lives. Some of them took the time to write to the newspapers, particularly *The New York Times*. Mujeeb R. Khan, policy coordinator of the Muslim Voters of America of Oak Park, Illinois, wrote a letter dated October 27, 2000, to the *New York Times* editor, "The American Muslim community will fight for and achieve recognition in our circumscribed democracy, like our African-American, Hispanic and Asian compatriots before us."

Robert M. Levine of Syosset, New York, raised an interesting question in his letter dated October 26th, "I was perplexed to read that Hillary Rodham Clinton is returning $50,000 in contributions raised at an event by a Muslim organization because she was offended by remarks attributed to members of the organization. Wouldn't it be more effective for Mrs. Clinton to announce that she will use the money to renounce the offending remarks and then do so?"

Then Nancy S. Dorfman of Belmont, from my home state of Massachusetts, characterized Mrs. Clinton's rejection of political contributions from AMA in her October 27th letter as "the most shameless form of pandering, not to mention hypocrisy, coming as it does from a person who prides herself on being a supporter of equal rights for people of all races and faiths."

Letters came as far as from London, England. Aly Rahim called it a "precarious time" for American Muslims. Aly wrote, "Her [Mrs. Clinton] actions further thrust millions of peaceful Muslim-Americans into an unwarranted abyss of public suspicion and prejudice."

Hillary Rodham Clinton, on October 29th, told reporters that she did not mean to offend Muslims in America when the funds were returned, and that she respected Islam. "I think every American deserves to be part of our political process," Mrs. Clinton said. *Dawn* of Karachi, Pakistan, on October 30th carried the same remarks under its headline "Hillary moves to appease Muslims."

Things were looking good for the first lady. Her campaign got editorial support from *The New York Times* and *Newsday*. *The New York Times* had editorially rebuked her opponent, New York Senatorial candidate Rick Lazio for his "attack politics," and described his conduct as "desperate," "unethical," "absurd" and "extreme." The newspaper the New York *Daily News,* that started the whole episode, came up with its editorial support as well, "Our choice is Hillary Clinton. Vote for her." The report concluded.

The Washington Post's heading of November 2nd, "Lazio's political pornography," caught the eye of many Muslims, especially since it was written by an American Jew: Richard Cohen. "The American Muslim Alliance is a mainstream group...equating the American Muslim Alliance with Hamas or Bin Laden's outfit because they are all Muslim and have a problem with Israel is like equating the Boy Scouts with the Nazi party, because they both dress up in uniforms and sing songs around a bonfire." Cohen concludes, "Now he [Lazio] has played the New York equivalent of the race card, plunging into the political sewer like a man attached to a pulley. The lower he sinks, the higher she goes."

And that's exactly what happened. Lazio found himself on

the defensive over the infamous ads and the "anti-Muslim bigotry" issue. American Muslims in New York were encouraged by their leadership to vote against Lazio. American Muslims decided to fight back. This became a door-to-door campaign. Shahid Ahmed Khan and other AMA members were busy going door-to-door, knocking on every Muslim's door in the neighborhood to go out and vote against Lazio. They did not sit out the election, but got out and voted. They were mad, but smart enough to get even.

The 800,000 Muslim New Yorkers succeeded in help defeat the all-weather bigot Rick Lazio by helping to elect the fair-weather liberal Hillary Clinton.

Jack Newfield of *The New York Post* outlined on November 8th ten reasons why Hillary Clinton beat Rick Lazio. The number one reason: "Lazio alienated moderate swing voters when his campaign insinuated Clinton condoned Arab terrorism against Israel and the United States." Newfield continued, "First, Lazio tried to exploit the overplayed *Daily News* story that linked Hillary's donors to Hamas…" Newfield chose the headline carefully: "How the 'carpet-bagger' cleaned his clock."

The minute Mrs. Clinton announced that she was going to return the money raised in Boston, and she did, thank you, it would have behooved Rick Lazio to keep his mouth shut. Had he done that, the estimated 800,000 Muslim New Yorkers would have voted heavily against Hillary Rodham Clinton, probably joined by the 250,000 Christian Arabs and other similar coalitions, and Rick Lazio, not Hillary would be at the Hill today. But Lazio's anti-Muslim bigotry and xenophobic approach cost him the election. This divisive tactic backfired so badly that it did not even matter whether the allegation against Mrs. Clinton were true or not that she called a former campaign adviser "a f---ing Jew bastard" after her husband Bill Clinton early in his career lost a congressional bid.

David Rosen later revealed to me that, when Shahid Ahmed Khan had introduced me to him as the "chairman of AMA," he thought AMA was some form of a medical association. David sounded sincere in his confession, and I believe it to be quite true.

The Muslim vote, however, was issue oriented and not party oriented. Muslim-Americans voted for both Democrats and Republicans. Whereas, the Muslim vote for Democratic candidate Hillary Clinton was characterized by a strong sense of disillusionment over her opportunistic behavior, the vote for Democratic candidates like David Bonior in Michigan, Maxine Waters in California, Jon Corzine in New Jersey, and Marcy Kaptur and Dennis Kucinich in Ohio reflected strong sentiments of support for these candidates.

Before or since the Hilary-Lazio blowup, very few American newspapers have had the courage or the openness to publish the above quoted U. N. General Assembly Resolution 31-34 of November 1976. However, Dean Murphy of the *New York Times* reflected the diginity of his profession then on October 27, 2000 he told his audience, in pointing that the attacks on AMA and Dr. Agha Saeed were indeed a smoke screen to invalidate the Muslim bloc vote:

> "When Salam Al-Marayati read yesterday that Hillary Rodham Clinton would return $50,000 in political contributions from members of the American Muslim Alliance, he got a sinking feeling. It was happening again, Mr. Al-Marayati said. A prominent Muslim-American — in this case, Agha Saeed, who is president of the alliance — was being punished for pushing Muslim-Americans into the political mainstream, he said. "Agha Saeed was successful in unifying the Muslim vote and, for the first time, in creating a voting bloc."

All this activity brought to mind a story I heard during my childhood:

> *A man, losing all he had, became depressed and wandered aimlessly for a long time. He heard of a wise man living many miles away who might be able to help him. After many hours on foot, he reached the refuge of the wise man. Upon hearing the story of his loss, the wise man answered simply, "It must be for the best, something good will come of it." Angered by the response, the man decided to take out his revenge and went to the wise man's home to wait for him. He waited all night in vain for the wise man did not return.*
>
> *In the morning, the man climbed back to the refuge and found the wise man again. Upon asking why he had not returned home, the wise man explained he had been ready to leave; but he slipped, twisting his ankle and could not walk back to his home "It must be for the best, something good will come of it."*

If the intention was to stigmatize some Muslim organizations and to seek their exclusion from the political process, the unintended consequences led to: 1) further isolation and ultimate defeat of Rick Lazio, 2) brought national attention to Muslim voters and organizations which showed them to be quite modern, moderate and mainstream, and 3) refocused the question of equal access to politics.

Even today, most people do not recognize the implicit connection between the Muslim Bloc Vote and the electoral controversy in Hillary Clinton's senate election in New York.

Shuntler stands his ground; McGreevey pull a Lazio;

M.A. Quadeer-Siddiqui, member of the AMA national executive committee called me and asked if I could repeat a presentation, "AMA in the News," that I had given a few weeks earlier at the AMA leadership conference in Massachusetts. Dr. Siddiqui, chairman and professor of anatomy and cell biology at the State University of New York-Downstate medical center, had over 100 publications to his name and was included in the top 2,000 "outstanding scientists" of the 21st century. He reminded me of my cousin Dr. S. M. Farouq Ali, who was named as the world's best in his field of petroleum and minerals, fluent in 17 languages including German, Japanese, Spanish, French and Russian. During the voter registration drive he told me, "I am glad that Muslims are finally gettting politically organized. It is the correct thing to do." His words spoken to me on October 19, 2000 were still fresh in my mind – "It is very important that Muslims – usually indifferent – participate in American politics. Otherwise, others will decide their fate, and they will have to live by rules made without any input from them."

I agreed to oblige Dr. M. A. Siddiqui and do a presentation at the AMA conference in New Jersey on April 28, 2001. The keynote speaker was Bret Schundler, Republican candidate for governor. Speaking at the conference, I gave an account of the Hillary/Lazio flap. This time it took a little over a month for Schundler to find himself trying to explain why he attended the AMA function. Shai Goldstein, director of New Jersey's Anti-Defamation League was on his case, but unlike Hillary Clinton, Schundler stood his ground, offered no apologies, recognized that Muslims constituted nine percent of New Jersey's population, and said, "Why should I be asked to justify or disagree with board members' [AMA] comments?" Bret won the Republican primary over Bob Franks. Jack Kemp, former

GOP presidential candidate, called Bret Schundler's victory one "for the ideas of Mr. Lincoln, our founder and Ronald Reagan."

Round 2: Bret Shundler's Democratic opponent Jim McGreevey was not holding any punches, either. He openly criticized Bret for participating at the AMA conference in April. He used the same "inflammatory / sewer politics" tactic that Rick Lazio had tried in his race against Hillary Clinton. In July of 2001, Muslims were quick to show their resentment of this bigotry. The AMA was joined by other Muslim organizations in the area, namely: Majlis Ash-Shura, American Muslim Council New Jersey chapter, the American Muslim Union, the Islamic Public Affairs Council, the Arab-American League of Voters, the Muslim-American Society New Jersey chapter, along with the Islamic Institute and CAIR, both Washington D.C based.

In their joint statement, they clearly considered McGreevey's attacks repugnant "anti-Muslim bogotry." The statement also read: "The McGreevey campaign's statements are an affront to the entire Muslim community, as they encroach on the constitutionally protected right of American Muslims to fully participate in the political process."

Round 3: Week later, members from the McGreevey campaign met with Muslim groups. The meeting resulted in a statement by McGreevey showing his regrets: "I regret any offense that may have been taken by the exchange of remarks between my campaign and individuals from the Muslim community. I, and I alone, am ultimately responsible for the statements and actions of this campaign."

When I got a chance to talk to M.A. Quadeer-Siddiqui that day, he appeared quite satisfied with the outcome of the meeting with McGreevey's campaign officers. He could appreciate what some of us had gone through with the Lazio/Hillary dispute. But McGreevey's statement appeased the Muslims who, in turn, sought an opportunity for meeting with McGreevey. I reminded Siddiqui that, since he was spearheading this effort on behalf of all of us, the AMA would have to be invited to these meetings as well. He was confident that there could be no meaningful talk without the AMA in the meeting. "We'll look forward to this opportunity so we can explain to him AMA's stance."

A week later Siddiqui got a call from McGeevey's office inviting him for a meeting with Jim McGreevey, along with 15 heads of the

Muslim organizations. "I asked M. Ali Chaudry to accompany me. He [McGreevey] said that he was sorry, not once but repeatedly, and said that his remarks were unwarranted; he wished he had done his homework," Siddiqui told me. "I told Jim McGreevey that we will help him and encourage those Democrats who were holding off, now to vote for him."

Siddiqui did just that in a statement that was published in leading newspapers and Muslim periodicals. M. Ali Chaudry, an activist who came to America over 25 years ago was also perturbed by this xenophobia and made several statements. The crux of his message was in alignment with those of other Muslims tired of bigotry: that Muslims had every right to participate in U.S. politics, without being intimidated or marginalized. M.A. Chaudry later was elected to a city office.

Bret Schundler issued his own statement praising McGreevey for his action. "I'm pleased that Jim has recognized his need to apologize for his statements and actions with regard to New Jersey's Muslim community."

Round 4: Regardless of how the Muslims voted, Jim McGreevey won the New Jersey gubernatorial race. He was probably not sorry for saying "sorry."

To Endorse or not to Endorse...

Meanwhile, the mayoral race in New York, between Democrat Mark Green and Republican Michael Bloomberg, was not free of its own surprises, either. That too was proving to be embarrassing for Muslims. However, there was an interesting twist here. Both candidates were Jewish, and Muslim organizations were backing the candidates, but not without controversy. The endorsement for Mark Green by a coalition of Muslim organizations - The Muslim Political Coordinating Committee (MPCC of New York) - was jeopardized, as Assemblyman Dov Hikind criticized Green for accepting the Muslim group's support. AMA was again a target, and, frankly, it sounded like a broken record.

Ali A. Mirza, speaking for the coalition, blamed Hikind for using the endorsement to hurt Green. In this confusion, some of the members of the coalition reportedly withdrew the endorsement. The headlines in New York papers indicated that the endorsement was indeed withdrawn by the Muslim group. The disparity among the

Muslims was damaging to any unity of purpose. This hasty action was quickly corrected as the MPCC scrambled to put out a statement reasserting their endorsement for Mark Green, as well as for City Councilman Sheldon Leffler of Queens, Councilman Pedro Espada of the Bronx and Ken Fisher of Brooklyn.

Bloomberg took the oath of office on New Year's Day, 2002, with Former Mayor Rudy Guilliani presiding.

It had become quite clear by now that American Muslims were politically savvy, in significantly large numbers. Smearing Muslims for political gain was a thing of past.

I concur with Paul Findley who wrote on page 69 of *Silent No More:* "I doubt that the term 'Emersonism' will make it into the dictionary, but through *Jihad in America,* Emerson had damaged American society more permanently than did McCarthyism."

But the term "Pull a Lazio," as a deterrent to smearing Muslims in the political arena, had made its debut noticeably - within the minds of Muslims and other ethnic groups.

CHAPTER 11   *After the Bloc Vote*

[The debates shift from whether or not we should participate and whether or not we should vote to whether or not we should have voted for Republican].

The Rosemont Convention Center in Chicago, Illinois, on September 1, 2001, was packed with mostly American Muslims who had traveled across the States and around the globe to attend the 38th annual ISNA convention.

Sayyid Syeed had a huge task ahead of him. He realized that the convention hall was packed to the aisles, and he had to repeatedly warn people not to block any of the exits. He was concerned for their safety, but at the same time one could see that he was also pleasantly excited. He knew that this indeed was a proud moment for him and for ISNA when he asked, "Do you all remember what we nick-named Chicago at last year's convention?"

"Yes," came the audience answer, "Chicago *Shareef.*"

"Your immense presence today is a testimonial to that fact." There are always a few unsung heroes. Sayyid Syeed may fall well into that category. But then, there are always one or two individuals who are considered the backbone of an organization. That person may not be a member of the executive committee, yet he or she serves as the guiding light. Sayyid Syeed is one of them.

When we talk about ISNA, the first name that comes to mind is that of Sayyid Syeed. In the same way, when we talk about the American Muslim Council (AMC) the name that pops into the mind is that of Abdurahman Alamoudi, who served as its secretary, not its president. Nihad Awad's name has become synonymous with the Council for American-Islamic Relations (CAIR). Then there are others who stand out, each in their own way — Sirhaj Wahaj, Yusuf Islam (known to the Western World as Cat Stevens) and many others. Sayyid Syeed was born in Kashmir, a land that was at one time called "heaven on earth." Kashmir has now been made into hell on earth by outside forces, depriving Kashmiris of their autonomy.

"We are very large in numbers and we are diverse; people from different backgrounds, race and color. So we are diverse and we are many, but let me tell you one thing: we are weak, our community is weak. If we are not together, then we are weak." Those were the opening remarks offered by the outgoing ISNA president of four years Dr. Muzammil Siddiqi, as he welcomed the president-elect Sheikh Mohammed Nur Abdullah, originally from Sudan.

Siraj Wahaj, born in an African-American Christian family, embraced Islam in his early years. When he spoke, people paid close attention. With his heavy voice and forceful delivery, it was expected of him to get emotional during his ISNA speech, but at the same time maintain his composure, remaining in complete control of his thought process. It is a quality not many possess.

Siraj Wahaj, in making a point, recalled an incident that had happened in Washington, D.C. *Imam* Talib Rasheed was invited to a national Muslim organization meeting. He watched silently as the leadership prepared a list of ten items that they felt were important for the American Muslim agenda. Next, they assigned priorities to each item. At length *Imam* Talib Rasheed, a U.S. immigrant, was asked for his opinion.

The *Imam's* response was quick and precise: "What you listed as priority ten in your list is number one in my community. And what is number one on your list is number ten in our community."

Diversity can lead to diversity in priorities as well. "I love the Arabic language, but today I want to mention another language. It is universal. Have you seen a baby cry in Arabic, or French? It's a universal language, of a cry and smile," Sirhaj Wahaj went on to say. "I want every member of ISNA to learn this language. What is this language?" came his rhetorical question. "It is the language of the body - the body language.

"Upon entering his home, the wife of the Holy Prophet Muhammad, Hazrat Aisha, started to utter, "I repent to Allah and His messenger for what sin did I commit." Although knowing there was no sin committed, she said, 'I saw in his face disappointment.'

"But in his face was the 'body language'. And that's what I am talking about," Sirhaj Wahaj said in a high pitched voice. Wahaj is recognized a leader among Muslims in America.

Wahaj's message was clear: Muslim-American's must learn to use every facets of public speaking to be able to get their message clear across to those who cared to listen.

Hamza Yusuf, a familiar repeat speaker at the ISNA conventions, was very much impressed - like many of us - by the massive turnout at the convention. He emphasized the point well: "It is difficult for us to recognize 'global struggle.' We want to call this the truth, and the truth is the struggle."

Hamza Yusuf, born to a Christian family, embraced Islam early in his life. He had complete command of the language, and his delivery was unique. He knew his topic well and articulated it with ease. Listening to Hamza Yusuf speak as he did, I felt it was necessary to talk with him and get to know more of him. He stood like an island completely surrounded by the sea of men. Once I managed to swim across, I asked him what he thought was our divine destiny.

"Our divine destiny is to rise up and speak the truth in the presence of unjust government." That was more or less what he had said in his talk earlier.

"There is a lot of good in this country, but there is also much ignorance and wrong." Hamza Yusuf was very sincere about that. He did honestly feel that American Muslims have a critical role to play in the States. He wanted us to wake up to our historical reality. Islam might be moved to play its historical role again. Yusuf made a point that I felt required some elaboration. He blamed the United States for the recent economic bust. I was curious how he arrived at that conclusion. He rolled his eyes, gently stroked his 'goatee' beard and then told me, "There are people in Palestine praying that the government of United States suffers like them, because of the government [Israel] this supports. The prayers of the oppressed are being answered; that's why we are having an economic bust."

Yusuf or Mark Hanson as he was known before he converted to Islam at the age of 17 had a near-death experience involving a car accident and reading about Islam he found himself drawn to it.

Abdalla Idris, of Sudan origins and former ISNA president, made a fine point in his remarks, "Our American leaders need to be educated, so that they can educate the Muslim leaders of the world."

That evening professor Necmettin Erbakan, former prime minister of Turkey, received the ISNA Distinguished Service to Humanity Award.

The next morning I headed toward the room where I was among the speakers in the session "Muslim Participation in the Political Process," set up more or less like a workshop. As I stopped at the booth in the lobby of the Rosemont Convention Center, I noticed a soft-spoken, silver-haired gentleman in a black suit, explaining away to the lady at the booth. I was not sure whether she was trying to find his nametag or verifying his identity.

As I moved forward I recognized him and told the lady that this gentleman was none other than Paul Findley, the author of *They Dare Speak* and, quite recently, *Silent No More.* At that moment, the former congressman slowly turned his face toward me, and found my hand extended to meet his. We shook hands vigorously. I introduced myself. Although this was the first time we ever met face to face, Mr. Findley did not take long to recognize me.

"I remember you. You are the one who have been sending me all those wonderful articles by e-mail." I assured him that I was not done yet, and hoped that those had helped him in his writings. "Keep them coming," was Findley's reponse.

One of the reasons I had wanted to come to the convention was to get a chance to meet Paul Findley. Realizing that both of us were in a hurry to be at podiums in different sessions, we had to part, but not without a promise of getting together again before the convention was over.

I got to my podium just in time to meet Ryan Rockwood of TV's Public Broadcast Station, better known by its acronym *PBS.* Or the "Big Bird channel." As the *PBS* crew was busy setting up its cameras and other equipment, Ryan, neatly dressed and with distinctive yellowish hair, started to talk to me and asked if I were on the panel. As I told him, I was hoping to do a slide presentation and was concerned that the LCD projector was not yet set up (carrying the laptop gets pretty heavy at the end of the day). I introduced myself to Ryan as the former Massachusetts chairman of the American Muslim Alliance, and now a member of the AMA national secretariat. I started explaining to him the episode with Hillary Clinton's fund-raiser during my chairmanship, figuring that this was a good time to tell the public some of the lessons we had learned. After all, that was the stated theme of this workshop: our participation in politics, including dealing with the Islamic political paradigm.

At that moment, a lady made her way toward us. "Let me introduce you to my colleague, Kim Lawton," Ryan said. He paused for a second as if to mentally pronounce my name, and then added, "Ali will be presenting a slide show, 'American Muslims in the News.' "

Kim stepped closer, rearranging the scarf around her neck and, with a smile on her face asked, "That's nice. What aspects will you be covering?"

I told Kim and Ryan, that besides giving exact excerpts from various newspapers' coverage of the Muslim bloc vote process, I also wanted to talk about three things that needed special attention: education, organization and mobilization. I told them briefly of an episode that had occurred in my life almost 15 years ago.

My friend, Dr. M. Riaz Khan and I were at an auto store to buy a wheel hub. The owner of the store, just to make conversation, asked us where were we from originally. On hearing our response, that we were from Pakistan, the first thing that the store owner interjected was: "You must be an Engineer, or a doctor or Professor." He was right on the money. I have a master's degree in electrical engineering from McGill University in Montreal, and Riaz Khan is a professor at the UMass Lowell. The reason I told this story is because a lot of American Muslims are highly educated, but most of us are almost illiterate when it comes to politics. So when I said I was to speak on education, I really was talking about political literacy for an educated people. It would be our organization's contribution to American Muslim society to tell our audience today that they should understand politics, understand their rights as citizens of the United States, and stand up for their rights if they feel those rights have been usurped.

The first panel speaker was Mahdi Bray, political advisor to the Washington, D.C. and Los Angeles, California based Muslim Public Affairs Council. He recalled an incident that took place in the White House, during the "faith based" briefing.

"We were all cleared, including Abdullah Al-Arian, the son of Sami Al-Arian who is sitting in the audience," Mahdi Bray started, "when some jerk, let me repeat that—when *some jerk* said that Abdullah had to leave. I looked across the room and said, 'Then we all have to leave.' We all walked out of the White House briefing, just like that."

This was an incident that had made it into the news. Even President Bush conveyed his apology. The faith based briefing, however, did resume, once Abdullah Al-Arian was readmitted and accepted the apology. Dr. Sami Al-Arian was then a professor at the University of South Florida, and his brother-in-law Mazen Al-Najjar had made the news in respect to the secret evidence act. Professor Al-Arian was also going to be in the news before 2001 was over.

Judy Genshaft, the president of the University of South Florida, made a decision on December 19, 2001, to dismiss the professor from his tenured position. The dismissal, according to a statement released by the Tampa Bay Coalition for Justice and Peace was "politically motivated and unconstitutional." Apparently, Dr. Al-Arian's appearance on Fox News September 26th and off-campus speeches he had made were alarming for the university, because one of the reasons she gave to rationalize her sudden decision was that Dr. Al-Arian had failed to make it clear that the views in his speeches reflected his own and not those of the university. He was dismissed even though the speeches in question were made off-campus, and the professor never once claimed to speak on behalf of the university. He made that clear also on October 4, 2001, in his open letter to the community when he stated: "I also told [the Fox producer] that although I was on the faculty of USF, I'd like to be introduced as chairman of the coalition that was established to defend civil rights and political freedom."

I do not recall Sami making any reference to his profession during the past year's speech he gave at the ISNA convention, either. Sami and I were panelists on one of the sessions, under the topic "Muslims and Civil Rights." Nor do I ever remember any of the many friends I have in academia — or any professor — giving off-campus speeches on a topic unrelated to their educational institution, to clearly indicate whether the views expressed by them were their own or those of the institute where they were teaching.

Mahdi Bray, born in the town of Norfolk, North Virginia, in 1950 told me that he had embraced Islam 27 years ago. My next question was direct: "Why?"

"I tried everything else...I saw the most segregation at church on Sunday," Mahdi Bray explained. "Islam knows no ranks. In a Mosque, rank is determined by what time you arrive for prayer, as opposed to your race, color or income. The poorest of the poor will be in the first rank in prayer line. The richest if he arrives late will be at the back row."

At that note, when I started drawing an analogy with Malik Al-Haaj Shabaaz (a/k/a Malcolm X), Mahdi responded hastily, "This never hardened my heart. That aspect of racism never got into my head. Because even as a Christian, I always believed that God changes and controls destiny, not man."

I then asked him to give his account and his observations on lessons he and the American Muslims learned by participating in the political process.

Mahdi, as if anticipating the question, was well prepared to give me his opinion: "Bad—The process was not as inclusive as it could have been."

I had to agree with him on this; we *did* fail to include or mobilize our efforts with African-Americans.

"You discuss and ask for support on issues *before* the candidate is elected, not after he is elected." Mahdi Bray then recalled what he had said in his speech about "fluff and stuff."

"And even some of the congressional candidates who were approached, even the members in the delegation had no idea what the issues were—and therefore knew nothing *about* the issues. You collect a few community leaders to show clout, then you end up talking about your organizations and how well they have been doing, and never address the issue. And just when you are leaving or it's time to leave, you ask the candidate or incumbent, "By the way, could you look at HR so-and-so." That is fluff. No substance, accepting symbolic gestures without substance. As compared to stuff: you decide on the talk points, you bring the Imam or a leader from his district. You present him or her, I do not want to be discriminatory, with a package that contains support letters, writings from his or her district. Preferably that address some of the points that align with the issue or issues that you want to discuss. Then talk about the issue and, like a salesperson, close the deal."

I handed him a glass of water, noticing that his voice was breaking up.

"But we took the first step. We endorsed Bush." Mahdi gave us that, but not without pointing out: "Right process, but wrong candidate. Not that Gore would have been better. Gore did not earn our endorsement. He ignored us."

"Bush was the pragmatic choice." I said.

"Bush has an agenda which goes against the African-American brothers. But we encouraged everyone to support the 'united vote'—the bloc vote, for the good of the Muslim Community, to maintain unity." Mahdi said proudly.

Mahdi Bray, his group and others like him did not let personal ambition get in the way.

"You know, the big 'I' leads to the big 'E'—ego,' " Mahdi Bray said as he walked toward Kim Lawton of *PBS*, who was patiently waiting for him for an interview.

I thanked Kim and *PBS* for broadcasting the fine documentary "Islam, The Empire of Faith." "I cannot take credit for that," Kim said. Then she started to talk about my presentation and what she thought about it. "I can see you put a lot of effort into it."

Suhail Khan, a young lawyer, is a good role model for the Muslim community. We need more Suhail Khans. If we cannot find them, then we need to cultivate them. He has been instrumental in and the force behind the recent White House briefings with the Muslim community, the one that I attended and have already written of, and many more that I could not attend.

He belongs to the next generation. He was born in Colorado. I am hoping by the time this book is at the publisher's, he is a member of the White House staff, in the capacity of "Muslim Liaison." It is an appointment under consideration by the administration, a fact that Suhail does not want to reveal, until confirmed.

It was for the same reason that he respectfully declined the invitation to be interviewed by Kim that day. He had talked about an episode early in his life when he was an intern at Congressman Campbell's office in California.

"A few years back a couple walked into my office, Sami Arian and his wife." He paused momentarily and pointed in the direction where Sami Arian was sitting, in the third row. "Sami's brother-in-law; Dr. Mazen Al-Najar had been arrested, supposedly on an immigration violation. Under the Secret Evidence Act, they or his attorney had no access to whatever evidence, if any, there was against him. After that experience, Sami and his wife had done their homework. They had brought me all the necessary papers, documents and related stuff pertaining to the secret evidence law. I presented that to my congressman, and he told me, 'Suhail, let's work on preparing a bill. Contact David Bonior and we will present something together. I think we have something here.' "

The secret evidence law is now discussed at high national levels.

"But remember, it started with a husband and wife," Suhail wanted me to remember. "And that's what I am talking about. It takes initiative like these people had to get the ball rolling."

Suhail introduced me to his mother and his sister. "And that's my big younger brother," he said. His younger brother was even bigger than Suhail.

I walked out of the room with the family and told Suhail's mother how proud we were of her son.

" So are we." His mother completely agreed with me on that. She told me they were from Madras, India. I bade farewell to the family and headed toward the Hyatt Regency, where my daughter Uzma was staying with her friends.

A most intriguing scene that leaves a lasting impression on anyone, is the sight of many Muslims on the street, women in full Hijab, men in their Islamic attire. This part of Chicago turns into a Muslim camp over the Labor Day weekend.

On the way to Hyatt hotel, I bumped into one of Uzma's close friends, Zareen Mushtaque, the daughter of anesthesiologist Dr. Mohammed Mushtaque. "She is still in her room," Zareen assured me. "She was getting ready to go to the convention center. You might catch her in the lobby if you hurry."

The Hyatt lobby was full of Muslim students, men and women. The Muslim Student Association (MSA) was holding its annual conference at the same time, a part of the ISNA annual convention.

Uzma was in the hotel lobby accompanied by her friend Amane Abdul Jaber, both of whose parents were from Palestine. Amane noticed my ISNA speaker badge and could not help asking, "when is your session?" When she learned it was over, she turned to Uzma. "What kind of a daughter are you, that you did not go to your father's session?" As Uzma searched for the appropriate words to get her out of this embarrassing moment, I came to her rescue and told Amane that Uzma had already seen the presentation in Boston. I had indeed given a similar presentation and talk—at the Muslim Heritage Council Conference sponsored by Rhode Island University's Professor Mohammad Sharif, and held at the Massachusetts Institute of Technology (MIT) in Cambridge, as well as at the Regional AMA Leadership Conference, held at the Wyndham Hotel in Westborough, Massachusetts.

My first encounter during the convention with Dr. Muzammil Siddiqi was outside the Hyatt Regency in Chicago. Dr. Siddiqi is a soft-spoken, very humble person. I wanted to share my thoughts on his recent article on stem cell research. According to the article, the research appeared to be Islamically acceptable as long as done for medical research and to help save lives. He admitted that it was a controversial subject, and his views not necessarily agreed upon among many Islamic scholars. I reminded him of the following *Hadith* [sayings of Prophet Muhammad pbuh], that he could refer to in support of his views. Dr. Siddiqi eyes widened in agreement as he thought about the quote:

On the authority of Abdullah bin Masud, who said narrated to us: "Verily the creation of each one of you is brought together in his mother's belly for forty days in the form of seed, then he is a clot of blood for a like period, then a morsel of flesh for a like period, then there is sent to him the angel who blows the breath of life into him and who is commanded about four matters: to write down his means of livelihood, his lifespan, his actions, and whether happy or unhappy. By Allah, other than Whom there is no god, verily one of you behaves like the people of Paradise until there is but an arm's length between him and it, and that which has been written overtakes him and so he behaves like the people of Hellfire and thus he enters it; and one of you behaves like the people of Hellfire until there is but an arm's length between him and it, and that which has been written overtakes him and so he behaves like the people of Paradise and thus he enters it."

It is clear from the above *Hadith* that the stem cell extraction process is done well before the advent of the angel who blows the breath of life into the cell.

My second encounter with Paul Findley was at the Hyatt Regency. He was heading for the convention hall with a slow gait.

"Tahir," he greeted me, "let me introduce you to Mrs. Haque."

I told Paul that I recalled him introducing Dr. Naz Haque in the beginning of his book, *Silent No More*. I turned to Naz and confessed that Paul had paid a lot of tribute to her. "She is the queen," Paul said loudly and proudly.

I asked Paul if I could assist in any way. "Get my book in the hands of non-Muslims," was his quick reply.

I reminded him that we were handing out the book to all the congressmen. Paul replied, "I want someone who reads books, not someone who collects them."

I was sure he meant that as a joke—he himself was a U.S. congressman at one time. I asked Paul if there were any advice he could give the American Muslims. "Sure. Come along and listen to my lecture, coming up next", he said. I had to take a rain check on that. Alas! I had a plane to catch.

I was homebound.

Not realizing that ten days later, all hell would break loose. And we would all be watching the president of ISNA, Dr. Muzammil Siddiqi, participating in a prayer in the National Cathedral in Washington, D.C., a prayer that would be shown on CNN and almost all the other national TV stations. A prayer to be heard all over the world. A prayer to be recited in the presence of all the living presidents of the United States save Ronald Reagan. A prayer that would be offered in the presence of members of House of Representatives and House of Senate.

And Hamza Yusuf would be invited to the White House to advise President Bush on the 9/11 crisis. He would then deliver a speech outside the White House saying. "Islam was hijacked on September 11, 2001, on that plane as an innocent victim,"

America was under attack.

CHAPTER 12   *America under Attack*

"Arif, it's after two in the morning. When are you coming to bed?" whispered Cindy Blair Khan carefully, so as not to wake her sleeping four-year-old daughter.

It was nearly 3:00 a.m on the morning of September 11, 2001 when Gary Schkedy and Arif Khan decided to call it a day and log off their computer.

Cindy and Arif lived in Edison township of New Jersey and had been happily married for over six years. The 33 year-old Arif Omar Khan had come to America from Pakistan with his parents, and two siblings. Cindy's parents, originally from Jamaica, had come to America from London, where Cindy had been born.

Both Arif and his colleague Gary worked at a brokerage firm on 5th Avenue and 46nd Street, and were debating whether or not to skip a morning seminar at the World Trade Center and go to the firm instead. Both were scheduled to attend a three-hour training beginning at 8.00 a.m on the 106th floor of the World Trade Center, on the same floor where the Cantor Fitzgerald trading firm was. Arif climbed into bed quite exhausted around 3:30 a.m.

The next morning Arif and Gary decided to go straight to work. Arif was on a train and Cindy was driving to work, when she heard the news on her radio that a plane had crashed into one of the World Trade towers. She called Arif on her cellular phone to inform him of the breaking news. Before she could hear Arif's voice, his train went into a tunnel and the line went dead. The worst fears popped into Cindy's mind. She wasn't sure where Arif actually was. Did he decide to go to the seminar?

Arif's cellular phone started to ring as soon as the train pulled out of the station. The connection was much clearer this time. Cindy was utterly relieved when she learned that Arif did not keep his appointment at the World Trade Center.

Meanwhile, Eric Vickers, a former candidate for U.S. Congress and the executive director of the AMA, was pounding on the bathroom door of room 516 in D.C's Hotel Washington. In the shower, Agha Saeed faintly heard Eric saying something about a plane crashing into the twin towers in New York City.

Yahya Mossa Basha, president of AMC, was in another room in

the same hotel, halfway through dressing when he saw smoking images of the north World Trade tower. "I was still watching TV when the second plane went into the other tower," Yahya told me. "I stood motionless for a minute."

Arif got another call from his wife to inform him of the second plane crashing into the south tower. "I got off the train near work and watched, in horror, the building burn and fall. Police quickly barricaded 5th Avenue all the way up to 46nd Street. We could see the inferno from our office building," Arif said. "It did not even dawn on me that we were supposed to *be* in that building until someone watching over our shoulders pointed that out to us."

Agha Saeed got out of the shower and realized what had transpired. "It did not connect for me to what Eric was trying to tell me earlier, until I saw the images on TV," he recalled. It would be difficult to realize the gravity of the situation on hearsay.

Basha told me that he could not take his eyes off his television, "It was a unique sight. In front of me were live images of burning towers on my television screen, and behind me, from a window overlooking the White House and Pentagon, I could also see smoke coming out of the Pentagon. No one was allowed to exit or enter the hotel. We were asked to stay in our rooms."

Saghir Tahir, a New Hampshire state assemblyman who was watching CNN in Pakistan, could not believe his eyes either: "I was sitting at the edge of my bed, and when I saw the plane fly into the world trade center, I just slipped onto the floor," Saghir renacted slipping off his bed in his hotel room when I visited him in his room at the Wyndham Garden Hotel in San Jose on October 13th, 2001 - the venue where the 6th National AMA convention was held. Both of us had come to San Jose to attend the convention.

Eric one more time came knocking at Saeed's door and told Saeed that the police and secret service were all over the place and they were asking everyone to evacuate the building - "NOW." Within half an hour, the hotel guests were out on the street. Because of the high alert, the streets were secured systematically, then buildings in close proximity of the White House were secured. Agha Saeed and Eric found themselves a hotel 20 miles away from the White House. Yahya accompanied Omar Ahmad, president of CAIR, to the organization's headquarters. Subsequently, Dr. Muzammil H. Siddiqi, president of the Islamic Society of North America, and other Muslim-American leaders also had to make alternate arrangements.

They had come from all across the States and were making their way to the hotel café for breakfast and preparations for a 3:00 p.m. rendezvous with the president of the United States.

A month later Eric Vickers summarized the events of that day at the 6th AMA national convention in San Jose. "The surreal events of that morning started to unfold dramatically. People running through the streets in near panic, and police and military personnel first sealing us in the hotel and then forcing us to evacuate. I could see vanishing before my eyes all the work we had done over the years to encourage the eight million Muslims living in America to become active participants in this country's political and civil life.

"Although that morning there was not a clue as to the identity of the terrorist perpetrators," Vickers said, "I knew instinctively that the religious faith of over one billion persons around the globe would face blame. It seemed that in an instant all of America's progress in knowing and understanding Islam would give way to the prejudice and bigotry borne of fear and ignorance.

"Suddenly and ironically," he observed, "what was to have been a momentous afternoon meeting with the president to discuss domestic and foreign issues of concern to Muslim-Americans turned into an encamped week in the capitol filled with intense efforts to mute an anti-Muslim backlash. But in the crucible of that week, Islam became forever imbedded in the fabric of American life."

This kind of meeting with President Bush was a direct result of the Muslim-American bloc vote. The meeting was not just a mere "thank you for your bloc vote," but rather was to be more substantial. This was a time to make good on campaign promises, "and manners and procedures in which these promises could be fulfilled," Saeed explained.

Hence, by that assumption two items were sure to be on the agenda: one, a new initiative that would include U.S. support for the creation of Palestine State, and second, lifting of the Secret Evidence Law.

Muslim-Americans quickly realized that, after the colossal damage due to September 11, all bets were off. The emphasis and focus were more toward first rescue and relief, then, secondly toward healing and harmony. The meeting with the president obviously could not take place, but Saeed and others marched to the nearest Red Cross center and donated blood.

As America was coming in grips to the 9/11 reality, American

Muslim organizations like CAIR, AMC, AMA and Islamic centers were scrambling to get their statements out – all unanimously condemning the act in the strongest terms. In a communiqué that I sent to the press on behalf of the Islamic Society of Worcester as its designated spokesman, I termed these vicious attacks cowardly, and against both divine and human laws. This was a tragedy of unimaginable proportions. No matter how you looked at it, the senseless acts against innocent civilians could never be justified, no matter the grievance against anyone. Most statements called for "swift apprehension and stiff punishment of the perpetrators."

Massachusetts Cardinal Bernard F. Law, archbishop of Boston, and other interfaith groups joined on September 13 to collectively condemn the acts of 9/11. Dr. A. Karim Khudairi and Dr. M. Riaz Khan represented the Islamic Council of New England, I the AMA and ISGW. While Khan recited in Arabic the verses 5:32 from the Qur'an, Khudairi translated them: "If anyone kills one human being, it would be as if he had killed all humanity, and if any person saves the life of a human being, it would be if he saved the life of all humanity."

Toward the end of his talk, Khudairi cautioned citizens against any backlash by saying, "If the destruction of the World Trade Center in New York is compared with the bombing of Pearl Harbor, then we should not repeat history, when mistakes were made against Japanese Americans."

The following day, Dr. Muzammil Siddiqi of ISNA, Dr. Agha Saeed and others who had come to meet with the president but were now stranded in D.C. with all commercial air traffic grounded were invited to join in the national day of prayer at the *National Cathedral* in Washington D.C. The nationally televised service captured Dr. Siddiqi's reciting and translating verses from the Qur'an, along with his unequivocal condemnation the horrific acts of 9/11.

Saeed told me later, "that what may not have been clearly evident was that besides President Bush, the service was largely attended by members of Congress, former presidents – Bill Clinton, Gerald Ford, George Bush senior and Jimmy Carter. In fact I was pleasantly surprised when Jimmy Carter greeted us with '*Assalaam-O-Alaikum*' as he extended his hand towards us."

Nihad Awad told reporters in a press conference held by CAIR – and I heartily agree – that no one should be judged by their looks or last names: "We may have come to this country in different ships, but we are all in the same boat." Nihad and other Muslims stood silently with President Bush as he said, "Like the good folks standing with me, the American people were appalled and outraged at last Tuesday's attacks. And so were Muslims all across the world. These acts of violence against innocents violate the fundamental tenets of the Islamic faith. And it's important for my fellow Americans to understand that."

These words and others that followed echoed in prayer hall of the D.C. Islamic center. Bush became the second U.S. president to visit the Islamic center since its inauguration by former President Dwight Eisenhower in 1957.

Bush's visit and his address from the pulpit became both a historical landmark and a shot in the arm of the ailing Muslim-American spirit. An important step Bush took was meeting with American Muslims, thus winning and restoring confidence between himself and Muslim-Americans. In this hour-long meeting with Muslim-Americans representatives of various Muslim organizations were present, to name just a few: Dr. Jamshed Uppal, representing AMA; Yousuf Saleem of the Muslim American Society; Dr. Hassan Ibrahim of MPAC; representatives from the Ministry of Imam Warith Deen Mohammad (son of Elijah Mohammad, the founder of Nation of Islam), including Prince Bandar bin Sultan the Saudi-Arabian Ambassador to the United States.

Three days later on September 20th, in an address to a joint session of Congress, Bush condemned harassment of American Muslims fueled by anti-Muslim hysteria.

According to reports gathered by CAIR and ADC, Bush's speech had an immediate effect: a dramatic decline in hate crimes, reportedly "from 95 percent negative remarks to 80 percent favorable."

Most American Muslims at this point had realized the great impact the Muslim bloc vote carried. President Bush did make good on his promise. He reinvited the Muslim delegation to meet with him on September 26, 2001.

I called Yahya Mossa Basha in October to get an account of the "historical" visit. A radiologist by profession, originally from Daman, Syria, Yahya lives in Michigan with his wife Samar Basha – also from Syria and their seven children. Initially, the president was to meet with Yahya, Muzammil Siddiqi, Talat Usmani and Amanullah Khan in the *Oval* office, then an invitation was extended to George Salem of AAI and lobbyist Khalid Saffouri, as well.

The meeting in the Oval Office was a more cordial and relaxed atmosphere. Yahya told me, "It was a private meeting to get to know each other. The president and his staff were very courteous and made us feel right at home."

This meeting was a preparation for the next scheduled meeting in the *Roosevelt* room, where a dozen American Muslims were waiting to meet with the president. It was in this meeting that the Muslim guests wanted the president to make a distinction between terrorists and refrain from using the term Islamic terrorists, but rather identify the terrorist or 9/11 perpetrators by the country they had come from.

"We respectfully pointed out to the president that the media did not call Timothy McVeigh a 'Christian terrorist,'" Agha Saeed revealed to me. "When I introduced Eric Vickers to the president and mentioned that he was the first Democrat to endorse the bloc vote for Bush, the president embraced Eric and asked his staff photographer to take our picture."

"Uh-huh," I responded. "Not in the same manner Hillary Clinton pulled me closer to pose for her photographer after I presented her with a plaque. Let's hope Eric's and Bush's isn't put on TV by Bush's political adversaries, in the same manner in which our [Mrs. Clinton's and my] photo was used by her opponent Rick Lazio to upset her bid for the New York Senate seat." Saeed was apparently amused by the analogy, joining me in laughter then adding, "The meeting with the president provides ample proof that participation in mainstream public affairs does matter. It is now under the worst possible circumstances that American Muslims are beginning to realize the significance of the Muslim bloc vote."

The following joint statement that was released presents the essence of the meeting:

"We Arab-American and American Muslim leaders, who have just completed a meeting with President Bush, wish to thank the president and his administration for setting a tone of unity, resolve and respect.

"We once again condemn these horrific acts, express our sincerest condolences to the victims' families, and join with all Americans in pledging our full support for the president at this critical time in his efforts to establish peace and justice in the world.

"We especially appreciate the president's leadership in articulating the message that Arab- and Muslim-Americans are full and active participants in American society, and have been victimized by this tragedy like all Americans.

"We thank the president for his outreach to our community, and for his steady and wise leadership during this national crisis."

Bush's pluralistic approach to the 9/11 tragedy was indeed admirable.

CHAPTER 13 *Guess Who's Coming to Dinner*

"Auntie, your friend is in town and she wants to meet you." When Humaira Kirmani of Lexington, Massachusetts, heard these words, she recognized the familiar voice over the other end of the phone line as Bilal, the son of Perwez Musharraf, president of Pakistan. The Kirmanis are good family friends of the Musharrafs. The friendship between Mrs. Kirmani and Mrs. Sehba Musharraf, the president's wife, goes back to their days as college classmates. When Mrs. Kirmani told Bilal Musharraf that she would come and visit his mother, she was pleasantly surprised by the response that his parents were coming to see *her* instead, and might have dinner at *her* place.

The rest of that day, February 11th, 2002, for the Kirmanis might have come from a scene in a movie. Shortly after that phone call, members of the secret service were at her door. Explaining to the family what to expect. Instructing them that only her husband Maarij Kirmani and she would receive the president and the first lady. Then many questions were asked: how many people would be in the house? Where would the president sit? What was the name of the food caterer? Let the neighbors know that they were expecting a high official without revealing any identity, so the neighbors would be prepared to expect a police-escorted motorcade of a dozen cars.

It was the right thing for the secret service to do. "What would the neighbors have thought otherwise, when a barrage of police-escorted vehicles were at the family's door, especially after the post 9/11 trauma?" I told Humaira.

"The secret service was surprised when I told him that there was no caterer, and that I would cook the food," Humaira told me. "But I emphatically told him that the man was not coming as a president; he would be one of my guests, just like anyone else. This was an informal family gathering."

I myself was amused when Humaira started to explain to me that the secret service noticed how calm and relaxed she was. It isn't every day that one of the most prominent figures in the world, recognized throughout the world as being in the vanguard in the war against terrorism, comes to dinner at your place—and you are not nervous, not stressed at all.

"How shall I react? I asked him." Humaira was very humble in my opinion, and the secret service commended her on her simplicity.

"And Tahir *Sahib*, I told him this is the kind of people we are."

I agreed with Humaira. I wish this side of Muslim life were displayed more often in the United States instead of the open calumny heaped on Muslims. An overzealous newscaster or a political candidate is ever willing to utter any banal cliché to placate unaware listeners.

Humaira and Maarij have lived in the U.S., mostly in Massachusetts, for over 25 years. They belong to that generation of Muslims which has rightly earned the status of pioneers. I came to know the Kirmanis through Maarij's brother-in-law Sami Ullah, who was well known for his community service, in the same league as Dr. Karim Khudairi. They were both founding members of the Islamic Council of New England (ICNE). They and others all served as guiding lights for the growing Muslim community. The Kirmanis are among those who remain as icons in the Muslim community. Maarij's main concern today is the formation of a Muslim database, a project that he pioneered in Chicago a couple of years back. I remember meeting the Kirmanis in the early nineties, when they were both busy mustering support for John Silber in the gubernatorial race.

The reason President Musharraf was in town because his official visit to meet with President George Bush was two days away, starting on Wednesday the thirteenth. This was his second official visit to the States.

General Pervez Musharraf, chief executive, Islamic Republic of Pakistan, the second of three brothers, was born on August 11, 1943, in Delhi, India. After the creation of Pakistan, the family chose to settle in Karachi. His father, the late Syed Musharaff-ud-Din, was a career diplomat retired in 1974, while his mother successfully devoted her time between caring for her family and serving the International Labor Organization, and retired in 1987.

He joined the Pakistan Military Academy in 1961 and was commissioned into an elite Artillery Regiment in 1964. He saw action in the 1965 war as a young officer. He was awarded the *Imtiazi Sanad* for gallantry. He also participated in the 1971 war as company commander in a commando battalion.

As a promising young captain, he got married to Sehba Musharraf on December 28, 1968. He remains a devoted family man and a loving father to their two children, Ayla and Bilal. They are both happily married and Ayla has brought her parents their first granddaughter, Mariam.

General Pervez Musharraf took oath as president of Pakistan on June 20, 2001.

Pervez Musharraf had distinguished himself at the Royal College of Defense Studies in the United Kingdom. A comment in the report on his performance remarked, "A capable, articulate and extremely personable officer, who made a most valuable impact here. His country is fortunate to have the services of a man of his undeniable quality."

Pakistan is really fortunate to be led by a man of his integrity. His leadership capabilities became more prominent after the way he handled the post-9/11 situation after the shocking acts. He not only absorbed the shock, but also came out shining with his resolve and clear thinking. There are 1.5 billion Muslims on this planet; his actions must have made the majority of them feel proud of themselves. I am one of them, and the Kirmanis are a family more.

Humaira and Maarij were also feeling very sad, "because we wanted to invite the community to meet him, so that they could tell him how good they feel about the work he is doing. But his movements were so restricted. Our hands were tied."

I could understand how they felt, because Maarij and Humaira were known for their warm hospitality. Present that day were old acquaintances of the honored guests, the families of Salman Dar, Nadeem Akram, Riaz Khan, Hassan Usmani, Raheela Chowdhary, Minhaj Kirmani, and Imran and Rubina Khan.

"President Musharraf told us that he believed that 'our biggest strength' comes from the Muslims living in U.S." Maarij Kirmani recalled President Musharraf articulating that point very well. "He told us that Pakistan is going through an evolution of democracy in the same way United States had, a few hundred years ago."

This was an enjoyable evening, both for the hosts and the honored guests. They spent over three hours together.

"I felt sorry for the 15 or so secret service personnel, so I ordered pizza and dessert for them. They appreciated the concern and were admittedly not expecting it, so I told them—This was part of our culture, too," Humaira concluded.

Maybe what the Kirmanis felt that cold Monday night in February of 2002 was not quite the same as what the Draytons felt on a warm day in California, for there was no pigmentation problem here, but one thing was sure: they must have been Kafkaesque moments for both. I wonder if Stanley Kramer knew the words "I think your daughter is optimistic. I'll settle for secretary of state," uttered in 1967 jokingly by Sidney Poitier playing Dr. John Prentice, could really become true someday.

A couple of days later, on February 13, I found myself on a flight heading toward Washington, D.C. Maleeha Lodhi, the Pakistani Ambassador to the United States, had invited my wife and I to a Pakistani community dinner in honor of the Pakistani president. Labiba decided to stay home with Uzma. The three of us had had the pleasure of having dinner with President Musharraf a few months back in New York City. I was scheduled to have a one-on-one with the president the day after the dinner, before he was scheduled to visit "Ground Zero." But, due to the unfortunate airline crashes, (American Airlines Flight 587 that crashed in Queens on November 12) the president's whole schedule was canceled that day. This time I was hoping that we could fulfill the appointment in D.C. Asad Hayauddin, press attaché of the Pakistan Embassy had been ever so kind and helpful in arranging for such a meeting. Asad spoke highly of President Musharraf and believed that the steps he took to join the United States in the fight to uproot terrorism was a "wise move." I found Asad very articulate and well informed on any issues that came up in discussion. This time, I was hoping that we could fulfill the appointment with President Musharraf in D.C. with Asad's help.

"Look for a tall, handsome fair-colored young man in the audience, and that will be Bilal." This is how Mrs. Kirmani described Bilal Musharraf to me, so that I could easily recognize the president's son at the dinner reception in D.C. She was right. Bilal did stand out. I approached the table where he was sitting with his wife and family friends. Maarij had evidently talked to him about me, because Bilal had no problem relating to me and was well aware of my desire to talk to his father. He promised to make that happen if possible, as did Rashid Qureshi, second in command after President Musharraf, his right hand. The secret service was thick around the president, thus the encounter with him was very brief, but not without a promise to have a meaningful dialogue with him in Pakistan.

President Musharraf had very constructive meetings with President Bush and his cabinet members concerning the bright future relationship between Pakistan and the United States, and you would think after that his address to the Pakistani-American community would be short. But when he started to talk he went on and on, in a way that reminded me of the *Energiser* bunny. The audience knew that the president was at ease, not feeling any pressure. President Musharraf could judge for himself that he was among friends and well-wishers, so time was never an issue in either his or the listeners' minds.

Making good on his promise to take on the *madrassas* (religious schools) that had been under scrutiny, accused of producing "Islamic militants," Musharraf declared what he called a *Jihad-e-Akbar* ("the Great War") against the madrassa system in Pakistan. He acknowledged their importance and characterized them as "one of the best children's charity organizations in the world." The madrassas reportedly took orphans and children of poverty-stricken families off the streets, provided them with much-needed food and shelter, and with teaching (mainly recitation) of the Qu'ran. It was these images of Muslim children that were repeatedly shown in the West – a group of children diligently and dutifully reciting Qu'ranic verses while rigorously swaying back and forth in a manner similar to the worshippers at the Wailing Wall. Musharraf's *Jihad* was to overhaul the Madrassa curriculum to include mathematics, science and English. The change was necessary, for it gave students the opportunity to go for higher education and compete for better jobs. Thus, by replacing the culture of despair, hopelessness and poverty with the culture of hope and prosperity, he aspired to eliminate the breeding ground for religious extremists like Osama bin Laden.

The president completed his speech by addressing the "Kashmir" issue: "and we will continue to politically, diplomatically and morally support the just struggle of Kashmiris."

The growing border tension between Indian and Pakistani forces over the Kashmir region was a concern. Maybe U.S. mediation was warranted.

President Bush, on the other hand had declared a "hands-off" stance when he earlier rejected Musharraf's request for U.S. mediation on the standoff over the disputed border region of Kashmir. "The only way this issue is going to be solved is if the Pakistani (and Indian) government sit down and have serious, meaningful dialogue." Bush said.

U.N. Secretary-General Kofi Annan called on India and Pakistan to exercise full restraint, "to avert a further escalation of tensions." The tension between India and Pakistan escalated so much over the next three months that war between the two "nuclear-armed" countries appeared inevitable. Verbal exchanges between the two leaders were reminiscent of those surrounding the two wars India and Pakistan fought in 1965 and 1971.

President Musharraf told CNN on June 2002 that he did not believe either side would fire its missiles. "I would even go to the extent of saying one shouldn't even be discussing these things, because any sane individual cannot even think of going into this unconventional war, whatever the pressures," he told CNN.

Most Muslim-Americans, particularly of Pakistani origin, realized that even though Musharraf played down fears of a nuclear war with India, going to the extent to a call for de-nuclearization of South Asia, it would not really mean much if India's Prime Minister Atal Bihari Vajpayee was not paying enough attention.

"He [Pervez Musharraf] is a great president and a strong U.S. ally", Andrew Card, the White House Chief of Staff told me at a fundraiser for President Bush on March 25, 2004. The kind comments were made by Card when I thanked him for publicly acknowledging Pakistan's and especially President Pervez Musharraf's staunch resolve in fighting the war on terrorism.

CHAPTER 14   *New Challenges and New Debates*

[Meeting with President Bush on September 11, 2001 that couldn't take place. Meeting with President Bush on September 26, 2001. The Patriot Act, NSEER Registration, Interrogation of 11, 000 Iraqi Americans during the recent Iraq War, Incarceration of Prof. Sami Al-Arian and others; also, appointment of Daniel Pipes].

The big question remained unanswered for some time: Who was really behind the heinous attacks of 9/11? Jeddah-born Saudi national, a millionaire-in-exile, Osama bin Laden and his organization *Al-Qaeda* [the base] became the prime suspects, but not without cause. The 1998 bombings at the U.S. embassies in Kenya and Tanzania also were the work of Osama and his group, according to U.S. intelligence. He was linked to the suicidal attack on the USS Cole in Yemen in year 2000. But then Rick Lazio linked Hillary Clinton to the USS COLE attack in 2000, but for a different reason altogether. Osama Bin Laden, or "The Contractor", a nickname he picked up in the 1980's during his construction endeavors that included hospitals and orphanages, was fighting alongside the U.S-supported Afghan resistance fighters, mostly *Pushtoon*, against the Soviet Union and the Northern Alliance, comprised mostly of *Tajeks*. A new term, "Afghan Arab," was thus coined. In later years, a generation beyond the Afghan resistance or the *Mujahideen*, these people took the name "*Taliban*." [students].

After the fall of the Soviet Union, Osama established his base in Sudan, with a mission to compromise U.S. interests in any country, according to U.S. intelligence reports released by the U.S. State Department.

John Walter Lindh, an American who adopted Islam as his religion early in his life, decided to join the Afghan resistance to fight the Soviet Union and the Northern Alliance. He was unaware of the fact that later the U.S. would switch sides, and he would end up fighting on the wrong side - branded a traitor and conveniently labeled as "the American Taliban." In a similar manner when Adam Shapiro, when he acted as a human shield to protect Palestinians from Israeli army, was labeled as "The Jewish Taliban"

The *Pushto* tribe, considered as brave warriors, is also known for two other things: First, the life of their guest is dearer to them than their own. (We saw their adamant and staunch refusal in handing over Osama bin Laden to the West – and now, even with a handsome Reward for his capture, allegedly he remains at large). And second, vengeance is inherited. If we are to be blamed, then we should be wary of any uprising of the remnants of the generation left behind by the *Taliban*, in whatever form, shape and identity they assume. To them, any American, including Muslim-Americans like myself, is the enemy. It is in this context that I appeal to the reader, and the U.S. government to take a good hard look at our foreign policy and to sustain civil liberties within our own borders.

FBI's press release on September 27, 2001 stated, "The Federal Bureau of Investigation is today releasing 19 photographs of individuals believed to be the hijackers of the four airliners that crashed on September 11, 2001, into the World Trade Center in New York, the Pentagon, and in Stony Creek Township, Pennsylvania."

Some notable discrepancies appeared on the FBI "suspect list," for example Waleed Alshehri and Adnan Bukhari were actually alive. Similarly, the Saudi Arabian embassy verified that Saeed Alghamdi, Mohand Alshehri, Abdul Aziz Alomari, Salem Alhazmi, and Al-Mihdhar also were alive.

Two days after 9/11, CNN reported that Adnan Bukhari was in Florida, had "passed an FBI polygraph and was not considered a suspect." In the same news bulletin CNN also stated, "Ameer Bukhari died in a small plane crash last year." Ameer Bukhari was on the FBI list.

Waleed Alshehri turned up alive in Casablanca, reported on September 24, 2001 by The *Daily Trust (Abuja)* (http://allafrica.com/stories/200109240325.html). Waleed by his own submission did attend flight training school at Dayton Beach in the United States as reported by the FBI. "But, he says, he left the United States in September last year, and became a pilot with Saudi Arabian Airlines, and is currently on a further training course in Morocco." *The Daily Trust* reported.

However, the FBI had articulated that point well in its press release: "It should be noted that attempts to confirm the true identities of these individuals are still under way."

The CNN Web site in reference to WTC and 9/11 casualties carried over 2800 names; none of the names of the alleged hijackers were to be found in that list either. There *were* other Muslim names, but these were victims. I could recognize 32 Muslim names were of those who lost their lives either in the World Towers at the time of the attack or those who were among the passengers on the planes. Waleed Iskandar was a passenger on *American Airline* flight 11, Norma Khan on *American Airline* flight 77, and notably Rahma Salie on *American Airline* flight 11.

The Islamic Society of Boston (ISB) in Wayland, Massachusetts held a memorial service on September 16, 2001 for Rahma Salie and her husband Michael Theodoridis, who also was on the *American Airline* flight 11. The 28 year-old Salie lived in South Boston with Michael, and was seven months pregnant. Ysuff and Haleema not only lost their daughter but also their future grandchild. "Let me set the record straight. Rahma should be counted as two Muslim lives lost on that flight," Rahma's father Ysuff told me. I found Ysuff eager to talk about his daughter's accomplishment, blinking constantly to hold back tears. Both parents, who came from Sri Lanka in 1993, and now residents of Newton, showed no animosity or anger toward anyone; rather they sought comfort knowing that they were not alone in their sad moment. Muslims, fellow Christians and Jews that visited the Islamic center were mourning alongside them.

Mohammed Salman Hamdani was also on the list. He was a member of the police corps. Minutes after the attack, when he saw the towers on fire, Hamdani did the only thing that he was trained to do; he instinctively darted toward the burning towers to save lives. Save lives he did, and he lost his own in the process. Unfortunately, instead of giving Hamdani a burial befitting a hero, his photo had been circulated around on a poster "wanted by the FBI." It took a few months for the authorities to realize that Hamdani's beng a Muslim did not make him a terrorist. Hamdani was finally recognized for his selfless deed and was accorded a hero's burial. More than 1,000 area Muslims, and the newly elected Mayor Michael Bloomberg of New York City, along with members of the police corps, attended the hero's funeral and paid him proper homage. Mayor Michael Bloomberg joined the police commissioner in consoling the family.

"We have an example of how one can make the world better," he said. "Salman stood up when most people would have gone in the other direction. He went in and helped people."

It was not difficult to realize that Muslim-Americans were in an awkward position, and backlash was inevitable. Many of us will adhere to California's 15th Congressional District representative Mike Honda's advice not to change our "names" and be proud of our heritage. Representative Honda, the keynote speaker in the American Muslim Alliance's (AMA) 2001 national convention in San Jose, told the predominantly Muslim-American audience that he did not change his name or identity even though he "spent his early childhood with his family in an internment camp in Colorado during World War II." It was no doubt a humiliating episode for him, his Japanese parents, and other Japanese-Americans living in America when Pearl Harbor was attacked. The California-born representative proudly asserted to a standing ovation, "This Honda is made in America."

The Council on American Islamic Relations (CAIR) remained focused mainly on collecting data on any incident that affected Muslims in the States. CAIR put out a report documenting each of these incidents. The abstract of the report is as follows:

"The fallout from the September 11 attacks continues to impact Muslim daily life in several ways, especially at airports and ports of entry. FBI agents and other local law enforcement authorities have sometimes responded to hearsay reports, and conducted raids and interrogations of legal immigrants and citizens. While the government has defended such actions as necessary for national security, none of these actions led to the arrest of terror suspects. Instead they disrupted the ability of thousands of Muslims to practice their religion freely, negatively impacted the careers and hopes of many individuals, and threatened democratic freedoms and the rule of law."

The report grew bigger as complaints came in. Tariq Omar Ahmed, a name that resembled someone on the "Watch List" of terrorists, was subjected to a humiliating experience in Madrid, Spain. His parents, Ann Theresa Gacquin, originally from Ireland, and Zubair Ahmed originally from Pakistan, both worked in the *New Victoria* Theater just outside Victoria Station in London, England before being married. For them it became an instant nightmare, but eventually they were successful in clearing their son's name.

"The main concern that I have is that if our son who is a born U.S. citizen can be subjected to such scrutiny just because he happens to have a Muslim name, what will happen to American Muslims, immigrants and student alike?" an emotional Zubair of Randolf, Massachusetts asked me rhetorically.

For some it was a Kafkaesque moment: Dr. Agha Saeed had flown to Washington, D.C. to meet with the President on September 11. Because of the events that unfolded that day, the meeting was never held. Dr. Agha Saeed who was stranded for five days in DC after September 11, 2001 managed to get a seat out of Baltimore flying back to California. But when he arrived at the airport to catch his flight, five FBI agents stopped him and started interrogating him. When they asked Saeed what was his business in Washington, he replied that he was there for a meeting. They asked with whom and he replied, "With the President of the United States." Dr. Saeed told me, trying to re-enact the scene, "The agent looked at me from head to toe." When the agents verified his story Dr. Saeed was on his way back to his home in California.

Soon after 9/11 the FBI decided to pay a visit to Hamza Yusuf's home. Hamza Yusuf's wife told the FBI agent that Hamza was with President George Bush. The FBI agents, finding it hard to believe decided to make a few phone calls. They discovered that Hamza Yusuf was indeed with the President. Hamza, who is known in the Islamic scholarly circle, had been invited to the White House to advise the President and his staff on the 9/11 crisis.

It goes without saying that everyone and his brother in the United States was affected or influenced, in one form or the other, by the impact of the 9/11 attacks. For Muslims living in America, it was a double-edged sword. On one hand, they had to find ways to comfort themselves and prepare for the obvious backlash that would follow. On the other hand, equally important, was what was needed to be done to disprove and repudiate the growing negative sentiment toward Islam. Muslims in America found themselves constantly facing bias attacks, but in the midst of all this inconvenience, they also discovered an increasingly tolerant American society. However, the attacks on Islam were not limited to the hate-mongers, bigots and ignorant alone, but emancipated even from the pulpit – Rev. Jerry Falwell, evangelist Pat Robertson, Rev. Franklin Graham, son of evangelist Billy Graham, Rev. Jerry Vines, the former president of the Southern Baptist Convention, just to name a few. Whereas slurs may be characterized as meaningless, emotional outbursts, the attack on the religion of Islam was purposeful. At the outset, it appeared that some people of authority and others of similar mind perpetuate false stereotypes of Islam.

Now the Muslim-Americans were faced with another challenge, and that meant simply protecting their religion. Most everyone got involved, some at an individual level and some at a community group level. Many members of various church groups and synagogues joined with their Muslim brethren at this moment of crisis. In turn, Islamic societies, not only initiated but participated heavily in interfaith activities, in nearly every state.

The Islamic Society of Greater Worcester (ISGW) is a community-based organization that provides a wide range of services for its members and for the community at large. The center is currently located at 57 Laurel Street in Worcester, Massachusetts. The members of the Islamic Society of Greater Worcester (ISGW) were busy in such activities on their own as well. I was then the designated 9/11 spokesperson for the Islamic society. Just after a couple of days of the destructive attacks on the Twin Towers and the Pentagon, we were busy outreaching and participating in vigils and related activities, because this was our grief as well. The first three-month post-9/11 activity of our society is included in Appendix [VIII]; this synopsis is a reflection of what transpired in different parts of Massachusetts and other parts of the states.

On September 13, 2001 for instance, Cardinal Bernard Law, archbishop of Boston, and other members of various churches organized a vigil in Boston Plaza. Dr. M. Riaz Khan, represented the Islamic Council of New England (ICNE). I represented AMA and ISGW. Other Muslims were also invited to participate at the vigil. I thanked Attorney General Tom Reilly for honoring our request for a press release "that violence against the American Muslims" will be dealt with the law.

Dr. M. Riaz Khan recited the Qu'ranic verse (5:32) from *Surah Hujrat* while Dr. Karim Khudairi of the Islamic Council of New England (ICNE) delivered a befitting speech, which was widely broadcast by the media. Dr. Khudiari said, "God has given life to humans and He is the One who has the right to take it away. The Qur'an 5:32 says that, 'If anyone kills one human being – it would be as if he had killed all humanity, and if any person saves the life of a human being, it would be as if he saved the life of all humanity."

Dr. Khudairi added, "These are the teachings of true Islam, human life is sacred and should not be for sacrifice".

On October 6, 2001 ISGW had an Open House to discuss the theme: "Islam, Perception and Reality in the light of current events". The panelists included representatives from other Islamic centers as well. Approximately 500 people showed up for the Open House. Guest speakers included: U.S. Congressman, James P. McGovern; Raymond Mariano, Mayor of Worcester; along with clerics from various Islamic centers, churches and synagogues.

Hinna Mushtaque, a member of the ISGW youth group, spoke about her experiences at the Open House: "I feel proud to live in a society, which celebrates and supports multiculturalism. I was extremely disheartened when I first learned about the backlash against Muslims, and people of Middle Eastern and South Asian descent as a result of the tragic events on September 11. At first, this was not my major concern. I, too, along with the rest of America, was utterly overwhelmed and shocked by the horrendous tragedies that occurred that fateful Tuesday morning. I, as well as the entire Muslim community, have received an amazing outpour of support from our neighbors, friends, and community members. I am extremely pleased that through this difficult time, many national officials have also clearly stated that Islam and Muslims are not to blame for this tragedy.

I strongly believe that something should be done to account for the events of September 11th, but not at the expense of the values that we Americans treasure", Hinna concluded.

During this interfaith activity and interaction with members of various denominations, a clear understanding was being fostered between the Muslim community and the following leaders of faith, but not limited to: *Auxiliary Roman Catholic Bishop of Worcester* - The Most Rev. George E. Rueger, the Rev. Thomas Schade of the *First Unitarian Church*, Rabbi Seth Bernstein of *Temple Sinai*, the Rev. Mark Beckwith of *All Saints Episcopal*, Cantor Sally Neff of *Temple Emmanuel*, the Rev. Wanda Martinez-Diaz of *Iglesia Hispana Unida de Cristo*, the Rev. Michael P. Bafaro of *Our Lady of Mount Carmel/St. Ann*, the Rev. Dr. Barbara Merritt of *the First Unitarian Church Second Parish*, the Rev. Allyson D. Platt of *Worcester County Ecumenical Council*, Robert Adler of *Jewish Federation*, Directors Catherine Loeffler, of *Catholic Charities Worcester County*, the Rev. Dr. Richard Wright of the *Emmanuel Baptist Church*, the Rev. Jeffrey R. Newhall of the *Greendale People's Church*, Laurie Shane Burke of *All Saints Church*,

Fran Manocchio of *NCCJ,* the Rev. David Miller of *First Unitarian Church,* Project Coordinator Wendy O'Leary of Unitarian Universalist Church, Debra Sprangler, of *Catholic Charities Worcester County,* Dir. Frank Kartheiser of *Worcester Interfaith,* Rabbi Jordan B. Millstein of *Temple Emmanuel,* and Cardinal Bernard Law, archbishop of Boston.

The interfaith activity continued almost endlessly into 2002 and beyond. Most of the major national Muslim organizations like the Islamic Society of North America (ISNA), CAIR and others were busy trying to put out as much literature about Islam as they possibly could, in an effort to remove any misconception or poor taste lingering in the minds of the American people about Islam. Even new organizations were founded to provide an insight into Islamic values. One of such was *"Bridging the Gap, Inc."* Founded by Rafia Syeed of Indiana who tried to explain her organization's manifesto in one sentence. "The main purpose of the organization is well spelled out in its name. We are trying to bridge the gap between the three major religions," Rafia told me during ISNA's Interfaith unity banquet in August 2003. "One way to achieve this goal is by reaching out to concerned people striving to find common ground through recognizing and celebrating common values." Rafia was able to find time to provide outreach and promote this program in local schools while taking care of her six children. She took pride knowing that her husband, Sayyid Syeed, the secretary general of ISNA, fully supported her outreach program. "In today's world of instant communication, more than often, facts are sacrificed for instantaneity, leading to misunderstanding through misinformation and misconception about many cultures and values." She added.

Similarly, Ms. Samina Faheem of California started a forum called the American Muslim Voice (AMVOICE) as a vehicle for Muslim and non-Muslims alike, to voice their opinions on any current issues. Abdus Sattar Ghazali, author of several books, including *"Hegemony of the Ruling Elite in Pakistan",* joined Faheem as co-moderator of the message board. Ghazali is also an editor for the online magazine *American Muslim Perspective.*

As in many other parts of the United States, similar activities helped to an extent to bring followers of the three *Abrahamic* religions much closer to one other. They also raised the level of support and understanding among one other to a higher plateau. This did not, however, free the American society of bigots, anti-Semitic or anti-Muslim sentiments or hate crimes. But when such would occur, sporadic as it may be, we all got together and denounced it in public. In August 2002, Representative James McGovern's office was asked if the ISGW would like to make a statement denouncing anti-Semitism. The previous night or very early that morning, someone had painted the Swastika and anti-Semitic graffiti on a wall in front of McGovern's office in Worcester and on the walls of Worcester City Hall. Congressman McGovern and the newly-elected Worcester Mayor, Timothy Murray had called a press conference at the city hall. Representatives of various religions were invited, and they all denounced this kind of bigotry in front of television cameras. Elected leaders and officials stated clearly that intolerance was divisive and unacceptable. That day we stood alongside our Jewish brothers and declared that intolerance toward any religion cannot be tolerated in this society.

Less than two months later conservative preacher Jerry Falwell made some inflammatory remarks against the Prophet Muhammed (peace be upon him) on *CBS's '60 Minutes'* on October 6, 2002. Every Muslim in the nation and the world over took notice to these offensive remarks. The statement made by the Islamic Society of North America, more or less reflected our sentiments:

"We express our profound sadness, pain and anguish. We urge all people of faith to condemn acts and all statements, which disparage sacred symbols, scriptures and personalities of all religions. Such statements have no place in American society where people of different faiths live together in peace and with tolerance and respect."

This reflected the main point we had made at Worcester City Hall. We made note of the fact then that over the past year ominous signs had appeared signaling a diminishing concern for religious tolerance both locally and nationally. Some religious, academic and political leaders had made highly inflammatory remarks directed against Islam and Muslims. While some media outlets and religious leaders had condemned this bigotry, most politicians and officials had failed to stand up and condemn these outrageous sentiments. The U.S National Council of the Churches of Christ, representing 36 churches and over 50 million U.S Christians, however, unanimously passed a resolution on October 7, 2002, which stated in part: "We affirm to our brothers and sisters in Islam that we condemn and repudiate Jerry Falwell's hateful and destructive statements delivered on CBS's '60 Minutes' October 6, 2002, and we call upon President George W. Bush to repudiate and condemn Falwell's remarks"

On October 18, the ISGW called for a press conference to condemn hate and intolerance from the pulpit and to encourage a dialogue and discussion to inculcate and mitigate misconceptions about Islam. This time around, statements were read from Congressman McGovern and various religious denominations, including *All Saints Church*, the *Unitarian Church*, *The Jewish Federation*, and organizations like the American Civil Liberties Union *(ACLU)*, *Worcester Peace Works*, and *the Worcester Rainbow Coalition*.

Gordon T. Davis, of the Worcester Area Rainbow Coalition said, "The Coalition opposes the anti-Islam hate speech of national and local so-called leaders. We have opposed the racist swastika graffiti found in Worcester earlier this year and we have opposed racist profiling by the government and others." Davis concluded by saying, "We must shout down and drown out the hate speech with speech for justice."

This nation wide interfaith among Christians, Jews and Muslims must have been seen as a threat of some magnitude to some, for hardly a month had passed when the televangelist Pat Robertson commented in view of the mid-East conflict that Muslims' attitudes toward Jews were "worse than the Nazis".

Ibrahim Hooper, spokesperson for CAIR responded in the same manner that we objected to Jerry Falwell: "We would call on elected leaders and religious leaders to repudiate these kinds of comments. Time and again we see attacks on Islam go unchallenged."

Hooper also called on President Bush to specifically repudiate these attacks. Bush needed to realize that these inflammatory remarks were doing incredible damage to America's image in the Muslim world, and the timing was critical because America needed allies in the war on terrorism. Bush's visit to the Islamic Center of Washington and his meeting with Muslim representatives just within a week of September 11 were indeed appreciated by the American Muslims. The meeting was seen as an attempt to promote tolerance toward Muslims. But Bush's failure to openly criticize remarks made by Falwell, Robertson and others that followed was clearly seen as a shortcoming on his part. But this was to change in the weeks that followed. Bush finally took notice of this reaction. On November 15,

2002 in a meeting with U.N. Secretary General Kofi Annan, he said: "Some of the comments that have been uttered about Islam do not reflect the sentiments of my government or the sentiments of most Americans. Islam, as practiced by the vast majority of people, is a peaceful religion, a religion that respects others." He also added: "By far, the vast majority of American citizens respect the Islamic people and the Muslim faith...Ours is a country based upon tolerance...And we're not going to let the war on terror or terrorists cause us to change our values."

Muslims reacted positively to remarks by President Bush that renounced rhetorical attacks on Islam by evangelical leaders. Ibrahim Hooper of CAIR added: "It is encouraging to hear President Bush address the issue of Islamophobic rhetoric in our society. We hope the president's rejection of anti-Muslim hate speech will be followed by similar statements from other elected officials and from mainstream religious leaders."

American Muslims, however, felt really betrayed when the man they helped put behind the desk in the Oval Office, issued a so-called "recess appointment" for Daniel Pipes to the board of the United States Institute of Peace (USIP).

Daniel Pipes, in addition to his work as director of the Philadelphia-based Middle East Forum and on a Defense Department Special Task Force on Terrorism, has taught at the University of Chicago, Harvard University, and the U.S. Naval War College. He is also well known for his discursive stance on almost everything having to do with Islam, its followers, and the Palestinian/Israel conflicts in the Middle East.

CAIR again took the lead and urged President Bush to rescind his nomination of an "Islamophobe." CAIR also sent a letter to Dr. Richard Solomon, the president of USIP and urged him to reject the nomination of a 'Muslim-basher' – "an inappropriate choice" to its board of directors. The institute's board of directors is appointed by the president and confirmed by the Senate. But before an anticipated heated debate could took place in the U.S Senate, President Bush took the back-door approach to circumvent the normal approval process in the Senate and issued a "recess appointment". Pipes' appointment ends in January 2005.

Nihad Awad, CAIR executive director, presented the following "logical argument" that resonated well among the Muslim community: "Unfortunately, no credible Muslim leader in the United

States or around the world could cooperate with an organization in which Pipes has a decision-making role. For example, it would be extremely difficult for Muslim representatives to take part in USIP's Special Initiative on the Muslim World if Pipes joined the board. Instead of 'increasing the prospects for long-term understanding between the Western and Islamic worlds,' Pipes' bigoted views have been instrumental in widening the divide between faiths and cultures." Some U.S. Senators were clearly opposed to Pipes' nomination as well. On July 23, 2003, CAIR posted the following statement to that effect:

> "Senators criticize Daniel Pipes in committee meeting, Kennedy, Dodd, Harkin speak out against controversial USIP nominee
>
> *Alhamdulillah,* (praise be to God) Several U.S. senators today came out strongly in opposition to the nomination of Daniel Pipes to the board of the United States Institute of Peace. The senators expressed that opposition during a meeting this morning of the Senate Health, Education, Labor, and Pensions Committee, the body that must take the initial vote on Pipes' nomination. A vote had been scheduled, but was postponed because too many senators left the meeting to maintain a quorum.
>
> "We thank the thousands of people who e-mailed, faxed or met with committee members to express their concerns about Pipes' bigoted views," said CAIR Board Chairman Omar Ahmad. "The political momentum to block his nomination is building on Capitol Hill."
> During the discussion of Pipes' nomination to the USIP board, Sens. Edward Kennedy (D-MA), Christopher Dodd (D-CT) and Tom Harkin (D-IA) described Pipes variously as a "provocative" and "highly controversial" candidate whose "decidedly one-sided" views would be in "direct contradiction" to USIP goals.
>
> Sen. Harkin, who said he took the time to investigate the nominee, spoke at length about Pipes' statement warning of the "dangers" posed by the enfranchisement of American Muslims and of his web site (www.campus-watch.org) that sought

to create "dossiers" on academic critics of Israeli policies.

Harkin said the ongoing controversy generated by Pipes' possible confirmation would "overshadow" the work of the institute. He also said Iowa is home to the oldest operating mosque in America in Cedar Rapids and that Muslims are a vibrant segment of that state's population. "[Daniel Pipes is] not the person that ought to be on the United States Institute of Peace board," said Harkin.

Sen. James Jeffords (I-VT) said the fact that Pipes would stimulate debate was "hardly a reason" to support his nomination. Only Senator John Ensign (R-NV) offered a cautious defense of the nominee, saying he agreed with Pipes' position on peacemaking needing to be backed up by strength.

"We view the outcome of today's meeting as a victory for all those who reject bigotry and, unlike Daniel Pipes, seek negotiated resolutions to international conflicts," said CAIR Executive Director Nihad Awad. "It is clear there is little enthusiasm for Pipes' confirmation, even among his political supporters. Republican senators need to join their Democratic colleagues in reconsidering this divisive nomination."

It was not only Muslims who were protesting; a joint statement was released by several Jewish-American organizations had the same issue: "JEWISH GROUPS OPPOSE DANIEL PIPES NOMINATION

> (WASHINGTON, DC, July 30, 2003) - A broad coalition of Jewish peace groups today called upon President Bush to withdraw his controversial nomination of Daniel Pipes to the Board of Directors of the United States Institute of Peace....."

> Jewish Groups endorsing the statement included:

> Jewish Voice for Peace (San Francisco)
> Jews for Peace in Palestine and Israel (Washington, DC)
> Philadelphia Jewish Peace Network (Philadelphia)
> Not In My Name (Chicago)

Jewish Voice Against the Occupation (Seattle)
Jews Against The Occupation (New York)
Visions of Peace With Justice in Israel/Palestine (Boston)
Jewish Women for Justice in Israel/Palestine (Boston)

The five-month protest by American Muslims and Jews against Pipes' nomination was put to rest on August 22 when President Bush issued the recess appointment. But the many American Muslims, Jews, Arab–American, Christians, and all those that openly opposed Pipes' nomination saw the "recess appointment" as moral victory. First and foremost, without Senate approval, Pipes' appointed term is just 18 months rather than a four-year term; second, the president clearly had to resort to this "back-door" tactic in anticipation of the Senate's rejecting the nomination.

My own encounter with Daniel Pipes prepared me to easily relate to the relentless opposition he faced. Just two months earlier I had a chance to listen and talk to Daniel Pipes when he lectured at Worcester's College of the Holy Cross on February 6, 2003. The title of his lecture, "Militant Islam and the War on Terror," was reason enough to draw local Muslims, including myself, to the lecture, and to raise a few eyebrows. Pipes' "bigoted" reputation had evidently preceded him; a few days before the lecture, he drew protesters, including college faculty, students and peace activists from the group Worcester Peace Works. The protest stemmed largely from Pipes' web site, which lured students to report teachers whose political views were anti-Israel. The web-site, www.campus-watch.org, is designed to maintain what it calls "dossiers" on professors and academic institutions. For this reason, some of the protesters put tape or gags across their mouths. Muttasem Razzaq of the ISGW and Imrana Soofi of American Muslim Communication Link (AMCL) had brought the news about the "controversial" visit, and we joined in with the protest already underway. A Clark University student held a sign that read "Blacklists are un-American." Some of us had already registered our complaint when we called upon the administration of Holy Cross, and also the Jewish Federation, who had helped organize the lecture. We reminded the Jewish Federation of the time when the Worcester Muslim community stood at their side denouncing bigotry and intolerance when anti-Semitic graffiti was written on official buildings in Worcester. We also reminded them that with the same zeal, Robert Adler (then the president of the Jewish Federation) denounced bigotry coming from behind the pulpit in reference to Rev. Falwell's disrespectful remarks about the Prophet Muhammad.

The *Worcester Telegram*'s coverage of the protest reported comments made by Muslims who joined the protesters. Holy Cross senior Awais Ahsan said Mr. Pipes has written some "very derogatory depictions of Muslims. Imrana Soofi of AMCL pointed out, "We experience bad things by what he says," and Boston lawyer Imran Nasrullah said, "His is a collective grouping of Muslims of various shades and levels of belief. He never says what is the standard to declare a person an Islamist or a fundamentalist."

The next day's lecture drew over 200 people, including a dozen area Muslims, notably Dr. Ashraf Elkerm, the president of the ISGW, Isa Mujahid, the vice president of the ISGW, Randah Saleh, the president of the Muslim Student Association MSA of Clark University, AMCL's director Imrana Soofi, Mohamad El-Rafai, Haytham Hussein, Amane Abdel Jaber, Muttasem Razzaq and myself. Pipes' lecture and comments drew applause as well as boo's and hisses. During the question and answer session, Haytham made his objections loud and clear when he called Pipes a liar, after Pipes distorted the meaning of the word "Jihad." Imrana Soofi got her message across when she asked the lecturer why he was not talking about militants in Judaism and Christianity, to which Pipes dismissed these two militants as not a threat to the United States. Pipes was put on the defensive numerous times when the general public started to challenge his views. Some hurled insults at him, saying that there was "no difference between you and the Nazis." Others called his speech "very one-sided." Some, elaborating on the fact that Saddam and Osama bin Laden were supported and trained by the U.S., asked: "How do you explain the $43 million that were given to the Taliban by the U.S. in March 2001?" Because of these reactions, the *Worcester Telegram* reported the next day: "Mr. Pipes struck a nerve with members of the audience, some of whom shouted for him to leave or accused him of not telling the truth. He responded with insults of his own, saying that interruptions did not speak well of Holy Cross. Mr. Schaefer [the moderator] also joined in, telling one man who continued to interrupt that he would be escorted out by campus police if he did not stop." Unfortunately, the *Telegram* failed to report that the behavior of David L. Schaefer, Holy Cross' political science professor, also did not speak well of the college when he shouted hysterically at the man to sit down and adding in a derogatory manner, "Go back where you came from."

I am sure I was not alone in thinking and Schaefer may have been under the same impression — that the man who spoke with an accent was from an Arab country. But it came to my utter surprise when Randah Saleh, the president of MSA at Clark University, pointed out to me that the person was of a Jewish faith. I was to learn almost nine months later when the headlines in the *Hartford Courant* on 11/5/03 made even more sense to me as it read; PIPES DOESN'T SPEAK FOR ALL JEWS

That protest was to occur by an interfaith coalition of Jews, Muslims and Christians, their statement clearly stated:

> "We wish to voice our profound concern over the inclusion of Daniel Pipes in the two-week Jewish Book Festival sponsored by the Greater Hartford Jewish Community Center.
>
> His writings reflect a lack of tolerance for the very ethnic and religious diversity that has so enriched our nation. In fact, it was exactly because of his narrow, overgeneralizing views that the Senate's Health, Education, Labor and Pensions Committee, in its first round of hearings, energetically opposed his nomination by President Bush to the board of directors of the U.S. Institute of Peace, which Congress created to promote peaceful solutions to world conflicts. He obtained the position only as the result of President Bush's congressional recess appointment because it was apparent that the full Congress would reject his nomination. Daniel Pipes' track record of inciting hatred against American Muslims and American Arabs has been the hallmark of his life's work... "

At the end of the question-and-answer session I approached Professor Schaefer, who apparently was expecting me since I had called earlier in my capacity of National American Muslim Alliance (AMA) to register my objections and concerns about the controversial speaker. Schaefer, who had apparently briefed Pipes about me, introduced me as such. I confronted Pipes and inquired in front of reporters why he had distorted the meaning of "Jihad" — especially when he claimed that he knew Arabic. "I was talking about the political meaning," he retorted. I told Emile Astell, the *Telegram Ga-*

zette reporter, that I am a Muslim and believe that I was more patriotic than Pipes. Emile ended her article quoting me: "Tahir Ali, a Westboro engineer and a Muslim, told a reporter after the speech that he objected to Mr. Pipes' sweeping statement that both violent and nonviolent militant Islamics are dangerous. "I am more patriotic than he is," he said."

I do, however, credit Pipes for giving an honest and accurate historical account of the Muslim era. Whereas most of his lecture was offensive to say the least, he managed to say a few good things about early Islam, Islamic culture and civilization. "The first 600 years went very well," he said, and added that the vastness of the Muslim empire spread as far as "Spain into the West, and India into the East." And surprisingly enough he went to the extent of admitting that, "If there were Nobel Prizes in 1003, a good portion would have gone to the Muslims" because he honestly believed that, "they were blessed, not only in a spiritual way, but also in a mundane way." Somehow, none of this was reported in the article, probably due to lack of space. Pipes for the most part remained focused on "Militant Islamist." He substantiated his point by comments such as "Militant Islam pushed over the Shah and took over Iran." The birth of Militant Islam, according to Pipes, is not a result of "poverty" but rather the other way around. "One needs a certain attainment of economics before going to militant," he says. Daniel Pipes was not short of offering a solution either: "We defeat militant Islam, we strengthen Modern Islam." He contradicted himself later in his speech, saying, "It is the Muslims themselves who must come up with a solution." Furthermore, his definition of Modern Islamist is one who finds no fault in drinking alcohol and adopts Western ways.

Another impact of the dreadful day of September 11, 2001 is depicted in the headline appearing in the December 26, 2003 issue of the New York *Daily News:* "Conversions to Islam on rise in U.S." Tamer El-Ghobashy wrote, "Experts say the number of people converting to Islam, especially whites and Latinos like Rivera actually has risen since Sept. 11, 2001. "

The report summarized: " Last January, [Marisol Rivera] converted to Islam - joining more than 30,000 Americans who make the same leap each year, helping make Islam one of the fastest-growing religions in the United States."

Within a year of September 11, 2001 the *Boston Globe* echoed a similar account in its headlines, indicating that new conversions to Islam had "quadrupled" since September 11.

The reason for such a dramatic change can be attributed in my opinion only to the fact that after 9/11 many people wanted to know more about the religion that "allegedly" promotes violence. Rather than relying alone on the media, many came directly to the source to learn about Islam. They came to the people who actually practiced Islam. The church took it upon themselves to visit Islamic centers in their area, and the American Muslims went to their congregations to explain Islam. This interfaith dialogue was one of the main reasons for many to learn about Islam, and most realized that there was not much difference between Christianity, Judaism and Islam. The Qu'ran became the "best seller." The *Boston Globe* highlighted this fact well in the headlines on October 5, 2001; "Bookstores Selling Out Their Copies of Koran – Interest in Islam on Rise after Sept. 11 Terrorism"

> "Sales of the Koran, the holy scripture of Islam, have quin-tupled in the United States since Sept. 11, according to the book's main US publisher. Penguin Books is attempting to airlift reprints of the Koran in from the United Kingdom to meet demand for the book, sometimes spelled Qur'an," re-porter Michael Paulson wrote.

Several articles were written regarding the new "converts." New Muslims are commonly referred to as "reverts" in view of the belief that everyone is born a believer, hence, the new Muslims were merely returning to the faith they were born with.

Karen Schwartz, of the *Michigan Daily* reported October 22, 2003, how Islam changed Michael Dann's life. Dann "was raised as a Chris-tian, going to church and Sunday school in Amherst, Mass., as was his family's tradition. But four years ago, he decided he was des-tined for a different path. Dann converted to Islam." The report went on to say, "Dann said he went from being involved in "the drug culture" and party scene in junior high school to looking for some-thing more in life thanks to the example set by his tennis coach, a black Muslim man from New Jersey."

Joeseph Sweat of *Nashville Scene* reported in November 2003 that "Islam is the second-largest religion in the world, and it's bringing new people to the faith — including some local Christians."

An *ABCNEWS* telephone poll conducted between September

4 and September 7, 2003 among a random national sample of 1,004 adults, summarized the results in part as follows:

> Nearly two-thirds of Americans feel they don't have a "good basic understanding" of the religion, essentially the same as it was in October 2001.
>
> Significantly, people who feel they do understand Islam are much more likely to view it positively.
>
> Among Americans who feel they do understand the religion, 59 percent called it peaceful and 46 percent thought it teaches respect for the beliefs of others.

There were three related news items that caught my utmost attention. The February 24, 2004 edition of the UK-based *The Guardian* gave a detailed account of how the Qu'ran changed a "hard-drinking, hard-nosed news reporter [Yvonne Ridley] until her capture by the Taliban and subsequent conversion to Islam." Ridley dismissed the notion that her conversion was a result of the Stockholm syndrome. The second item from the *Associated Press* in 2002, reported that a devout Jew, Joseph Cohen, arrived in Israel from the United States in 1998, "but within three years he had converted to Islam and become Yosef Mohammed Khatib, according to a report broadcast Thursday on Israel TV. Wearing the white skullcap and robes of a religious Muslim, Khatib denied his Jewish past, insisting that he is 100 percent Muslim." Reportedly his American Jewish wife Luna of 10 years, also a devout Jew, accepted Islam as well. The third was the following article that appeared in the magazine *The Message* in July 1996, under the caption, "Digging for the Red Roots" by Mahir Abdal-Razzaaq El, a Native American Muslim. I had no idea until then that Islam found its way to the Cherokee tribe, long before Christopher Columbus set foot in North America. Apparently Muslims and non-Muslim alike discovered quite a bit after September 11, 2001.

> "My name is Mahir Abdal-Razzaaq El and I am a Cherokee Blackfoot American Indian who is Muslim. I am known as Eagle Sun Walker. I serve as a Pipe Carrier Warrior for the Northeastern Band of Cherokee Indians in New York City. There are other Muslims in our group. For the most part, not many people are aware of the Native American contact with Islam that began over one thousand years ago by some of the early Muslim travelers who visited us. Some of these

Muslim travelers ended up living among our people. For most Muslims and non-Muslims of today, this type of information is unknown and has never been mentioned in any of the history books. There are many documents, treaties, legislation and resolutions that were passed between 1600s and 1800s that show that Muslims were in fact here and were very active in the communities in which they lived. Treaties such as Peace and Friendship that was signed on the Delaware River in the year 1787 bear the signatures of Abdel-Khak and Muhammad Ibn Abdullah. This treaty details our continued right to exist as a community in the areas of commerce, maritime shipping, current form of government at that time which was in accordance with Islam. According to a federal court case from the Continental Congress, we help put the breath of life in to the newly framed constitution. All of the documents are presently in the National Archives as well as the Library of Congress.

If you have access to records in the state of South Carolina, read the Moors Sundry Act of 1790. In a future article, Inshallah, I will go in to more details about the various tribes, their languages; in which some are influenced by Arabic, Persian, Hebrew words. Almost all of the tribes vocabulary include the word Allah. The traditional dress code for Indian women includes the kimah and long dresses. For men, standard fare is turbans and long tops that come down to the knees. If you were to look at any of the old books on Cherokee clothing up until the time of 1832, you will see the men wearing turbans and the women wearing long head coverings. The last Cherokee chief who had a Muslim name was Ramadhan Ibn Wati of the Cherokees in 1866.

Cities across the United States and Canada bear names that are of Indian and Islamic derivation. Have you ever wondered what the name Tallahassee means? It means that He Allah will deliver you sometime in the future."

The above account of Mahir Abdal-Razzaaq El, a/k/a Eagle Sun Walker, was an eye-opener for me. This set me in the direction of finding out what really motivates some people to leave their religion to follow another. I started to look for answers by talking to people in my own community that had accepted Islam.

Isa Mujahid, an Afro-American born and raised in Massachusetts, converted to Islam from Christianity very early in his adult life. Born to Baptist parents in rural Alabama on August 1, 1949, his birth name was Isaiah Evans.

According to biblical scholars, Isaiah was a scribe, the first literary man to become a prophet. "I'm the youngest of five brothers and sisters. I grew up under cruel oppression in the racist South." Isa told me. "I attended all black schools. The South has only been integrated for about 35 to 40 years. I also grew up during a time of change: the Civil Rights Movement, Black Nationalism, Vietnam, the Sexual Revolution."

Isa was always proud to be an American, just like any born citizens, or immigrants who became American citizens. This should be true of all Muslim-Americans, except lately the Bush administration's foreign policy in Afghanistan and the Middle East [and now the Iraq war, and the passage of the PATRIOT Act which infringes on civil liberties] has put doubts into the minds of many Muslim-Americans. Many who at one time or the other felt proud to be called Americans were really feeling ashamed of that term.

Isa has a lot to show for his patriotism to America. He is a decorated vet, and served in the Air Force during Vietnam. "I served in the Army National Guard. I also served as a First Officer in *FOI* of the Nation of Islam," Isa was proud to say. As a graduate from Becker College, Isa converted to Islam in 1973 for the simple reason that it, "made good sense with regard to the concept of God and religion, religion being a complete way of life. That idea hit me right in my brain. I had always wanted to be religious, but the concept of God in the church did not make sense. I have two sons they are both practicing Muslims."

Isa had his own reason for his name change. "I consider it to be a curse for an African American to have European surname. These names were forced upon us during the cruelty of slavery. These names identify us as property of the slave master, so that's why I got rid of it.

"My family never had any issues with my conversion to Islam. Many of them admire me for what I stand for. Others say they would become Muslims if they did not have to give up pork." Isa told me with a big smile on his face.

Isa believed strongly that the bloc vote was a good idea. In retrospect, the choice may not have been the best under the circumstances, he agreed, but he well understood that the voting block idea is very powerful, and that it sent a strong message: we know how to maximize political assets.

Isa had been an integral part of the Muslim vote process. The biggest task that one can undertake would be to get all the Muslims in the world, estimated between 1.2 and 1.5 billion to be united on one thing. I do not mean on a religious viewpoint, but rather on a political perspective. Isa Mujahid was able to articulate this point very well and convey the force of these numbers in an interview with a reporter from the *Worcester Telegram & Gazette* on the fate of Jerusalem in the wake of the Middle-East violence that erupted in September, 2000. "There are 1.25 billion Muslims in this planet, and Jerusalem is sacred to all of them. So don't ask me how I feel about the future of Jerusalem."

"My advice to America is this, Islam is your friend, not your enemy. Islam is an asset to America. Islam is a powerful force that can help save America from moral decay. Islam will help America become a better America. I will say it again - Islam is your friend not your enemy."

Isa Mujahid hoped for his message to reach out to as many Americans as possible as he uttered those words. He honestly believed that Islam is the final answer to a peaceful world.

My meeting at the ISGW with Christopher Safford on a warm day in August 2002 was a mere coincidence. He was a new face, and I wanted to welcome him to the Islamic center and learn more about him. Christopher, an African-American was, only 22 years old, and lived in Worcester. He had come into Islam just a month and a half before, he told me. He told me that the events of September 11, 2001 had nothing to do with his accepting Islam. " I believed in Islam 3 to 4 years ago – on my own." Christopher Safford, born to Craig and Brenda, was originally from Texas and was raised as a Christian. He claimed that the church and the Sunday Bible study class did not give him the answers he was looking for. "Just have faith" was not the answer he was looking for. When he stopped going to church his mother told him that she had raised him to follow morals. "Follow your heart," she said. He started reading all books like the Torah, old Testament, and the Qu'ran. " I use to read the Qu'ran during my lunch break, and found that it gives you proof before it tells you to have faith."

That same evening we had invited Om Salama, her son Zakariya Hassan and daughter Roqiyyah Wright Yarrow to our house for dinner. Sally Keller changed her name to Om Salama about two years earlier when she accepted Islam. Both her grandparents came to the United States from Northern Ireland. Her father's family came from Germany. Her slim-built son Zakariya stood a good six feet tall and appeared even taller in the traditional Islamic attire he was wearing. Before changing his name from Zachary Wright. A graduate of Stanford with a degree in African studies, Zakariya had traveled to Sengal in Africa to learn more about his major. He met Shiekh Hassan Cisse, a devout Muslim, and spent most of his time in African American study with the Sheikh. Zachary noticed that Sheikh Hassan Cisse was "living the religion". It was here that Zachary realized, "Islam is the true religion – for I always had problem with organized religion." Recalling an incident in his life Zakariya told me, "Islam came together with me in a different way. I had a Hindu roommate who used to meditate in the morning for half an hour. I found that cool. I asked my roommate if I could meditate, and he told me that I need a *Muntra* to be repeated in my mind, and that *Muntra* has to be two syllables and should end in a vowel. So I recited "Allah" and through meditation I found God." He laughed.

Zakariya had no difficulty convincing his mother to accept Islam. Om said that she had raised her children not believing that Jesus was a son of God, but a prophet. Om Salama, who was an active Congregationalist and an evangelist, had no difficulty in leaving her Protestant denomination.

Her 24 year-old daughter Roqiyyah had accepted Islam six months earlier when she visited Africa and spent some time with her brother and Hassan Cisse. "I actually initially had planned to stay no longer than a week, but ended up staying for a month and a half," she explained. She talked about her experience learning in Hassan Cisse's school. She remembered the hardness of the concrete floor that she used to sit on along with 60 other kids cramped in a small hut in a hot day, "with flies all over you, if you can concentrate there then you can concentrate anywhere." Her mother proudly declared that they came from an athletic family. Zakariya was a runner who participated in national races, her elder son was a skiing champion, and her brother was an All-American football player. "However, my running days are over." Zakariya interjected jokingly.

The case of Steven Shakir was different. He had joined the *Nation of Islam* in 1974 when he was just 19 years old. Born to Helen and Joseph Boykin, when he replaced his Protestant name Boykin to Shakir, he was following what Fard Mohammed had taught Elijah Mohammad. As a result of his teachings, Elijah founded and became the leader of the *Nation of Islam*. Fard, who had come to the United States from the sub-continent in 1930, was either unable to impart the full knowledge of Islam, or somehow his teachings remained incomplete. It was much later in Steven's life when he started to read the Qu'ran and accepted "true Islam." The Islamic center in Worcester was established in early 80's, and since then Shakir had become a regular visitor. Shakir and his family remain regular active members. While Shakir oversees the interfaith and prison program, his wife Aquilah teaches in the Islamic school. Aquilah embraced Islam when she was 18-year old. Shakir was also elected the president of the ISGW in the 90's. "My mother was nervous when I joined the *Nation of Islam.* She became okay as years went by. If she didn't have to wear long dresses she would become a Muslim, she would say jokingly."

However, Latino Chris Botelho, son of Jackie Botelho, would come to the Worcester Islamic center just to give company to his friend Maher M. Taufeeque. Pakistan native Maher ran a business in Worcester and was in close proximity to the center. Chris accepted Islam on November 21, 2003 after only a few visits to the center. He enjoyed sitting with the Muslim community and paid a lot of attention to what Hamid Mehmood, the *Imam* [cleric] of the center was saying in the sermons that were so eloquently delivered. "I saw how things were done here – lots of attention [was given] to detail," Chris told me. Chris, who went to the Seminary at Horizon School of Evangelist, wanted to become a minister. He came to know more about Islam during the war in Iraq during George Bush's presidency, and Operation Desert Storm when he was a tank driver. Chris then continued to say, "I felt good after the first visit to the Islamic center. So I returned the next day. I had absolutely no intentions of becoming a Muslim. I still had my fear as a Christian. I was told that if I do not worship Jesus I would go to hell. But toward the end of the day all the fear was gone. Everything had changed, including my name. You may now call me Abdullah Ali."

I reminded him that Jesus was respected in Islam as a prophet.

The Qu'ran was very clear on this subject, and that it has a whole chapter dedicated to the Virgin Mary and the miracle birth of Jesus.

What I told him next really came as a pleasant shock to him. A year earlier at the ISNA convention I met with Yusuf Estes, a former ordained minister, his father also an ordained minister, and their Catholic priest friend Rev. Peter Jacoby, all accepted Islam as their new religion. I confessed to Abdullah that I wanted to ask Yusuf to find out what it takes to convince a person to convert to Islam, especially people whose very job is to preach Christianity. I got a chance when I met with Yusuf in the halls of the convention center in Washington, DC at the ISNA convention in August 2003. As I stood in the shadow of the huge man all dressed in white that matched the color of his long beard, waiting for his reply, one of his followers gave me the address of Yusuf's web site that had the story of his conversion to Islam. His entire story in his own words is included as Appendix [VII]. The interesting part in this was how it all started. Yusuf wanted to convert to Christianity a Muslim who was living with his family at the time. Yusuf thought between his father, himself and Rev. Jacob they could save the Muslim's soul. But in this process it was Yusuf and his friend Jacob who learned more about Islam, and one day to Yusuf's utter surprise he learned that Jacoby had become a Muslim, then Yusuf himself, followed closely by his wife, then his father. Yusuf mentioned a few more instances like these: "A Baptist seminary student who also came to Islam after reading the Holy Qu'ran while in Baptist seminary college. A former Catholic priest who had been a missionary for eight years in Africa accepted Islam. A former archbishop of the Russian Orthodox Church gave up his position to enter Islam."

When I asked his opinion about the American Muslim bloc vote, Yusuf shrugged off the question. American politics, he admitted, did not interest him much. I could understand and appreciate his stance much more after going over his web site.

Yusuf summarizes his accomplishment and mission in life well as he says on his web-site. "And since my own entrance into Islam and becoming a chaplain to the Muslims throughout the country and around the world, I have encountered many more individuals who were leaders, teachers and scholars in other religions who learned about Islam and entered into it. They came from Hindus, Jews, Catholics, Protestants, Jehovah's Witnesses, Greek and Russian Orthodox, Coptic Christians from Egypt, non-denominational churches and even scientists who had been atheists."

If there were any residue of fear of converting to Islam so suddenly in the mind of Abdullah Ali, the story of Yusuf Estes put him at ease.

Similar and interesting tales of new converts to Islam can be found almost everywhere, and they all have unique elements, as in the case of Abdur Raheem Green. During the first week of October 2002 the Islamic Society of Boston (ISB) in Wayland, Massachusetts invited Abdur Raheem Green, a very well known Muslim scholar from England, to speak at their community dinner. He shared one of his own experiences when he used to go to church in his early years, and recalled, "when they offered wine and referred to it as God's blood – it's a bit scary we are eating and drinking God, I thought." Green was often told that he looked like a picture of Jesus. He embraced Islam in the mid 1980's after being brought up as a Roman Catholic. He has since invited a great many people to Islam. He is especially known for his efforts at the renowned "speakers corner" in London's Hyde Park.

When I asked what made him come toward Islam, he replied in one word: "money," then added rather abruptly, "to get rich." He knew that I could not let him get away with short ambiguous statements, so he continued this time seriously. "I wanted to get rich quick, and I even pursued 'get-rich-quick schemes' but to no avail. So I looked around to see who and where the richest men in the world were. Americans – they worked from ground up, no. The Japanese – forget it, all they do is work. The Saudis – they are rich, and they sit on their camels all day. And that's why I picked Islam because God must be pleased with them. There's got to be something in the religion, I thought, and that is what got me to pick up the Qu'ran."

He confessed he never got rich, but he found many answers in the Qu'ran that he was confused about as a Christian. "In Islam, religion and politics are one. In democracy [and by that he meant Western democracy] religion and politics are separate. The future of the Muslims in the Western world depends upon the Muslim parent."

The conversions to Islam became almost a regular feature. For instance, on a cold Sunday afternoon, March 14, 2004, 27 year-old Mariam, who had recently arrived from Iowa as Kari Lindeman of the Mormon faith, repeated after the ISGW *Imam* [cleric] Hamid Mehmood the *Shahada* [declaring faith] first in Arabic then in English: "I bear witness that there is no god but Allah, and I bear witness that Mohammed is His Messenger." With those words Mariam converted to Islam. The women started embracing Mariam, and the rest of us greeted her with the appropriate chant *Allah-O-Akbar* [Allah is Great]. Mariam, seemed very comfortable in wearing the *Hijab* (head scarf that covers the head and side of the face - an Islamic attire for women). I was anxious to find out what motivated her to embrace Islam. Did she have a teacher or a Muslim friend? Then came her reply in a single word, "The Internet." Mariam managed to navigate on the Internet and visited many web sites that talked about Islam and it's teaching. The more she read, the more her interest in learning about Islam grew. Eventually she ended up in a Muslim chat e-mail group where she met other Muslim friends. One of her "email friends" Lena Najar Zegers, who was from Massachusetts, suggested she come to Boston. "Please come to Boston, she said." Mariam said with a smile that could not be hidden entirely even through her *Hijab*, and added, "And I said yes." Lena, or Stacey Zegers her given Catholic name, of Dutch-heritage, converted on September 27, 2000, when she was not even 17 years old. "My dad was in the Air Force, so we moved a lot in Turkey and other parts of Europe. That's when I started to read about Islam. I compared it with other religions and found Islam to be a more balanced religion," Lena told me. Glancing at Mariam she added, "She is a good example of Islam on line." We took leave of each other laughingly.

It is important to make a point that Muslims believe that there is absolutely no difference between Allah, God or YHVH [Jewish name for the Creator]. He is one and the same – the Creator of the Universe. In other words, the name *Allah* is analogous to the Semitic term *Eloh*, means "*God*," like *Dios* in Spanish and *Dieu* in French.

Mariam had just left the building when I noticed a Caucasian male in the assembly, thinking he was Mariam's brother or a relative. I approached him to introduce myself. I soon found out he was not related to her, but he was really moved by what had just transpired, and this was the first time he visited the Islamic center or any other Islamic center for that matter. Dan Landers, 21, had recently moved to Worcester. His real exposure to Islam started a year and a half earlier when he took a six-month vacation trip to Europe. He was living in the outskirts of Weisbaden, Germany, where he met and spent some "quality" time with Muslims that he befriended in the area, and then in Turkey. "I was much impressed by their way of living," Dan told me. "I wanted to learn more about their religion. That turned out to be really a vacation from my old lifestyle to a holy lifestyle."

Dan spent most of his life in small Orangeburg, South Carolina and did not have any Muslim friends. He told me, "I had only $40 on me, and I wanted to invest it in the best possible way. I went into the *Wonder* book store and brought a copy of the Qu'ran." Dan started reading and studying the Qu'ran on his own. He could not locate any Mosque in the area where he lived. What Dan did not know that there was a small Mosque in Orangeburg, but it was obscure. Dan had no idea the closeness I felt with him as I told him that it was the members of that Mosque that helped us locate the Muslim cemetery nearby, and helped bury my son Yaser Ali nearly 10 years earlier when he succumbed to leukemia.

"What was it about Islam that appealed to you?" *Imam* Hamid Mehmood asked. "Humble yourself to God," Dan added. "It showed me the way of life, how to live a life, and that's when I started to appreciate it more. I looked at the present religions including Christianity and Judaism. I soon realized that those religions did not represent me. I completely agree that the Qu'ran properly shows how to go about your life."

I wanted to know if the events of September 11, 2001 influenced him in any way. Dan's eyes widened as he said, "Personally I do not believe that the Muslims had any thing to do with 9/11. In that case, my view of Islam did not change negatively. If anything, 9/11 set me on a course to Islam. You would want to know why someone would like to do what the media, and let me repeat, what the media and the government were indicating that Muslims had done. In the process I ended up learning more of the true Islam, which was completely in contradiction to how it was being portrayed in the media."

Dan started to confess that he did not know any of the "prayer" rituals and what to say or how to pray when he offered his prayer behind us. He had just picked up some simple stuff there and then talking to Dave Silva, who himself had converted to Islam about four years earlier from a Catholic and strong Portuguese family background. Dave showed him the basics like taking off your shoes before entering the prayer area, not to lay the Qu'ran on the floor — little things like that he was unsure of. He was afraid whether he had offended anyone.

The *Imam* comforted him."Call on your Lord in your own language, do not worry about the rituals. Glorify God in your own language. In the meanwhile, learn at your own pace, no need to rush." I asked him if he wanted to take the *Shahada* just like Mariam had done so. He had no second thoughts on that, and Dan Landers, a carpenter by trade, raised in an Irish Catholic house, offered the *Shahada* right there at that moment.

Elizabeth DeMarco, a 21-year old junior at Worcester State College born to Catholic parents entered the Islamic center in Worcester on April 18, 2004 with one thing on her mind. She wanted to embrace Islam. Elizabeth too repeated the *shahada*. She told me that her draw toward Islam was a natural phenomenon, the only help she received was reading about Islam on the Internet.

Lynn Manning, of a strong Irish Catholic background, did not convert to Islam when she first married Khaled Ibrahim, originally from Egypt. It was nearly a year into her marriage with Ibrahim when she accepted Islam in November 2003. "My husband provided me Islamic literature, including the Qu'ran," Lynn told me. "I felt at peace when I read the Qu'ran. It was as if God is talking right to you. I did not want to put it down." Lynn Ibrahim, attired in *Hijab*, added that she found it "ironic" that while she observed prayer five times a day her husband was not able to.

Ibrahim Kalin received his Ph.D. from Washington University in 2002. He is a professor of Islamic studies at Worcester Holy Cross College and a Research Affiliate at the Center for Middle Eastern Studies, Harvard University. Kalin came to the United States eight years ago from Turkey. He was a guest speaker at the ISGW on May 1st, 2004. The theme of his talk was "The meaning of being a religious community in the U.S. today". He entertained a number of questions from the audience. Kalin remembered seeing me talking to Daniel Pipes at the Holy Cross College where Pipes lectured on February 6, 2003. Kalin thinking loud told me, "The U.S. Government has not made use of the potential of the American Muslim community in improving its relations with the Islamic world."

After his talk, Kalin summoned one of his students, Renee Chachakis who was in the audience to come forth. She stepped in front of the community and recited the Shahada in Arabic. Renee, of an Irish-English-Scottish Catholic background, embraced Islam on May 1st, 2001. She was born on April 1st, 1980. She too had been reading about Islam on-line for a couple of months. Renee explained to me how she learned about Islam "I read up on it on-line and basically found the words of Shahada and put it as screen-saver on my computer. So the Shahada scrolled across the screen when the computer went in its idle mode."

"Apparently when your computer was idle you were not", I hastily interjected. She went blank for a moment then burst into laughter as she ascertained my remark, then added, "The main reason for my conversion is my wonderful roommate Momena; she has been the best role model for me."

Momena Sayed, a student at Holy Cross, president of the Muslim Endeavor to Create Culture Awareness (MECCA) was born in Khandahar, Afghanistan. Momena and her parents migrated from Afghanistan to Pakistan when she was four years old and ten when she came to Portland, Maine with her parents. "I don't know how I can inspire people to convert to Islam. It is the will of Allah, not I", the modest 21-year old Momena insisted. Renee is the third person Momena introduced to Islam.

So where were the increased number of new converts to Islam coming from? The answer may lie after meeting Kunta Kunte. Alex Haley, the author of *Roots,* gave rise to the popular 1980 epic television series of the same name. Kunta Kunte became a household name, and the African Americans soon realized that before their ancestors were forcefully brought to the United States on slave ships from Africa, their religion was Islam. But in the United States they were gradually converted to Christianity. It was with this notion that Haley's 61 year-old grandson, living in Worcester revealed that he had very seriously been thinking of converting to Islam.

To an extent, then, the steady flow of African Americans toward Islam can largely be attributed to Alex Haley and his genealogy research and epic drama Roots. But after September 11, 2001 it was also white Americans who joined in and increasingly read more about Islam, learned more about Islam, and for the first time saw Islam in a more positive way with an open mind.

But whenever I asked any of the above-mentioned converts about the Muslim bloc vote, they mostly agreed that it was good in one sense, but it was bad in the sense we chose the wrong guy. Their advice was based on their living experiences that the leadership has to have more vision and insight about any candidate. We cannot choose someone because we may think he or she might help. But they all agreed that it is good to show the ability that you have the power of the bloc vote.

CHAPTER 15   *History and Destiny: Legacies and Lessons*

Indeed, there is a cause for worry. President Bush may want to re-negotiate renewal of the "expired items" in the Patriot Act. Many agreed to allow it to pass the first time, arguably out of fear. What will be interesting to see in the days to follow is how much resistance President Bush gets this time. The Patriot Act, many will admit goes against the grain of the U.S. Constitution. I wonder if Bush will have to resort to the level of asking of his "trusted" cabinet friends to find him an excuse to get the Patriot Act through, again.

Muslim-Americans faced and overcome many challenges and will continue to face even more. The use of Secret Evidence Law will be sufficient enough to deport or incarcerate in some cases. The disproportionate or selective use of Patriotic Act will penetrate deeper to make a case for others. In this regard, the cases against Professor Sami Al-Arian and Abdurahman Alamoudi are of keen interest.

The National Liberty Fund (NFL), is a nonprofit, legal defense organization established in April 2003 in Washington D.C. NFL was established with the mission to defend the rights of Muslim political prisoners in the United States. NFL is analogous to the NAACP. The alliance between Wells-Barnett and Fredrick Douglas helped found the NAACP in 1877. The NAACP scored a major victory in 1954, when Thurgood Marshall was successful in overturning the *Plessy v. Ferguson* ruling of 1896 that upheld Jim Crow law. Until today, the NAACP challenges racist and discriminating law and practices.

Since 1986, Dr. Sami Al-Arian, a professor at the University of South Florida has been incarcerated on charges of supporting terrorism.NFL is focusing its resources on the case of Dr. Sami Al-Arian and co-defendants, Hatim Naji Fariz, Ghassan Zayed Ballut, and Sameeh Hammoudeh. The NFL's position is well articulated in one of their pamphlets made available to public, reproduced here in part as follows: "After nine years of a highly public investigation, the government has yet to provide solid evidence to support their claims against Dr. Al-Arian and his co-defendants. Meanwhile, the case had already been intensely politicized by years of misinforma-

tion and lobbying by pro-Israel groups. The government's indictment, which relies heavily on innuendoes and guilt-by-association,
is based largely on old allegations that have already been debunked."

The American Civil Liberties Union (ACLU) of Florida in its open
letter of August 21, 2003, stated " The justice system and the state of
Florida had investigated Dr. Al-Arian and his relatives and associ-
ates repeatedly without finding cause for indictment, until the USA
Patriot Act was passed.

Dr. Al-Arian has not been accused of overtly or directly being
responsible for any violent crime, yet he is being treated as if he had
been found guilty in a court of law. He is inflicted with prison procedures usually reserved for the most violent, bad-actors in the penal
system. Dr. Sami Al Arian has been denied justice." The statement
concluded with the remark, "Dr. Al-Arian is being treated more se-
verely because he is a Muslim, a Palestinian, and most importantly
an outspoken political activist at odds with the ideology of his ac-
cusers."

Dr. Agha Saeed, National Chairman American Muslim Alliance,
once again stepped up to the plate. It was time to walk the walk and
he did testify on behalf of Dr. Sami Al-Arian, on March 21, 2003. "I
told the court that Sami Al-Arian was my friend and I had known
him for more than ten years, and during that time we have worked
together to mainstream American Muslim politics." Dr. Saeed also
told the court that Dr. Al-Arian and he had been working together
to replace the culture of despair with a culture of hope, and the culture of bullet, with the culture of the ballot.

Dr. Saeed added "It was during the cross examination that I got
my two cents worth in. I was asked what I thought of Sami Al-
Arian, 'now after having read the indictment'. I gladly answered the
question: 'The legal system in this country is founded on the belief
that a person is innocent till proven guilty. The Justice Department
has made very serious allegation against Prof. Arian but at this stage
these are mere allegations. And they will remain so unless and until
he is proven guilty in an open court and under open evidence."

The trial is expected to begin in January 2005, until that time Dr.
Al-Arian and his co-defendants remain incarcerated in a maximum-
security federal penitentiary.

CAIR issued a press release. CAIR Board Chairman, Omar Ahmad made a valid point, "We are very concerned that the government would bring charges after investigating an individual for many years without offering any evidence of criminal activity. This action could leave the impression that Al-Arian's arrest is based on political considerations, not legitimate national security concerns."

Abdurahman Alamoudi, a leading activist and founder of the American Muslim Council (AMC), was arrested on September 28, 2003. He was charged with illegally accepting $340,000 from the Libyan government. Stanley Cohen, one of Alamoudi's lawyers labeled this as another "witch-hunt". Maher Hanania, also Alamoudi's lawyer, strongly believed this action to be "politically motivated", a penalty levied on Alamoudi because of his pro-Palestinian stance.

The underlining issue in both cases is the number of years they remained under surveillance and the guilt-by-association factor. Simply put, any one that came in contact with Dr. Al-Arian or Alamoudi while they were under surveillance could also be found guity-by-association. Nine years of surveillance is a long time. It remains to be seen at what point in time the term "innocent until proven guilty" is applicable.

While we all cherish the U.S. constitution which guarantees its constituents, freedom of speech, gender equality, due process under the law, equal justice, and minority rights – it was beginning to be clear these rights might not be equally applied to Dr. Al-Arian, Alamoudi and other similar cases or their cases would be tried behind closed door, and on the basis of secret evidence.

Another, but a more serious danger to Muslims, is the opinion and power of ideas, among some American intellectuals — including Samuel Huntington, Henry Kissinger, Bernard Lewis — that Islam itself is somehow to blame for the terrorist attacks. Their auctorial pursuits were focused on making the assumption and to prove their theory that the secular states of the West are on a collision course with the Islamic states of the East.

What I would submit to you is the crisis of civil rights and how the power of ideas and power of choices have gone into making of this crisis. We can start in 1987-88 when the Cold War between the Soviet Union and the United States was coming to an end. People were beginning to wonder what would happen since the Soviet Union would no longer be the prime enemy around which, against which and at which American foreign policy, Cold War policy, and the economic and military policies were directed. The concerns were two fold, one, what would fill the vacuum once the global enemy no longer existed and, two, how would the world economy be affected. This is where the power of ideas began.

The first piece that came to public evidence was Francis Fukuyama's famous article called "The End of History?" (Francis Fukuyama's "The End of History?" when it appeared in the summer 1989 issue of *The National Interest.*) At that time he was the Deputy Director of the U.S. State Department's Policy Planning staff. In his article "The End of History?" he said, using German philosopher Hegel's [G. W. F. Hegel] model, that history evolves to a competition of ideas. He argued that there were three main idea systems in the 20th century - Fascism, Communism and Capitalism. With Communism and Fascism fallen by the wayside, he argued that the history had come to an end in Hegelian sense because there was no competition of idea and no further evolution of thought. Things had come to a standstill in that sense and he said did not mean there would be no more wars, conflicts or disputes but they would be of the same conceptual flavor. So by what he meant by end of history where all events will come to be located in a single paradigm or a single conceptual flavor need not have concerned us too much.

From this argument he derived other arguments which were very relevant. He said with the end of the Cold War we changed from a geo-political phase to a geo-economic phase. He said in the name of geo political what counts is your military, and in the name of geo economics what counts is your economy. We entered a different phase in which countries would be seen, measured and judged in relation to each other on a totally different basis. In another very important point he said we had no global enemies – the last global enemy was Soviet Union. We had entered a relative age of peace; therefore, the whole world, principally, the United States, should reap the benefits and dividends of peace. Finally, he said Islam is not the enemy. Iran and Iraq, he said, may be local irritants but they lack the capacity to be global enemies for two reasons; one, they don't have an ideology that appeals to people outside of their own world; and, second, they don't have the military means to project their power beyond their borders.

No sooner had he finished his article and it had published the first person to dispute him was Henry Kissinger, who said that Fukuyama does not understand any of these complex international issues. He is obliviously wrong. We continue to have global enemies. Kissinger did not say but hinted at the Muslims.

Then came another individual, Bernard Lewis, who in his book "Islam in the West", argued, among other things, we do have the making of a global enemy within the Muslim world. Muslims are a civilization that have been left behind. They are suffering from the "rage of impotence" and, therefore, they are going to be our new enemy and we have to be prepared to deal with them.

The power of ideas: Internationally established scholar Samuel Huntington in his famous article "Clash of Civilization" argued that he was inspired by Bernard Lewis. One person's basic idea inspired a well-known, internationally established scholar who came up with his own thesis. In that thesis he claimed Fukuyama misunderstood the flow of history. History actually had gone through four phases and each age had its unit of conflicts. He claimed the unit of conflict was civilization – and ultimately the conflict of two sets of civilization; first, Islam and the west; second, between Confucian state (China) and Islam on one side and the west on other.

Now this was a very powerful and I would like to suggest that it continues to be a paradigm that, by and large has, been accepted by the American establishment with few exceptions. There were two major efforts to stem or limit this paradigm which makes Islam as the global enemy of the West. And the first one was made by Anthony Lake who was the national security advisor to Clinton who was prior to that a professor at Amherst College in Massachusetts who is again a professor at Amherst now.

In his very famous speech "From Containment to Enlargement" he said from 1945 to 1990 for 45 years American concern was to contain Communism, by military, economic, cultural and political means. Now he said in 1990 and onwards, that we had entered a new phase because we had nothing to contain. We had entered a phase of expanding things – what do we need to expand - two things; democracy and market democracy. Since our idea is the only idea in the world - we are the only show in town. Hence, selling the idea was no problem. He also said in that speech, "We neither have arrived at the end of history nor are we facing a clash of civilization". A very important point that we need to know because this is an idea and a fair idea and Muslims need to know about it and talk about it. He also said, that we had no conflict with Islam. We may have questionable Muslim states. He named a few of them, which he called the rogue states or outlaw states.

What Lewis and Huntington had done was find a religious category to looking at the world. What Lake tried to do to was restore a legal category to understand international issues.

CHAPTER 16   *Muslim Americans Cross the Rubicon, But...*

I was walking rather vigorously in order to stay warm on a fairly cold evening on March 25, 2004. The destination a few blocks away was the Park Plaza Hotel in Boston where a fundraiser for President George Bush was being held. The venue was significant as it brought some fond memories of the "controversial" AMA fundraiser for former First Lady Hillary Rodham Clinton that was held in the same hotel almost four years ago on June 13, 2000. Expectedly, all roads leading to the hotel were police barricaded, and at each barricade there were both demonstrators [mostly protesting the Iraq war] and Bush supporters. You could hear both derogatory as well as praising slogans directed toward Bush and his Administration. Many in the crowd held signs that read:

> *"Drop Bush Not Bombs"*
> *"Blood For Oil"*
> *"Be Patriotic Vote Bush Out"*
> *"A Vote For Bush is a Vote For Freedom"*
> *"Four More Years"*

After going through a routine credential and security check, I was escorted to the hotels' ballroom that was decorated in red and blue hues appropriate for the occasion. The names on the fundraiser co-chair list included Martha Chayet and William Weld, the former governor of Massachusetts. Sharing the stage with the president and the governor of Massachusetts Mitt Romney was Richard J. Egan, the former Ambassador to Ireland.

"We have two people running for president, and one of them is a strong leader." Romney said as he introduced President Bush to the cheering supporters. Bush in return praised the governor and had a few laughs at the governor's expense about Romney's own national political ambitions. Bush noted the telephone conversation he had a few days earlier during the traditional St. Patrick's Day political roast in South Boston. "When I called in, I had the feeling they were going to ask me about a Massachusetts politician who had his eyes on the White House – so I addressed the issue as directly as possible: I told Mitt the job was filled until 2008."

Justifying his re-selection of Dick Cheney as his running mate, the president said, "Dick Cheney is the best vice president the United States has ever had." He paused slightly as he glanced around the ballroom then added jokingly, "My mother said wait a minute."

Bush spent a great deal talking and defending his position in Iraq. He also outlined some of the lessons that could be learned from September 11, 2001. "We saw a war and grief arrive on the morning of September 11."

Bush criticized his presidential opponent, John Kerry, several times. "My opponent says he approves of bold action in the world, but only if other countries do not object. America must never outsource America's national security." I am not sure about others in the ballroom, but the words that came instantly in my mind were, "How about, America must never outsource America's jobs."

Words that followed after were comforting as the president stressed the point well that America will not stand for "discrimination against people of faith," and "we believe in a culture that every person counts and every person matters." Soon thereafter I turned to Card, the White House Chief of Staff who was talking to John J. Monahan, a *Telegram and Gazette* staff reporter. I wanted to thank Andrew Card for publicly acknowledging Pakistan's President Pervez Musharraf's staunch resolve in fighting the war on terrorism. President Musharraf narrowly escaped at least two assassination attempts on his life, but that has not discouraged him in abandoning the hunt for Osama bin Laden or *Al-Qaeda* top operatives that may be still hiding in the rugged terrain near the Pakistan and Afghanistan border.

"He is a great president and a strong U.S. ally," Andrew Card added. This resounded well with the statement that Dr. Condoleezza Rice, National Security Advisor, read two weeks later on April 8, 2004, in front of the National Commission on Terrorist attacks: "He [President Bush] recognizes that the War on Terror is a broad war. Under his leadership, the United States and our allies are disrupting terrorist operations, cutting off their funding, and hunting down terrorists one-by-one. Their world is getting smaller. The terrorists have lost a home-base and training camps in Afghanistan. The Governments of Pakistan and Saudi Arabia now pursue them with energy and force."

Andrew Card sounded sincere in his remarks about President Musharraf. He was eager to share information as he said, "You know his son lives right here in Boston."

"Bilal Musharraf," I responded quickly.

I reminded Card of the Muslim bloc vote that went to President Bush in 2000, but admitted that it would be difficult to mobilize the same force behind his boss in the upcoming 2004 U.S. presidential elections. He did not seem very surprised. I assured Card that the president's efforts to reach out to the Muslim community after the September 11 attacks did not go unnoticed and were much appreciated, with a case in point his visit to the Mosque in DC within a week of September 11. Andrew Card's eyes glittered as he said, "I was with the President."

In 2001 Elizabeth "Liz" Moore, a reporter of *NewsDay* in New York, asked me what was the population of American Muslims in the United States; my reply was seven million a figure former President Bill Clinton had used in one of his speeches. Whether that number had increased in 2004 is not of significance. What is more important is whether or not the number of American Muslim voters has increased. Those who were not of voting age in 2000 are now eligible to vote in 2004. These young, mostly American-born Muslim voters, seemed to have more political awareness than their immigrant parents.

Zeenat Khan who had recently moved to Boston from Ohio belonged to this category of young voters. She attended many of the AMA meetings in Massachusetts. Zeenat made an observation that our 2000 bloc vote was a good idea, but we selected the wrong candidate. "You all had your chance and blew it," she said, "Now let the new generation take over to form the 2004 presidential election plan." She and her family were instrumental in getting presidential candidate Dennis J. Kucinich to talk at the ISNA convention on August 30, 2003. After the talk, a private meeting was arranged with Dennis Kucinich, that was largely attended by ISNA's board: President Mohammad Nur Abdullah, Vice President Ingrid Mattson, Secretary General Sayyid M. Syeed, Sirhaj Wahaj.

Sayyid Syeed introduced me to Dennis Kucinich as one of the architects and implementors of the 2000 bloc vote. Where was the American Muslim vote going this time.

Dean's Last Stand - The American Muslim Dilemma" continues.
General Armstrong Custer's reckless behavior at West Point, led to many reprimands and disciplinary actions been taken against him.

Surprisingly enough, it may have been his unorthodox methods that led him to many victories in the battlefields during the Civil War and then later in the untamed frontier. The Battle of Little Big Horn, however, was his "Alamo". Facing 5000 warriors led by Chief Sitting Bull and Chief Crazy Horse, Custer and his 264 men gallantly, vigorously and courageously put up a fight to the end.

Doctor Howard Dean and his "internet-buildup" army fought vigorously in Wisconsin, but neither was John Kerry sitting idle, nor was John Edwards crazy enough to surrender. Completely ignoring Dr. Dean's DNR orders, his well-wishers continued to resuscitate him until February 18, 2004 when he was officially pronounced "politically" dead. His wife, Judith Steinberg was at his side.

In the year 2000, American Muslims made history. They created and executed a bloc vote that made the difference and helped put Bush in the White House. Why did it happen? Because the Democrats, at their own peril, completely ignored the American Muslims.

After 9/11 things were never the same for American Muslims. This included, but was not limited to, any and all campaign promises becoming volatile. The important issues in the mind of the American public, besides the economy and healthcare are: The attack on their civil liberties [the unpatriotic "Patriot Act"], and the "senseless" Iraq war. Elect-ability may very well be based on how the Democratic candidate confronts Bush on those issues. Senator Kerry will have a hard time attacking Bush on those issues since he voted for them - the pot calling the kettle black. So we are back to square one - either Bush or Kerry - a dilemma in the making.
From the Muslim perspective we have a caveat in the sense that it may be possible to create inroads through Shahid Ahmed Khan, who is well placed within Kerry's campaign staff.

American Muslim favorite - Ohio Congressman Dennis Kucinich received Arab-American endorsement in the Primaries. "My Mom won the spot for first delegate from our district," Zeenat said proudly, "She will not be going to the Democratic National Convention as an Ohio delegate because Dennis didn't get 15% in our district - if that makes sense." Zeenat Khan added with a sigh.
Our bloc vote in 2000, was a huge success; first, we were able to put Muslim issues on the American presidential debate. The proof of that is the second presidential debate when Bush came out and said that he was opposed to profiling of Arab Muslims and that he supported the repeal of Secret Evidence law. We had told him that he

would have to take that position in the presidential debate in order to get our votes. Second, we put Muslims on the political map. The very fact that two presidential candidates, Senator Carol Moseley Braun and Congressman Dennis Kucinich came to the 40th annual ISNA convention on August 30, 2003 is because we have placed ourselves on the critical map. It is the power of that bloc vote that brought them there.

Third, the bloc vote, which is now a matter of record, and Dennis Kucinich testified to the fact when he said to the audience of over ten thousand Muslim Americans at the ISNA convention on August 30, 2003, "You have political power, you demonstrated that in the past. You helped elect a president in 2000. And you can do it again in 2004 to set America on a new path. You can make all the difference in the Democratic primaries. The bloc vote of this community can change the outcome in any election, can help take America on a new path, for this country and the world, to take us away from war, to take us away from discrimination."

What happened after that was 9/11. Fourteen Muslim leaders living in the U.S. were invited to meet with President Bush on the afternoon of September 11, 2001. The meeting, obviously, had to be postponed. The President was going to announce the repeal of the Secret Evidence Act. When Muslim leaders finally met with him on the September 26, he indicated that all bets were off, and hereafter Arab men 18 and over would be profile

It is necessary to keep in mind, it was not a normal integration of the understanding within the complex structure of electoral politics; it was a major impact on the country. Now 9/11 and the Patriot Act has made it abundantly clear that we need to participate in politics more so. The only battle we have on these two fronts is the protection of civil rights and support for a candidate with an agenda for civil rights protection and solutions.

2004 Election Plan: One of the many lessons we learned during the 2000 presidential elections was that we were not inclusive enough. The first thing that needed to happen was to expand the American Muslim Political Coordinating Council (AMPCC) or replace it. Some of the key members and leaders of the existing national and local Muslim organizations met with this objective in mind. Meetings were conducted in various cities and different states to increase participation and diversity. The meetings took many forms, and everyone's opinion were taken into account. It was becoming clear in these meetings that the fallout of the September 11, 2000 attacks and the USA Patriot Act were an important factor in the minds of many. Therefore, the only battle we have on these two fronts is the protection of civil rights and support for a candidate with an agenda for civil rights protection and solutions. The apparent need for "community–based decision-making process" culminated into a new entity — "AMT" that stood for "American Muslim Taskforce on Civil Rights and Elections."

AMT, an umbrella organization is represented by the following Muslim organizations:
American Muslim Alliance (AMA)
Council on American-Islamic Relations (CAIR)
Islamic Circle of North America (ICNA)
Islamic Society of North America (ISNA)
Muslim Alliance of North America (MANA)
Muslim American Society (MAS)
Muslim Public Affairs Council (MPAC)
Muslim Student Association – National (MSA-N)
Project Islamic Hope (PIH)

The mission of AMT is to protect civil and human rights and to encourage American Muslims to be part of the mainstream American politics.

The statement sent to the American Muslim community by AMT outlined the following objectives, issues and strategy:

"Objectives
1) Become full partners in the development and prosperity of our homeland, the United States,
2) Defend civil and human rights of all,
3) Mainstream the American Muslim community, and
4) Develop alliances with like-minded fellow Americans on a wide variety of social, political, economic and moral issues.

Issues
In 2004 Election we will focus our efforts on a "Civil Rights Plus" agenda. By this we mean that 'civil rights for all' is the

main issue but not the only issue. We remain equally committed to education, homelessness, economic recovery, environmental and ecological safety, electoral reform, crime, and global peace and justice. Our 'Civil Rights Plus' agenda is broadly organized under three categories:

a) Civil and human rights,
b) Domestic issues of public good and general welfare,
c) Global peace with justice, prevention of war, and U.S. relations with the Muslim world.

Strategy
The AMT will organize strategic mobilization of the American Muslim voters at local, state and federal levels, with primary focus on key states and key races."

EPILOGUE

The 2000 presidential elections marked a significant change in the past voting practice of the American Muslim in that 76% of the national vote and 80% of the 80,000 Muslims in Florida voted for George W. Bush. If they have voted as in the past elections, most of those votes would have gone to Al Gore, the Democratic candidate. There would have been no need for a vote recount in Florida; hence the title of this book: "The Muslim vote counts and recounts."

Bush won by 537 votes Florida.* The approximate 64,000 Muslim votes were enough to tip the balance in favor of Bush. Therefore, the Muslim bloc vote was a major factor in electing Bush in Florida, which in turn was the deciding factor in electing Bush nationally.

[* *Source Federal Election Commission web site. Al Gore 2,912,790 and George W. Bush 2,912, 253*]

The bloc vote is not a new concept; it has been done many times before. But what Muslims and non-Muslims must realize is task of organizing the Muslim community in unison in a bloc vote on the basis of a clearly defined agenda and criteria, was a major feat on its own. The importance of this accomplishment is highlighted by the fact that Muslims come from all ethnic backgrounds and from all social classes, which each segment having its perspective on priorities. For example, to American Muslims of Pakistani origin, Kashmir is a burning issue, but for Muslims of Middle Eastern descent, Palestine comes first. But their ultimate agreement on seeking repeal of the Secret Evidence Act reflected conversions of ideas as well as maturity, sophistication and consensus building.

American Muslims need to cast their vote, not in anger, but based on reason. They must also recognize that they will have to align their issues with like-minded fellow Americans.

All Americans, Muslims, Christians, Hindus, Sikhs, Buddhist, Jews and Atheists alike, will have to take into account the affect of the Patriot Act on civil liberties. Everyone have to take into account the "outsourcing of jobs" when our Country has a very high unemployment rate. Everyone will have to take into account the Country's going from a surplus to a deficit. All of us will have to continue to question the credibility of the current Administration in the wake of former Treasury Secretary Paul H. O'Neill account in Ron Suskind's book, "The Price of Loyalty", former White House aide Richard A. Clarke's book, "Against All Enemies" and Washington Post's Bob

Woodward's book, "Plan of Attack." And finally, we will all have to take into account the tarnished image abroad after the invasion of Iraq, the fierce "insurgent" uprising in Fallujah plus the " Iraqi detainees abuse" scandal that will have dire consequences for generations to come.

I agree with Dr. Agha Saeed that our overall strategy must be premised on the belief that "Our vote is the best guarantee of our civil rights and the best expression of our citizenship".

Appendix I:
Bob Dole's letter to Agha Saeed for the Muslim Community
Oct.16, 1996
Dr. Agha Saeed, President
American Muslim Alliance
3550 Mowry Ave., Suite 302
Fremont, California

Dear Dr. Saeed,

As a candidate for President of the United States, I wish to express my firm belief that people of all faiths must recognize the contributions American Muslims have made, and continue to make, toward the goal of a family-centered, healthy and productive society. I truly believe that America draws strength from its churches, synagogues and mosques.

Throughout this country, American Muslims are our neighbors, classmates, and co-workers. Muslim families seek to promote strong moral values and a commitment to community responsibility. These universal values, coupled with community service, have been demonstrated to have a positive impact on problems such as crime, drug use and the breakdown of the family.

Since the end of the Cold War, many American Muslims have been the targets of stereotyping, bias and discrimination. This discrimination has been seen in the workplace, where Muslim workers were denied reasonable religious accommodation, in schools, and in the media, where our Muslim citizens are often unfairly associated with acts of violence.

American Muslims, like all citizens, wish to build a better America. As the Republican party platform states, I would oppose any legislation infringing on the rights of American citizens to freedom of religion, speech, press, assembly, or the right to judicial due process. While demanding increased security measures for the traveling public, I would oppose any discriminatory procedures for screening airline passengers based solely on race, sex, economic status, national origin, or political beliefs.

As a President of inclusion, I would seek to ensure that all Americans, irrespective of economic, social, or religious background, have all the rights and opportunities offered by a free society. I would also seek to open constructive dialogue with all Muslim countries working for peace, representing as they do, one fifth of humanity. A goal of my Administration would be to support a clear, long-term and even-handed foreign policy that is consistent with our nation's vital interests.

      Sincerely,
      Bob Dole
      810 First Street, NE, Suite 300
      Washington, DC 20002

Appendix II

Hillary Clinton's letter of 1998: AMA National Convention

The White House,
Washington, DC,

Oct, 1998

Dear Friends:

I am pleased to have this opportunity to send greetings to each of you attending the American Muslim Alliance Convention.

Diversity has always been America's great blessing—and our greatest challenge. We are a nation of immigrants, strengthened by many faiths, yet united by a common faith in democracy. As you come together today, you recognize the importance of offering members of your community the opportunity to learn from and support one another. As I have traveled throughout this country and around the world, I have learned that in too many places individuals are blocked from participating fully in the political lives of their countries. We choose not to hear the voices of many; and in too many places, there are those who never learn to project their voices. I commend you for your efforts to encourage others to work to make their voices heard in the present and for the future.

Please accept my best wishes for a wonderful convention.

Sincerely yours,

Hillary Rodham Clinton

Appendix III
Hillary Clinton's Thank You Letter: Boston Fund Raiser

Mr. Tahir Ali
Chair
Massachusetts Chapter
American Muslim Alliance
Suite x
46850 Warm Springs Boulevard
Freemont, California 94539

Dear Friends:

It was a pleasure to be a part of the Massachusetts Chapter meeting of the American Muslim Alliance. The plaque is a wonderful reminder of my visit. Please extend my appreciation and thanks to the entire membership."

With best wishes, I am

Sincerely yours,

Hillary Rodham Clinton

Appendix IV   *The American Muslim Population Question*

[It is conceivable that groups supporting Muslim political power in the United States may appear to inflate the numbers, while those groups of the opposite spectrum may try to deflate the numbers].

In the past several studies have been conducted to determine the Muslim population in the United States. For 2000, estimates vary between 2.8 to 8 million.

Tom W. Smith conducted a study for the American Jewish Committee (AJC). In the study, which was largely based on telephone survey, Smith concluded that the Muslim population could not be more than 2.8 million.[1]
The World Almanac reported a figure of 5.8 million.[2]
Dr. Ilyas Ba-Yunus, a professor of Sociology at State University of New York at Cortland, reported a figure of 6.7 million.[3]
According to the Council on American-Islamic Relations (CAIR), the figure is 7 million.
Zogby International, a polling and marketing firm, argued the figure for the Arab Americans segment to be more than 3.5 million, not 1.2 million as per U.S. Census 2000.

In order to reach a more accurate Arab Muslim population in the United States in years 2000 and 2004, we first have to take into consideration the Arab American population reported on the basis of ancestry. According to the U.S. Census 2000, the number of Arab Americans (which includes Arab Christians and Arab Muslims) is 1,202,871. This figure is an undercount, for reasons well documented in a report published by the Arab American Institute (AAI) on Arab-American demography. The AAI report states: "Estimates by Zogby International whose research projects population figures at least three times that of census data. The decennial Census identifies only a portion of the Arab population through a question on 'ancestry' on the census long form. Reasons for the undercount include the placement of and limits of the ancestry question (as distinct from race and ethnicity); the effect of the sample methodology on small, unevenly distributed ethnic groups," and the distrust or misunderstanding of government surveys among recent immigrants.

The U.S. Census of the Arab American population, therefore, increases to 3,500,354. Mohamed Nimer, a researcher and author at the Council on American-Islamic Relations (CAIR) looked at INS data from 1820 to 1997 and estimated that of the total immigrants from Arab origins 47% are Muslim.[4]

Arab Ancestry	Population
Egyptian	142,832
Iraqi	37,714
Jordanian	39,734
Lebanese	440,279
Moroccan	38,923
Palestinian	72,112
Syrian	142,897
Arab/Arabic	205,822
Other Arab	82,558
TOTAL	**1,202,871**

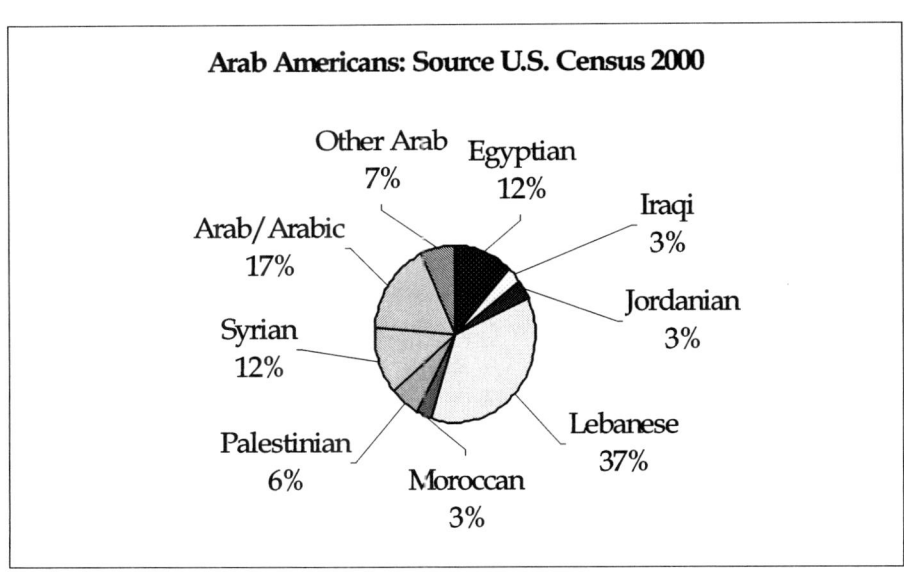

Arab Americans: Source U.S. Census 2000

Other Arab 7%
Egyptian 12%
Iraqi 3%
Jordanian 3%
Arab/Arabic 17%
Syrian 12%
Palestinian 6%
Moroccan 3%
Lebanese 37%

U.S. Muslim Population in 2004

Accounting for World Almanac's figure of (5.8 million), Ilyas Ba-Yunus's figure of (6.7 million) and CAIR's figure of (7 million), the largely reported estimated figure of 6 to 7 million of the Muslim population in 2000 appear sound. At the current annual growth rate of 6 percent [Source: 6% versus 0.9% for total U.S. – U.S. Census 2000, and Zogby 2000 survey], the Muslim population in the United States will exceed 8 million in 2004, but more importantly those American Muslims who were not of voting age in 2000 will be eligible to vote in 2004.

Electoral College and the 12 State Strategy:

The total of Elector College consists of 538 electoral votes. Each of the 50 States is allocated a number of Electors. A minimum of 270 Electors is required to win the presidential election. In each of the States, except Maine and Nebraska, the "winner takes all" rule applies. The candidate who wins the most popular votes wins the Electoral votes for the entire state. The majority of the Muslim population happen to be living in the following 12 states, listed in order of concentration. The electoral votes of the state is also shown in parenthesis: California (55), New York (31), Michigan (17), Florida (27), New Jersey (15), Texas (34), Ohio (20), Massachusetts (12), Illinois (21), Pennsylvania (21), Virginia (13), Maryland (10). The total Electoral Count in these 12 states is 276.

---

[1] Dr. Tom W. Smith, director of the General Social Survey at the National Opinion Research in Chicago, *"Estimating the Muslim Population in the United States."*

[2] The World Almanac and Book of Facts 2001, NJ, 2001 - Page 689.

[3] Dr. Ilyas Ba-Yunus, professor of Sociology, East-West University, Chicago, 1997 - *Muslim of Illinois, A Demographic Report* - Page 9

[4] The North American Muslim Resource Guide: *Muslim Community Life in the United States and Canada.* NY, NY: Routledge, 2002 - Page 25.

Appendix V   *"Muslim-American Activism"*

[Editorial: Washington Report on Middle East Affairs – AMC's 8th Annual Convention: Promises for a Stronger Muslim Political Participation].

Promises for "Stronger Muslim Political Participation [in U.S.]" at the AMC's 8th Annual Convention

July/August 1999, pages 104-115

Lobbying Session: On May 6, 1999 the American Muslim Council launched its 8th annual convention at the Cannon House Office Building in Washington, DC, where lobbying sessions were held with several AMC activists and congressional experts and assistants. In a briefing for the lobbying session, Randa Fahmy, counselor for Senator Spencer Abraham (R-MI); Suhail Khan, press secretary of Congressman Tom Campbell (R-CA); Leah Khaghani, staff assistant to Congressman David Bonior (D-MI); Kamal Nawash, legal adviser to the American-Arab Anti-Discrimination Committee (ADC); and Kosovo representative Bekim Hasani all advised would-be lobbyists of the American Muslim community on how to make their voices heard in American politics. On the specifics of the principal issue to be discussed with members of Congress, the speakers focused on the dangers of the unconstitutional use of secret evidence in 25 current cases of individuals being held in prison with no charges. Although they represent different members of Congress from both parties, Fahmy, Khan and Khaghani noted that all three congressmen stand very strongly against the use of secret evidence.

In a lobbying debriefing session, AMC director Aly R. Abuzaakouk asked members to call their representatives in Congress and ask them to support the return of Kosovar refugees to their homes and to request humanitarian aid be sent to Iraq. At the session, activists complained about the absence of an umbrella organization to work for both domestic and foreign issues that are of major concern to the American Muslim community in the U.S. In his response, Abuzaakouk confirmed the birth of such an organization (the American Muslim Political Coordination Council) and advised

AMC members to subscribe to the *Washington Report on Middle East Affairs,* where they can find the most recent coverage of Congress and of American Muslim activism in the U.S.

Congressional Dinner: At a Capitol Hill dinner, several members of Congress expressed their support for American Muslim concerns. "We have things in our history we are not proud of in this country," said House Democratic floor leader Bonior, referring to the use of secret evidence against members of the American Muslim community. Senator Abraham, a Christian Arab American, also criticized the use of secret evidence and airport profiling and expressed his support for NATO military action to protect the Kosovars and for sending humanitarian aid to Iraq. "We will continue to be there for your community," he said. Representative Campbell noted that "we [in Congress] have to recognize that there are people in Palestine who have the right to their own land." Rep. Janice Schakowsky (D-IL) said, "As a Jew, I am very much against ethnic cleansing." She promised to support sending aid to the refugees in Kosovo. Representatives Robert Aderholt (R-AL); John Conyers, Jr. (D-MI); John Dingell (D-MI); Rush Holt (D-NJ); Wayne Gilchrest (R-MD); Dale Kildee (D-MI); Jim McDermott (D-WA); Jim Moran (D-VA); Nick Rahall (R-WV); and Ciro Rodriguez (D-TX) all voiced support for the American Muslim community and its issues.

Iraq Policy: After a White House briefing with National Security Adviser Sandy Berger, the convention convened at the Sheraton Hotel in Crystal City, VA with a session on "International Policy on Iraq." Founder of Voices in the Wilderness, Kathy Kelly, told heartbreaking stories of Iraqi children dying because of the sanctions. "Sanctions themselves function as a weapon of mass destruction," she said. She invited members of Congress and the executive branch to join Voices in the Wilderness in a visit to Iraq. "Is there one congressman who will go over to Iraq and look at what eight and a half years of sanctions have done to the Iraqi people?" she asked. She criticized the cynicism of the U.S. government concerning the suffering of the Iraqi people. "Does killing people become easier for us day after day? Who taught Tim McVeigh to kill people?"

Former U.S. Ambassador to Iraq Edward Peck expressed his frustration with U.S. government policies in Iraq. "We in this country should be ashamed of what we stand for," he said. He argued that the "shameless embargo" on Iraq damages the reputation of the U.S. and the values it stands for in the world. He also criticized U.S. media for deceiving the American people by reporting one side of the story. "No one in this country is finding it bizarre that the press is only reporting that the Iraqis are violating the no-fly-zone," he said. "We behave as completely arrogant men."

Laith Kubba, from the National Endowment for Democracy, also criticized U.S. policies in Iraq. "Everything about Iraq has been reduced to Saddam Hussein and nothing is being told about the suffering of the people," he said. He said the U.S. should distinguish between the oppressor and the victim and that serious attention and concern should be shown toward the needs of the Iraqi people, who "harmed no one." Kubba argued that human rights are not the prime concern behind U.S. policy in Iraq. "Washington wants to see Iraq de-weaponized totally," Kubba charged.

Mazen al-Najjar: The session concluded with a dramatic scene of a 10-year-old girl crying over the imprisonment of her father. Yara al-Najjar is the oldest daughter of Mazen al-Najjar, a Palestinian resident of Tampa, FL who is currently imprisoned and facing deportation proceedings based solely on secret evidence. Yara read the following letter to the AMC attendees:

"Assalamu Alaikum. My name is Yara al-Najjar. I'm only 10 years old in 5th grade at the Islamic Academy of Florida in Tampa. My father, Mazen, has been in jail for two years. I was born here in America and was taught in my social studies to believe in the U.S. Constitution and all the freedoms it stands for. But this is quite difficult to do knowing that my dad has done nothing wrong. He remains a good citizen of the world. His only crime was to be a good father and a good Muslim. Every night before I go to sleep, I take out his picture, put it next to my bed, say a prayer, and wish him a good night. For those two years that he has been in jail he has missed seeing my daily maturity. He was the direct influence in my life to get straight A's in school. He was the one that would always read to us. He would read newspapers, classics, magazines, and bedtime stories to my two younger sisters and me every day.

I miss my dad, my sisters miss my dad not just because he is in jail but because he is in jail for having done nothing wrong. I miss my dad especially when I come home from school and when he is not there to help me. I miss my dad on the weekends when he has guided us on how to use our free

*time better. I miss my dad's scent every time he gave me a kiss on the cheek.
You can't get all these things through the glass window I see him through
the few times they allow me to visit. Why am I here today? To ask you to
write to your president, congressman, senator and representative and tell
them that Mazen al-Najjar is in jail because of secret evidence. And it is
time he is freed from the Manatee County Sheriff's Office in Bradenton,
Florida. He has done nothing wrong. Thank you for your time. May God
Almighty bless one and all."*

Election 2000: "A Muslim Agenda on the Road to Election 2000"
was the theme of a session held on Saturday morning. Atif Harden,
former director of the American Muslim Council, discussed issues
the American Muslim community should be working on for the year
2000 elections. He advised the community to work on issues that are
of primary importance to both Muslims and non-Muslim Americans such as day care, education, health care, women, independent
voters and children. "We as Muslims are the targeted numbers of all
the coming presidential candidates and that is why we should volunteer, give money and most importantly, vote," he said.

President James Zogby of the Arab American Institute noted
that it is critical for American Muslims to enter American politics.
"The first issue that should be on the Muslim agenda for the 2000
elections is to gain full respect and presence in American politics,"
he said. Dr. Zogby noted that 1996 marked the arrival of Muslim
activism in American politics when President Clinton and other Republican and Democratic leaders talked about "churches, mosques
and synagogues" in their speeches. "You need to be at every door
and recognized at every level as a full partner in the process," said
Dr. Zogby. He was not in favor of focusing on issues like Palestine,
Kashmir, or Kosovo for the 2000 elections. "Muslims are best served
in the Muslim foreign policy by not focusing on specifics but by over-
riding issues," he added. "The best agenda for a Muslim policy would
be combining American and Muslim values and make them export-
able," Zogby said.

President Agha Saeed of the American Muslim Alliance briefed
the audience on the development of Muslim activism in California
and the major role Muslims should be playing in the 2000 elections.
"There was not a single large mosque in California that did not participate in voter registration in 1998," Dr. Saeed said. "I am pleased
to tell you that we American Muslim organizations decided to come

under one umbrella organization called the American Muslim Political Coordination Council." He explained that the purpose of this
new umbrella organization is to develop a coherent strategy for the
2000 elections whereby every U.S. Muslim organization would work
for better American Muslim participation in American political life.
"To have a full impact, we have to unite Arabs, Muslims and Christians," he argued.

In a session entitled "Muslims and Domestic Issues," Suhail
Khan, press secretary and legislative assistant to U.S. Congressman
Tom Campbell, spoke about the significant impact Muslims can have
on domestic political processes. One such success centered on the
issue of the use of secret evidence by the Department of Justice and
the Immigration and Naturalization Services. As Khan explained,
both agencies use secret evidence to arrest, detain and deport individuals due to their alleged affiliation with groups designated as
terrorist organizations.

Khan told the audience about several Muslims within Congressman Campbell's district who approached him and explained that
family members were being held without being able to review or
challenge the evidence used to detain them, in direct violation of
Constitutional Amendment VI.

After learning of the situation, Congressman Campbell introduced legislation into Congress to repeal the use of secret evidence.
Campbell also circulated congressional letters to gain the support of
other members of Congress and held briefings to educate Congress
about the issue. After being signed by 17 congressmen the letter was
sent to President Bill Clinton and U.S. Attorney General Janet Reno.

"This was just one issue that was generated by Muslims at the
local level that will now be one of the legislative items considered in
this year's congressional sessions," Khan explained. "Furthermore,
Muslims can not only influence domestic policy, but can educate
their local representatives about international issues, such as Palestinian statehood."

According to Khan, most members of Congress are reticent to
discuss or support Palestinian self-determination. But Muslims in
Campbell's district urged him to travel to the West Bank and Gaza
Strip to assess the situation for himself. When Campbell traveled to
the West Bank and Jordan he visited several refugee camps and wit-
nessed for himself the suffering and impoverishment of the Palestinian people.

"Having come back from that trip and having met Muslims in our district who encouraged him to travel to Palestine, Congressman Campbell decided that the resolution introduced by Matt Salmon (R-AZ) denying Palestinians statehood was immoral and unjust," Khan said. And even though the resolution passed, several members of Congress who had voted to deny Palestinians statehood came to Congressman Campbell and said, "This time I couldn't vote with you. Next time I will be with you. I didn't know that we could do this and survive politically."

On the same panel Eric Vickers, a private attorney and board member of the American Muslim Alliance, offered his personal experience and feelings regarding the interaction of Islam and the American political landscape. "When I decided to run for Congress in 1994 I wrestled with what the real significance was of me holding an elected office. What difference would it make that I was a Muslim running for political office? And I came to the conclusion that if I were like every other politician running for office it would make no difference. That if my strategy was simply to be more mainstream, then I need not bother because the difference I could make as a Muslim in this country would only emerge if I put my faith before my politics, if I let my politics be driven by my faith."

The United States has a great deal to learn both about and from Muslims, Vickers said. "They don't know what we have to offer. When this country talks about family values being important, who is better to speak about that than the Muslims? When this country is trying to prevent the kind of thing that occurred in Colorado, where school children were murdered, who better to look to for answers as to how to raise your children, as to what to teach them, than us? When confronted with the problems of racism and hate-crimes, who better to teach America about this than us?"

Vickers said Muslim morality, family values, and tolerance are firmly grounded in the Qur'an, the Holy Book of Islam. For example, Vickers explained, the appreciation of difference is an injunction stemming directly from the Qur'an. "O you who have believed, let not a people ridicule another people...and do not insult one another and do not call each other by offensive names...O Mankind, indeed We have created you from male and female and made you peoples and tribes that you may know one another."

Vickers said that for too long Muslims have existed in the shadows of America, hoping that in many instances they would not be asked who they are or what they stand for. "The day has come when we must stand up as Muslims for this nation," Vickers continued, "because this nation needs guidance and leadership and God has given us through Islam the tools and faith to lead. It is incumbent upon us to use it for the betterment of this country and the world."

Vickers concluded by calling upon Muslims to use their education, their wealth, and their numbers to participate in the political process, to affect policy, and sow the seeds for new legislation. Vickers urged: "That is our obligation and that is how we must be involved in politics, not as Republicans, or as Democrats, or as Independents, but as Muslims, with our faith before our politics."

U.S. Foreign Policy: In the panel entitled "U.S. Foreign Policy and the Muslim World," Khalid Abdallah, chief representative to the United States of the League of Arab States, noted that the preponderance of power the United States holds enables it to influence through its actions the security, stability, and prosperity of nations around the world. The Arab world, therefore, has been trying to engage the United States in a constructive dialogue to further relations between the two regions, he said. "But as you know, it is not enough that one side is trying by action and behavior to make that relationship better. Rather," he continued, "it depends on both parties."

Mr. Abdallah suggested that to change the imbalance in this equation the United States could model itself after the Arab world in holding up the primacy of international law, respecting the norms of the international community, and in implementing U.N. resolutions. Mr. Abdallah cited two reasons for the diligence with which the Arab world has implemented international law.

"The first reason is that Arabs for many years were and are demanding that Israel respect international law and implement U.N. resolutions," he said. "So Arabs cannot decide when they do not like international law or U.N. resolutions to simply ignore them. Arab countries have accepted U.N. dictates to the point of implementing resolutions against fellow Arabs, as in Iraq and Libya.

"The second reason is that in order to survive in an international system Arab countries have adopted the philosophy that a bad law implemented equally is better than no law at all."

Citing the Nuclear Non-Proliferation Treaty signed in 1970 by 62 countries, Mr. Abdallah explained that in 1995, when the treaty came up for review, all Arab countries were prepared to sign it but Israel refused, as it had in 1970. Nevertheless, the Arab countries were promised by the United States and other U.N. Security Council members that if they would become signatories to the treaty, the U.S. would work to create a nuclear-free Middle East as outlined by previous U.N. resolutions. "However," Mr. Abdallah said, "the United States, contrary to its promise and in consideration of its relationship with Israel, refused to mention in a report regarding the Non-Proliferation Treaty a nuclear-free Middle East."

Also on the foreign policy panel Ambassador Petrit Bushati of Albania described the mass expulsion of ethnic Albanians from Kosovo, the mass killing of Kosovars, and the brutal rape of Kosovar women. What is happening in Kosovo, the ambassador charged, is a natural extension of the Serbian government's use of repressive tactics to fulfill the idea of a Greater Serbia.

The ambassador urged the audience to support the self-determination of ethnic Albanians and to understand that the Kosovars are not seeking to occupy other lands or to harass other nations. Rather, they are simply resisting against a repressive dictatorship in an effort to preserve their identity, dignity, and basic human rights.

Jesse Jackson Mission: Also on Saturday, former presidential candidate Jesse L. Jackson, president of Rainbow/Push Coalition, Inc., discussed his recent trip to Belgrade to secure the release of three American soldiers. Reverend Jackson complimented Dr. Nazir Khaja, president of AMC's Board of Directors, for the role he played in releasing the American soldiers, saying it was "very strong and effective." Jackson said that his group's meeting with Yugoslav President Milosevic was an attempt to build "a bridge of diplomacy" so that the pains of human suffering would end.

Jackson encouraged American Muslims to join the struggle as American citizens "to make this a perfect American union." He emphasized the significance of issues such as education, women's rights, labor, health care, equal opportunity and protection under the law. Citing the imprisonment in Florida on secret evidence of Dr. Mazen al-Najjar, he said, "We must fight together to release al-Najjar and make America a better place for all of us and leave no one behind…what makes America great is the right to fight for the right."

Lord Ahmed of Rotherham concluded the session with remarks about his appointment to the House of Lords in the U.K. In Britain, he explained, members of the House of Lords have only taken the oath of office using the Old Testament. When Lord Ahmed was appointed as the first Muslim member, he asked that he be allowed to take his oath using the Qur'an, and was given the right to do so. "As Muslims in the U.S. you do play a major role for the Muslims in the rest of the world," he said. "We have followed your footsteps in Britain as you have been the most important voice for Muslims in the world."

Appendix VI   *The Fatwa*

[People want to make sure that participation in politics was consistent with their ethical and moral beliefs – fatwa was one among many ways to gain that certitude].

As I lead to the Fatwa itself it is imperative to note the following saying of the Prophet:

Prophet Muhammad (s.a.w.) prophesied that there will be differences and factions among his followers after his death, and that of the four *'rightly guided Caliphs"*, who came after him. In these troublesome times when there would be turbulent factions, true Muslims were advised to stand firm as a rock by the *Qur'an, Sunnah* and the ways of the four rightly guided Caliphs. The saying reported by Irbad ibn Sariyah is as follows:

Book 40, Number 4590:

Narrated Irbad ibn Sariyah:

Abdur Rahman ibn Amr as-Sulami and Hujr ibn Hujr said: We came to Irbad ibn Sariyah who was among those about whom the following verse was revealed: "Nor (is there blame) on those who come to thee to be provided with mounts, and when thou saidst: "I can find no mounts for you."

We greeted him and said: We have come to see you to give healing and obtain benefit from you.

Al-Irbad said: One day the Apostle of Allah (peace be upon him) led us in prayer, then faced us and gave us a lengthy exhortation at which the eyes shed tears and the hearts were afraid.

A man said: Apostle of Allah! It seems as if it were a farewell exhortation, so what injunction do you give us?

He then said: I enjoin you to fear Allah, and to hear and obey even if it be an Abyssinian slave, for those of you who live after me will see great disagreement. You must then follow my *sunnah* and that of the rightly-guided caliphs. Hold to it and stick fast to it. Avoid novelties, for every novelty is an innovation, and every innovation is an error.

The Caliph was the head of the Muslim community. The four "rightly guided Caliphs" were successor to the Prophet. They are as follows: The First Caliph, Abu Bakr (632-634 A.C.), The Second Caliph, Umar bin Khitab (634-644 A.C.), The Third Caliph, Hazrat Uthman (644-656 A.C.), The Fourth Caliph, Ali bin Talib (656-661 A.C.)

"In the Name of Allah, the Most Gracious, Most Merciful

Fatwa concerning:
The Participation of Muslims in the American Political Process

By Dr. Taha Jaber al-Alwani, the chairman of the North American *Fiqh* [Jurisprudence in Islam] Council President of the Graduate School of Social and Islamic Sciences. "We have received from the American Muslim Council the following inquiry:

THE INQUIRY:

"You know that the American Muslim Council is in the midst of a voting registration campaign for the forthcoming American elections. In the course of this campaign, some American Muslims have expressed severe doubts as to whether it would be religiously permissible for them to participate in the political system of this country, The United States of America. Several reasons were cited for this doubt.

Some argue that participation would ally some Muslims with others they have little in common with in matters of belief. It may also divide Muslims in the United States, and harm the interests of the Muslim community. This would be in contradiction to the Qur'anic injunction that Muslims should support each other.

Others argue that participation in our system may be viewed as *rukun* (acquiescence) to the unjust. The Almighty said in the Qur'an: "And do not acquiesce to the unjust…".

Yet others argue that the participation of Muslims in our secular political system, which is increasingly denuding the public square from all symbols of faith, would desensitize Muslims into accepting the current status quo and interacting with it, to the detriment of all people of faith in this society.

Additionally, some Muslims, who escaped dictatorial regimes in their countries of origin or left to avoid bad economic conditions, live in the hope of going back to Dar al-Islam (Land of Islam) once the situation improves. This state of affairs is not uncommon among first generation immigrants, Muslim or otherwise. In our case, however, we are concerned about the fact that it leads to voting apathy. In particular, some Muslims in this group argue that voting can be justified only for extreme necessity.

We would like your Eminence to clarify this matter for us with a lucid statement, which, with proofs and arguments, may bring to an end the conflict among American Muslims over this vital issue.

May Allah reward you with His blessings.

Aly Ramadan Abuzaakouk
Executive-Director of the American Muslim Council

THE REPLY:

In an independent research entitled "Introduction to Minorities Jurisprudence: Founding Views" (the "Introduction"), to published this fall in a special issue on Islam by the Journal of Law & Religion, we dealt with the principles and rules that should govern the vision of the contemporary jurist (and the contemporary Muslim in general) on this topic. The connection of this *fatwa* to the Introduction is akin to that of a derivative principle (a branch) to a fundamental principle (a root), or of an example to the general rule. The understanding, therefore, of the Introduction and the orthodoxy of prevailing principles and argumentation contained therein, is necessary for a better understanding of this *fatwa* and the foundation on which it rests.

Overview of Basic Principles:

Among the legal and methodological principles we reached in the Introduction are the following:

1. All of humankind is one family that belongs in its entirety to Adam, and Adam is from earth. This Humanity is divided into two nations: "A nation that responds", and "a nation that summons".

2. Islam is a global religion, not restricted to any one ethnic group or geographical area.

3. The Qur'anic discourse is global and should not be restricted to a limited geographical place or a narrow social group.

4. The Muslim *ummah* is a benevolent one that evolved to bear witness to humanity.

5. The principle of "righteousness and equity, mentioned in the Holy Qur'an, is the greatest general principle by which to measure the relationship between Muslims and others. All other matters should concede to this principle.

6. We should avoid being limited by jurists' terminologies regarding the issue of international partitions. Terms, such as "*Dar al-Islam*" (The Land of Islam), were not mentioned in the Revelation in the geographical sense. They are but juristic and administrative terms, the use of which was imposed by the circumstances of the old science and the nature of relationships among countries, nations and peoples at that time.

7. To properly understand the particular examples found in the inherited body of jurisprudence, they should be examined in light of the general principles mentioned herein. By so doing, we can transcend the particulars and merge them into the general principles of the Qur'an, namely, its universal message and goals.

8. The existence of Islam in any country which is not part of the original Muslim World, should be viewed as a new and developing existence which falls in harmony with the universality of Islam and its message of hope.

9. The nature of contemporary international realities, which are characterized by both the interrelation and transcendence of borders, should be taken into serious consideration.

10. Current international legal instruments and domestic laws, which address human rights and civil rights, should be relied upon to protect and educate Muslim minorities. For example, Article 21 of the International Declaration of Human Rights states that each individual has the right to participate in the administration of his or her own country's public affairs, whether directly or via representatives.

11. The principles of justice included in such documents should be followed as they are in harmony with the sermon of the Messenger (Peace Be Upon Him) to his followers at his Farewell Pilgrimage and to "the alliance" which he attended at Ibn Jud'an's house. In addition, all legitimate means, including political participation, should be utilized to safeguard these principles of justice.

12. The lessons derived from the early Islamic experience, in particular the emigration to Ethiopia, should be fully understood.

13. There should be a transition from negative reasoning about what is permissible to positive reasoning in carrying the Message to the people of our society.

American Particularities

America has particularities that need to be considered in order to issue the most appropriate legal ruling. Among these particularities are:

1. The United States is a country of immigrants who are of different races and various cultures. It is not wholly identified by any one people or immigrant culture. In particular, American culture does not exclude non-Europeans.

2. The United States is a young country whose civilization and culture have an open nature, unlike ancient civilizations that tend to have definitively established characteristics. This makes the American culture more open to the contributions of Islam and Muslims.

3. The United States is a country of freedom that looks primarily after the rights of all of its citizens, of all religions and races, despite the problems in application that manifest themselves from time to time.

4. The United States has peoples among whom racism is relatively less manifested due to their intellectual background and the historical experience of its Protestant majority.

Based on these principles and particularities, we can deduce the following conclusions with respect to the participation of Muslims in American political life:

Conclusions:

First, it is the duty of American Muslims to participate constructively in the political process, if only to protect their rights, and give support to views and causes they favor. Their participation may also improve the quality of information disseminated about Islam. We call this participation a "duty" because we do not consider it merely a "right" that can be abandoned or a "permission" which can be ignored. It falls into the category of safeguarding of necessities and ensuring the betterment of the Muslim community in this country.

Second, every legitimate means or tool that helps achieve these noble goals is similarly judged. This includes:

1. The nomination of any competent American Muslim for election to any post where his or her presence may ensure either bringing benefits to American Muslims and other citizens or preventing harm to them. These posts range from those of mayor, state governor, and membership in educational and municipal councils, all the way up to membership in the U.S. Senate and House of Representatives.

2. Self-candidacy by an American Muslim, if the initiative for his/her nomination is not undertaken by the community, or if election laws require this form of candidacy. (Refer to the statement by Ibn Hajr on the question of becoming an *Amir* (or coming into power) in the "Introduction".)

3. Adopting a non-Muslim candidate if he/she would be either more beneficial or less harmful to the American Muslim community and the rest of the country.

4. Providing financial support to a non-Muslim candidate. God the Almighty has permitted righteous conduct and good relations with non-Muslims in exchange for nothing. So how much more so is such support permitted if clear and tangible benefits were to result from such behavior?

5. Obtaining American citizenship. Such citizenship emphasizes the true diversity of this country and is a necessary condition for participation in the political process.

6. Both registering to vote and participation in elections and voting are means to a goal. Hence, they are subject to the same legal ruling as their intended goal.

Limitations and Specifications:

1. Protection of Muslim civil rights in this country and the enjoyment of positive interaction with other Americans require American Muslims to engage in acts of deliberation to reach consensus on general principles, and to tolerate disagreement on particulars and disputed matters. We find a good example to follow in our ancestors who migrated to Ethiopia. They met and deliberated together about the best way to respond to the critical situation they faced.

2. The children of the Muslim minority must have a fair opportunity to develop and deepen their faith in God and Islam. Otherwise, their interaction with others may lead them to compromise on the basic tenets of their religion merely to keep up with a prevailing custom or sweeping current. Ja'far, by refusing to bow to al Najashi -The King of Abyssinia- (his two Quraishi opponents did as necessitated by custom) provides a good example for such situations.

3. The Muslim minority needs to have a fair opportunity to express clearly in its own voice the immortal truths of Islam and its advanced system of human values. The example of Ja'far helps in this regards. In his eloquent speech to al Najashi, Ja'far summarized the main

Islamic virtues and explained the difference between them and those of the pre-Islamic life (*the Jahiliyah*). By applying this method, Muslims not only gain the understanding of the rest of the people, but also their good will.

4. Both the art of persuasion and the science of public relations have an important role that should not be ignored. The words by which Ja'far ended his speech are appropriate here: "We came out to your country, we chose you from all others, we wished to be in your neighborhood, and hoped, O King, not to be treated unjustly in your country".

Objections:

As for the objections mentioned in the inquiry and raised by some of our brothers and sisters, they can be summarized in five points which are discussed as follows:

The First Argument:

Participation would ally some Muslims with others they have little in common with in matters of belief. It may also divide Muslims in the United States and harm the interests of the Muslim community. This would be in contradiction to the Qur'anic injunction that Muslims should support each other.

This argument is based on an incorrect presumption resulting from two errors:

First, The argument casts pragmatic considerations as matters of belief, although there is a vast difference between the two. The fair dealing of Muslims with others and their cooperation with them produce neither blind allegiance (*wala'*) to these others nor special exceptions (*bara'*) for them. For, this is not originally a matter of belief but is instead a pragmatic decision involving the proper implementation of the principles of "righteousness," "fairness and equity," success and constructive behavior.

Second, the argument confuses the limited meaning of the concept of "alliance" (*wala'*) referred to in the Qur'an, with a broader all-inclusive one. The type of alliance warned against in the Qur'an is that which harms the interests of the Muslim community. This meaning is mentioned repeatedly in the Qur'an in such a way as to leave no confusion.

The Almighty, threatening the hypocrites, said: "To the hypocrites give the glad tidings that there is for them (but) a grievous penalty. Yea, to those who take for *'awlia'* (allies) unbelievers (those who do not believe in God) rather than believers." (Qur'an 4:138-139). He then warned the believers: "O you who believe! Take not for *awliya'* unbelievers rather than believers." (Qur'an: 4:144). Confirming the warning in another verse, the Almighty said: "Let not the Believers take for *awliya'* Unbelievers rather than Believers."(Qur'an: 3:28).

But the meaning of specific Qur'anic verses is determined by various factors, including the context, reasons for revelation, other verses related to them, and even the *sunnah* of the Prophet . For example, we know that the Prophet befriended the Christian Ethiopian king al Najashi. We also know that the Prophet executed an alliance with the Jews of Madinah giving them rights similar to those of Muslims. Most importantly, we know that the Qur'an refers to Christians and Jews as "People of the Book," and not as "Unbelievers." So, even if the meanings of certain words are construed broadly, the above-cited Qur'anic verses do not prohibit Muslims from building alliances with the vast majority of Americans.

But to gain insight into the proper interpretation of the Qur'anic verses, it is important to examine the explanation provided by major scholars. In interpreting these Qur'anic verses, Al Tabari said: "This is a prohibition from God to his servants the believers, against acting like the hypocrites who take for *awliya'* unbelievers rather than the believers even where such behavior harms the interests of the community."(*Tafsir al-Tabari*, vol. 9: 336). Al Tabari added, that the verse means that believers should not take the unbelievers as back-up support and partisans, against their own community, showing them the vulnerabilities of the Believers."(*Tafsir al-Tabari* vol. 6: 303).

As stated in these Qur'anic verses, then, the blameworthy alliance is that which is given to support those who do not believe in God against the interest of one's own believing community. This is a far cry from the actions of those who cooperate with non-Muslims (believers as well as unbelievers) within the limits of "righteousness and equity" while continuing to work for the good of the Muslim community.

The Second Argument:

Political participation is a type of *rukun* (acquiescence) to those who do wrong. This is prohibited by the Qur'an where the Almighty warns against such acts by His words: "And do not acquiesce to the unjust …"(Qur'an: 11:113).

It is wrong to understand *rukun,* as used in the above verse, to include all types of cooperation. There is no evidence for that. *Rukun* in fact means "to acquiesce to the unjust" or "to be satisfied with their doings" or "to return to idolatry," These three meanings were derived by Al Tabari from the salaf (the worthy ancestors)." (*Tafsir al Tabari* vol. 15: 500-501). Again, these meanings are a far cry from an act of participation intent on promoting public interest and protecting the Muslim minority from injustice.

The Third Argument:

Participation of Muslims in our political system is an acceptance of the secular (i.e., faith-less, non-believing) status quo.

This argument is based on misunderstanding of the American system, as well as faulty logic.

First, the Framers of our American system did not intended it to be "faith-less" or "non-believing," but rather faith-neutral. Ideally, our political system is not intended to oppose religious values but to be unaligned with those of any one sect or religion.

Second, passivity and withdrawal from life are what brings about acceptance of the status quo by deed, which is far more effective than words. Positive participation, on the other hand, is what showcases Islamic values and morals to civil society. Indeed, it is what refutes any "faith-less" secular status quo by offering people an illustration of the blessings of faith.

The Fourth Argument:

Participation of Muslims in our secular political system, which is increasingly denuding the public square from all symbols of faith, would desensitize Muslims into accepting the current status-quo and interacting with it, to the detriment of all people of faith in this society.

Methodologically, this argument contains two errors:

First, it transfers a conceptual confusion that occurs in countries that have Muslim majorities to countries where Muslims are a minority. The two contexts are quite different and entail different obligations. While Muslims in Muslim countries, are obligated to uphold the Islamic law of their state, Muslim minorities in the United States are not required either by Islamic law or rationality to uphold Islamic symbols of faith in a secular state, except to the extent permissible within that state.

What is required of Muslim minorities in a secular society is the support of the Islamic existence of their community and the service of public interest through serious participation in public life. They are also required to work hard towards building a coherent, stable and flourishing Islamic community capable of properly representing Islam to the majority, and building bridges with other faith communities. Only then can the discussion of the place of faith within our secular society become possible.

Such was the methodology of the Prophets (Peace be upon them), and such was that of our Prophet (Peace be upon him) who began by building first the Islamic community, then the Islamic society, and then the Islamic system.

Second, this argument narrows the scope of participation to the political sense. It would be more precise to consider each contribution towards enhancing the values of truth, goodness, and justice as a brick in the construction of a fair and equitable system. If the Muslim minority, through its positive participation in the making or influencing of political decisions, manages to promulgate a law against the use of drugs, for example, then it would have promoted the values of truth and goodness shared by many. This is in accord with Islamic values that require Muslims to serve their communities.

The Fifth Argument:

Participation contradicts the intent of a temporary stay in this country and an eventual return to *Dar al Islam* (the Land of Islam).

This argument is based on historical perspectives and outdated juristic terms, such as "Dar al Islam "The Land of Islam" and *"Dar al Kufr* "The Land of Disbelief " or "Dar al Islam" and *"Dar al Harb* "The Land of War". We have shown in the "Introduction" that these terms stand on a weak foundation from a legal perspective and are not applicable to contemporary international realities whether from a realistic perspective or a *manaati* one (one based on the underlying cause upon which the legal ruling *hukm* hangs. Refer to the Introduction for further explanation).

We can also add here that this argument ignores the highly significant fact that Islam established its first society in a land of immigration, namely, *"Al Madinah al Munawwarah"*, and not in the original land of the Message (*"Makkah al Mukarramah"*). The Prophet (Peace Be Upon Him) did not agree to move to Makkah after his enemies lost their battles of aggression against him. He held on to the land of his immigration, and addressed its people who gave him support and victory, saying: "To live is to live with you and to die is to die with you".
1212 New York Ave. NW, Suite 400, Washington, DC 20005

Appendix VII
Conversion Story of Yusuf Estes, U.S. Federal Prison Chaplain

[The amazing tale of how an American former "born again" Christian and his father, both ordained ministers, plus their friend, a Catholic priest, all became convinced of the truth of Islam].

"Many people ask me how a preacher or priest in Christianity can ever go to Islam, especially considering all the negative things that we hear about Islam and Muslims everyday. I would like to thank everyone for their interest and offer my humble story, God Willing.

Actually, a very nice Christian gentleman asked me through email why and how I left Christianity for Islam. So this is more or less a copy of the letter that I sent back to him.

How It Happened
My name is Yusuf Estes and I am the National Muslim Chaplain for American Muslims, sponsored by a number of organizations here in Washington, DC. As such, I travel around the entire world lecturing and sharing the message of the Christ of the Quran in Islam. We hold dialogs and discussion groups with all faiths and enjoy the opportunity to work alongside of rabbis, ministers, preachers and priests everywhere. Most of our work is in the institutional area, military, universities and prisons. Primarily our goal is to educate and communicate the correct message of Islam and who the Muslims really are. Although Islam has grown now to tie Christianity as the largest of religions on earth, we see many of those who claim Islam as Muslims, that do not correctly understand nor properly represent the message of **"Peace, Surrender and Obedience to God"** (Arabic = '*Islam*').

Dear me, I am afraid that I got a bit ahead of myself. I was trying to give a bit of background on my own personal experience to see if it would in anyway benefit those who may being going through what I experienced while trying to resolve some of the issues in Christianity. This may seem quite strange, while we perhaps may share a few different perspectives and concepts of God, Jesus, prophethood, sin and salvation. But you see, at one time I was in the same boat as many folks are today. Really, I was. Let me explain.

I was born into a very strong Christian family in the Midwest. Our family and their ancestors not only built the churches and schools across this land, but actually were the same ones who came here in the first place. While I was still in elementary we relocated in Houston, Texas in 1949 (I'm old). We attended church regularly and I was baptized at the age of 12 in Pasadena, Texas. As a teenager, I wanted to visit other churches to learn more of their teachings and beliefs. The Baptists, Methodists, Episcopalians, Charismatic movements, Nazarene, Church of Christ, Church of God, Church of God in Christ, Full Gospel, Agape, Catholic, Presbyterian and many more. I developed quite a thirst for the "Gospel" or as we say; "Good News." My research into religion did not stop with Christianity. Not at all. Hinduism, Judaism, Buddhism, Metaphysics, native American beliefs were all a part of my studies. Just about the only one that I did not look into seriously was "Islam". Why? Good question.

Anyway, I became very interested in different types of music, especially Gospel and Classical. Because my whole family was religious and musical it followed that I too would begin my studies in both areas. All this set me for the logical position of Music Minister in many of the churches that I became affiliated with over the years. I started teaching keyboard instruments in 1960 and by 1963 owned my own studios in Laurel, Maryland, called "Estes Music Studios."

Over the next 30 years my father and I worked together in many business projects. We had entertainment programs, shows and attractions. We opened piano and organ stores all the way from Texas and Oklahoma to Florida. I made millions of dollars in those years, but could not find the peace of mind that can only come through knowing the truth and finding the real plan of salvation. I'm sure you have asked yourself the question; "Why did God create me?" or "What is it that God wants me to do?" or "Exactly who is God, anyway?" "Why do we believe in 'original sin?" and "Why would the sons of Adam be forced to accept his 'sins' and then as a result be punished forever. But if you asked anyone these questions, they would probably tell you that you have to believe without asking, or that it is a 'mystery' and you shouldn't ask.

And then there is the concept of the 'Trinity.' If I would ask preachers or ministers to give me some sort of an idea how 'one' could figure out to become 'three' or how God Himself, Who can do anything He Wills to do, cannot just forgive people's sins, but rather and had to become a man, come down on earth, be a human, and then take on the sins of all people. Keeping in mind that all along He is still God of the whole universe and does as He Wills to do, both in and outside of the universe as we know it.

Then one day in 1991, I came to know that the Muslims believed in the Bible. I was shocked. How could this be? But that's not all, they believe in Jesus as:

* a true messenger of God;
* prophet of God;
* miracle birth without human intervention;
* he was the 'Christ' or Messiah as predicted in the Bible;
* he is with God now and most important;
* He will be coming back in the Last Days to lead the believers against the 'Antichrist.'

This was too much for me. Especially since the evangelists that we used to travel around with all hated Muslims and Islam very much. They even said things that were not true to make people afraid of Islam. So, why would I want anything to do with these people?

My father was very active in supporting church work, especially church school programs. He became and ordained minister in the 1970s. He and his wife (my stepmother) knew many of the TV evangelists and preachers and even visited Oral Roberts and helped in the building of the "Prayer Tower" in Tulsa, OK. They also were strong supporters of Jimmy Swaggart, Jim and Tammy Fae Bakker, Jerry Falwell, John Haggi and the biggest enemy to Islam in America, Pat Robertson.

Dad and his wife worked together and were most active in recording "Praise" tapes and distributing them for free to people in retirement homes, hospitals and homes for the elderly. And then in 1991 he began doing business with a man from Egypt and told me that he wanted me to meet him. This idea appealed to me when I thought about the idea of having an international flavor. You know, the pyramids, sphinx, Nile River and all that. Then my father mentioned that this man was a 'Moslem.'

I couldn't believe my ears.

A 'Moslem?'

No way!

I reminded my dad of the various different things that we had heard about these people, how they are - **Terrorists; hijackers; kidnappers; bombers and who knows what else?**

Not only that but:

They don't believe in God
They kiss the ground five times a day and
They worship a black box in the desert.

No!

I did not want to meet this 'Moslem' man. No way!

My father insisted that I meet him and reassured me that he was a very nice person. So, I gave in and agreed to the meeting.

But on my terms.

I agreed to meet him on a Sunday after church so we would be all prayed up and in good standing with the Lord. I would be carrying my Bible under my arm as usual. I would have my big shiny cross dangling and I would have on my cap which says: "Jesus is Lord" right across the front. My wife and two young daughters came along and we were ready for our first encounter with the 'Moslems.'

When I came into the shop and asked my father where the 'Moslem' was, he pointed and said: "He's right over there."

I was confused. That couldn't be the Moslem. No way.

I'm looking for a huge man with flowing robes and big turban on his head, a beard half way down his shirt and eyebrows that go all the way across his forehead.

This man had no beard. In fact, he didn't even have any hair on his head at all. He was very close to bald. And he was very pleasant with a warm welcome and handshake. This didn't make sense. I thought they are terrorists and bombers. What is this all about?

Never mind. I'll get right to work on this guy. He needs to be 'saved' and me and the Lord are going to do it.

So, after a quick introduction, I asked him:

"Do you believe in God?"

He said: **"Yes."**

(Good!)

Then I said: **"Do you believe in Adam and Eve?"**

He said: **"Yes."**

I said: **"What about Abraham? You believe in him and**

how he tried to sacrifice his son for God?"
He said: **"Yes."**

Then I asked: **"What about Moses?"**
"Ten Commandments?"
"Parting the Red Sea?"
Again he said: **"Yes."**

Then: **"What about the other prophets, David, Solomon and John the Baptist?"**
He said:**"Yes."**

I asked: **"Do you believe in the Bible?"**
Again, he said: **"Yes."**

So, now it was time for the big question:
"Do you believe in Jesus? That he was the Messiah (Christ) of God?"
Again the said: **"Yes."**

Well now:*"This was going to be easier than I had thought."*
He was just about ready to be baptized only he didn't know it.
And I was just the one to do it, too.

I was winning souls to the Lord day after day and this would be a big achievement for me, to catch one of these 'Moslems' and 'convert' him to Christianity.

I asked him if he liked tea and he said he did. So off we went to a little shop in the mall to sit and talk about my favorite subject: Beliefs.

While we sat in that little coffee shop for hours talking (I did most of the talking) I came to know that he was very nice, quiet and even a bit shy. He listened attentively to every word that I had to say and did not interrupt even one time. I liked this man's way and thought that he had definite potential to become a good Christian.

Little did I know the course of events about to unravel in front of my eyes.

First of all, I agreed with my father that we should do business with this man and even encouraged the idea of him traveling along with me on my business trips across the northern part of Texas. Day

after day we would ride together and discuss various issues pertaining to different beliefs that people have. And along the way, I
could of course interject some of my favorite radio programs of worship and praise to help bring the message to this poor individual.
We talked about the concept of God; the meaning of life; the purpose of creation; the prophets and their mission and how God reveals His Will to mankind. We also shared a lot of personal experiences and ideas as well.

One day I came to know that my friend Mohamed was going to
move out of the home he have been sharing with a friend of his and
was going to be living in the mosque for a time. I went to my dad
and asked him if we could invite Mohamed to come out to our big
home in the country and stay there with us. After all, he could share
some of the work and some expenses and he would be right there
when we were ready to go to out traveling around. My father agreed
and Mohamed moved in.

Of course I still would find time to visit my fellow preachers
and evangelists around the state of Texas. One of them lived on the
Texas — Mexico border and another lived near lived Oklahoma border. One preacher liked to a huge wooden cross that was bigger than
a car. He would carry it over his shoulder and drag the bottom on
the ground and go down the road or freeway hauling these two
beams formed in the shape of a cross. People would stop their cars
and come over to him and ask him what was going on and he would
give them pamphlets and booklets on Christianity.

One day my friend with the cross had a heart attack and had to
go to the Veterans Hospital where he stayed for quite a long while. I
used to visit him in the hospital several times a week and I would
take Mohamed with me with the hopes that we could all share together in the subject of beliefs and religions. My friend was not very
impressed and it was obvious that he did not want to know anything about Islam. Then one day a man who was sharing the room
with my friend came rolling into the room in his wheelchair. I went
to him and asked him his name and he said that it didn't matter and
when I asked him where he was from he said he was from the planet
Jupiter. I thought about what he said and then began to wonder if I
was in the cardiac ward or the mental ward.

I knew the man was lonely and depressed and needed someone
in his life. So, I began to 'witness' to him about the Lord. I read to
him out of the book of Jonah in the Old Testament. I shared the story

of the prophet Jonah who had been sent by the Lord to call his people
to the correct way. Jonah had left his people and escaped by boat to
leave his city and head out to sea. A storm came up and the ship
almost capsized and the people on board threw Jonah over the side
of the ship. A whale came up to the surface and grabbed Jonah, swal-
lowed him and then went down to the bottom of the sea, where he
stayed for 3 days and 3 nights. Yet because of God's Mercy, He caused
the whale to rise to the surface and then spit Jonah out to return back
home safely to his city of Nineveh. And the idea was that we can't
really run away from our problems because we always know what
we have done. And what is more, God also always knows what we
have done.

After sharing this story with the man in the wheel chair, he looked
up and me and apologized. He told me he was sorry for his rude
behavior and that he had experienced some real serious problems
recently. Then he said that he wanted to confess something to me.
And I said that I was not a Catholic priest and I don't handle confes-
sions. He replied back to me that he knew that. In fact, he said: "I am
a Catholic priest." I was shocked. Here I had been trying to preach
Christianity to a priest. What in the world was happening here?

The priest began to share his story of being a missionary for the
church for over 12 years to south and Central America and Mexico
and even in New York's 'Hell's Kitchen.' When he was released from
the hospital he needed a place to go to recover and rather than let
him go to stay with a Catholic family, I told my dad that we should
invite him to come out and live with us in the country along with
our families and Mohamed. It was agreed by all that he would so,
he moved out right away.

During the trip out to our home, I talked with the priest about
some of the concepts of beliefs in Islam and to my surprise he agreed
and then shared even more about this with me. I was shocked when
he told me that Catholic priests actually study Islam and some even
carry doctors degrees in this subject. This was all very enlightening
to me. But there was still a lot more to come.

After settling in, we all began to gather around the kitchen table
after dinner every night to discuss religion. My father would bring
his King James Version of the Bible, I would bring out my Revised
Standard Version of the Bible, my wife had another version of the
Bible (maybe something like Jimmy Swaggart's 'Good News For
Modern Man." The priest of course, had the Catholic Bible which

has 7 more books in it that the Protestant Bible. So we spent more time talking about which Bible was the right one or the most correct one, than we did trying to convince Mohamed about becoming a Christian.

At one point I recall asking him about the Quran and how many versions of it there were in the last 1,400 years. He told me that there was only ONE QURAN. And that it had never been changed. Yet he let me know that the Quran had been memorized by hundreds of thousands of people, in it's entirety and were scattered about the earth in many different countries. Over the centuries since the Quran was revealed millions have memorized it completely and have taught it to others who have memorized it completely, from cover to cover, letter perfect without mistakes.

This did not seem possible to me. After all, the original languages of the Bible have all been dead languages for centuries and the documents themselves have been lost in their originals for hundreds and thousands of years. So, how could it be that something like this could be so easy to preserve and to recite from cover to cover.

Anyway, one day the priest asked the Mohamed if he might accompany him to the mosque to see what it was like there. They came back talking about their experience there and we could not wait to ask the priest what it was like and what all types of ceremonies they performed. He said they didn't really 'do' anything. They just came and prayed and left. I said: "They left? Without any speeches or singing?" He said that was right.

A few more days went by and the Catholic priest asked Mohamed if he might join him again for a trip to the mosque which they did. But this time it was different. They did not come back for a very long time. It became dark and we worried that something might have happened to them. Finally they arrived and when they came in the door I immediately recognized Mohamed, but who was this alongside of him? Someone wearing a white robe and a white cap. Hold on a minute! It was the priest. I said to him: "Pete? — Did you become a 'Moslem?'

He said that he had entered into Islam that very day. THE PRIEST BECAME A MUSLIM!! What next? (You'll see).

So, I went upstairs to think things over a bit and began to talk to my wife about the whole subject. She then told me that she too was going to enter into Islam, because she knew it was the truth. I was really shocked now. I went downstairs and woke up Mohamed and asked him to come outside with me for a discussion. We walked and talked that whole night through. By the time he was ready to pray Fajr (the morning prayer of the Muslims) I knew that the truth had come at last and now it was up to me to do my part. I went out back behind my father's house and found an old piece of plywood lying under an overhang and right there I put my head down on the ground facing the direction that the Muslims pray five times a day.

Now then in that position, with my body stretched out on the plywood and my head on the ground, I asked: "O God. If you are there, guide me, guide me." And then after a while I raised up my head and I noticed something. No, I didn't see birds or angels coming out of the sky nor did I hear voices or music, nor did I see bright lights and flashes. What I did notice was a change inside of me. I was aware now more than ever before that it was time for me to stop lying and cheating and doing sneaky business deals. It was time that I really work at being an honest and upright man. I knew now what I had to do. So I went upstairs and took a shower with the distinct idea that I was 'washing' away the sinful old person that I had become over the years. And I was now coming into a new, fresh life. A life based on truth and proof.

Around 11:00 A.M. that morning, I stood before two witnesses, one the ex-priest, formerly known as Father Peter Jacob's, and the other Mohamed Abel Rehman and announced my 'shahadah' (open testimony to the Oneness of God and the prophethood of Muhammad, peace be upon him).

A few minutes later, my wife follow along and gave the same testimony. But hers was in front of 3 witnesses (me being the third).

My father was a bit more reserved on the subject and waited a few more months before he made his shahadah (public testimony). But he did finally commit to Islam and began offering prayers right along with me and the other Muslims in the local masjid (mosque).

The children were taken out of the Christian school and placed in Muslim schools. And now ten years later, they are memorizing much of the Quran and the teachings of Islam.

My father's wife was the last of all to acknowledge that Jesus could not be a son of God and that he must have been a mighty prophet of God, but not God.

Now stop and think. A whole entire household of people from varying backgrounds and ethnic groups coming together in truth to learn how to know and worship the Creator and Sustainer of the

Universe. Think. A Catholic priest. A minister of music and preacher. An ordained minister and builder of Christian schools. And they all come into Islam! Only by His Mercy were we all guided to see the real truth of Islam without any blinders on their eyes any longer.

If I were to stop right here, I'm sure that you would have to admit that at least, this is an amazing story, right? After all, three religious leaders of three separate denominations all going into one very opposite belief at the same time and then soon after the rest of the household.

But that is not all. There is more! The same year, while I was in Grand Prairie, Texas (near Dallas) I met a Baptist seminary student from Tennessee named Joe, who also came to Islam after reading the Holy Quran while in BAPTIST SEMINARY COLLEGE!

There are others as well. I recall the case of the Catholic priest in a college town who talked about the good things in Islam so much that I was forced to ask him why he didn't enter Islam. He replied: "What? And loose my job?" - His name is Father John and there is still hope for him yet.

More? Yes. The very next year I met a former Catholic priest who had been a missionary for 3 years in Africa. He learned about Islam while he was there and entered into Islam. He then changed his name to Omar and moved to Dallas Texas.

Any more? Again, yes. Two years later, while in San Antonio, Texas I was introduced to a former Arch Bishop of the Orthodox Church of Russia who learned about Islam and gave up his position to enter Islam.

And since my own entrance into Islam and becoming a chaplain to the Muslims throughout the country and around the world, I have encountered many more individuals who were leaders, teachers and scholars in other religions who learned about Islam and entered into it. They came from Hindus, Jews, Catholics, Protestants, Jehovah's Witnesses, Greek and Russian Orthodox, Coptic Christians from Egypt, non-denominational churches and even scientists who had been atheists.

Why? Good question. May I suggest to the seeker of truth do the following NINE STEPS to purification of the mind:

1.) Clean their mind, their heart and their soul real good.

2.) Clear away all the prejudices and biases

3.) Read a good translation of the meaning of the Holy Quran in a language that they can understand best.

4.) Take some time.

5.) Read and reflect.

6.) Think and pray.

7.) And keep on asking the One who created you in the first place, to guide you to the truth.

8.) Keep this up for a few months. And be regular in it.

9.) Above all, do not let others who are poisoned in their thinking influence you while your are in this state of "rebirth of the soul."

The rest is between you and the Almighty Lord of the Universe. If you truly love Him, then He already Knows it and He will deal with each of us according to our hearts.

So, now you have the introduction to the story of my coming into Islam and becoming Muslim. There is more on the Internet about this story and there are more pictures there as well. Please take the time to visit it and then please take the time to email me and let us come together to share in all truths based on proofs for understanding our origins and our purpose and goals in this life and the Next Life.

And once again I thank you for your email today. If you hadn't sent it, I probably would still not have completed this task of putting down the story once and for all of how "Priest and Preachers Are Coming to Islam."

May Allah guide you on your journey to all truth. Ameen. And May He open your heart and your mind to the reality of this world and the purpose of this life, ameen.

Peace to you and Guidance from Allah the One Almighty God, Creator and Sustainer of all that exists.

Your friend,
Yusuf Estes
Chaplain Yusuf Estes
Visit the website of Chaplain http://www.todayislam.com/yusuf/priests_n_preachers.htm#story

Appendix VIII
The first three-month post-9/11 activity of the ISGW

[The Islamic Society of Greater Worcester (ISGW) is a community-based organization that provides a wide range of services for its members and for the community at large. The center is currently located at 57 Laurel Street in Worcester, Massachusetts. Faced with the challenge of a growing community, larger centers are under construction in close proximity, one on East Mountain Street in Worcester and the other on South Street in the neighboring town of Shrewsbury.

Lebanese born Ziad Ramadan, or "Papa Smurf" a nickname he picked up during the management of "Islamic Project"on East Mountain street, and Mairajuddin Ahmed, originally from India, joined with Ziad to complete the project on East Mountain Street, in Worcester. Farooq Ansari and Zahid "Iqbal" Ali head the project in Shrewsbury. With generous, monetary contributors like, Mohammed Moufid, Muzaffar Hassan to name a few plus the determination of Ziad Ramadan, Mairajuddin Ahmed, Zahid "Iqbal" Ali and Farooq Ansari, both "Islamic Projects"will be completed in a timely fashion].

9/13/01: BOSTON, MA: Cardinal Bernard Law, archbishop of Boston, and other members of various churches organized a vigil in Boston Plaza. Dr. M. Riaz Khan, representing the Islamic Council of New England (ICNE) and I representing AMA and ISGW. Other Muslims were also invited to participate at the vigil. I thanked Attorney General Tom Reilly for honoring our request for a press release "that violence against the American Muslims" will be dealt with the law. Reilly's press release was prepared from the ISGW Statement that was earlier sent to his and the Governor's attention. Dr. M. Riaz Khan recited the Qu'ranic verse (5:32) from *Surah Hujrat*, while Dr. A. Karim Khudairi of the Islamic Council of New England (ICNE) delivered a befitting speech, the event was widely broadcast by the media. Dr. Khudiari said, "God has given life to humans and He is the One who has the right to take it away. The Qur'an 5:32 says that, 'If anyone kills one human being – it would be as if he had killed all humanity, and if any person saves the life of a human being, it would be if he saved the life of all humanity."

Dr. Khudairi added, "These are the teachings of true Islam, human life is sacred and should not be for sacrifice".

9/15: Worcester, MA: On Friday prayer the ISGW invited members from various local churches and synagogues to the Center along with a representative from Congressman's McGovern office to read a statement. Media covered the event. This led to a meeting in Westboro with the congressman on Saturday, September 22.

9/17: Worcester, MA: The ISGW President Dr. Saleem Khanani and trustees, Dr. Khalid Sadozai, Dr. Khaled Abdul-Kader, and others participated at the open house (interfaith) at Islamic Society of Boston (ISB) in Wayland.

9/21: Worcester, MA: Vigil was held at UMASS Medical, ISGW was represented by Dr. Aisha Tahira Hameed, a psychiatrist by profession and Dr. Batool Tauseef. Dr. Hameed handed the ISGW statement that condemned the vicious and cowardly attacks on September 11. She also delivered a befitting speech titled: 'How to cope with this' and offered free counseling to those who deemed it necessary. Drs. Aisha and Tauseef reported that both of them were well received. The people thanked them and they received a bouquet of flowers. Dr. Hameed, recalling the enlightening experiences and the kind reception they got, said "after all, they said it with flowers".

9/21: Worcester, MA: The ISGW held a community open discussion night, titled: "Know your civil rights". Hussain Farrag, Vice President of the ISGW moderated the event. Instruction sheets were distributed that told the community what to do and how to deal with FBI and similar agencies when approached or visited by FBI at their residence or at work place.

9/22: Worcester, MA: A follow up of September 15 ISGW event, in conjunction with AMA: Meeting with Congressman McGovern in Westboro, a brainstorm session on what needed to be done at a National level. The Congressman agreed that a change in the current US Foreign Policy was required, especially in the Middle East. The Community demanded an even-handed Mid-East policy.

9/23: Worcester, MA: ISGW was well represented at a vigil at the Worcester City Hall. Call for prayer (*Adhan*) was made over the microphone for the first time and was heard by many. The evening prayer (*Maghrib*) was offered in public. The ISGW youth presentation, led by Samina Khan, went quite well. The Youth recited verses (*Surah*) from the Qur'an. Other speakers included clerics from churches, synagogues, and Congressman James P. McGovern. I introduced Fazal Rindhani, who was in his Marine Uniform to the crowd and declared that we have a Muslim who is ready to defend the country. Marine Rindhani presence was acknowledged with cheers.

September/October: Worcester, MA: Dr. Saleem Khanani was interviewed by FM 96.1. Khalid Sadozai, trustee, and Mohammed Yousaf, secretary of ISGW, and Dr. Riaz Khan were guest speakers on various radio talk shows, concerning the tragic events of September 11, 2001.
- Steven Shakir, former president of ISGW, attended several interfaith meetings on behalf of ISGW.
- Mansoor Khan, trustee ISGW and former president, represented ISGW in the meetings called by the attorney general in Boston.
- Samina Khan, former ISGW executive member, participated in a food drive in Boston.

Dr. Saleem Khanani, president of ISGW, contacted the Red Cross and offered to hold a blood donation drive, at the ISGW center. Many ISGW members signed up and were lined up and ready to roll up their sleeves when Red Cross arrived.

10/6/01: Worcester, MA: ISGW had an Open House to discuss the theme "Islam, Perception and Reality in the light of current events". The panelists included representatives from other Islamic centers as well. Approximately 500 people showed up for the Open House. Guest speakers included: U.S. Congressman, James P. McGovern; Raymond Mariano, Mayor of Worcester; along with clerics from various Islamic centers, churches and synagogues. Media, including NECN, CBS and Channel 5 and leading newspapers covered the event extensively.

Hinna Mushtaque, a member of the ISGW youth group, spoke about her experiences at the Open House: " My name is Hinna Mushtaque, and I am an American Muslim born and raised in the US. I've lived in Massachusetts my whole life, and graduated from Notre Dame Academy in Worcester in 1999. I'm currently a junior at Wellesley College.

As Muslims living in America, I believe that we are able to experience first hand what our religion is all about. I am one of very few Muslims women in the world who can practice Islam without any distortion caused by cultural restrictions, ancestral traditions and political motives which may take away from the true essence of this religion.

As an American Muslim, when I practice Islam, it is because this is the way of life I have chosen to follow.

A little less than a year ago, I made the personal choice to observe the head-covering, called hijab. The reason behind this was simple. As I took the personal initiative to learn more about my faith, I realized that this is something that is required of all Muslim women, for our own protection. I cover my hair not because it is enforced by the law or because someone else has ordered me to do so. I do it because this is what I am supposed to do, and this is what I have chosen for myself. A common misconception about the hijab is that it is a sign of oppression for women. In my own experience, the exact opposite has proven to be true. By wearing the hijab, I feel like I am truly free because this is a choice that I have made on my own free will. I can dress the way I want to, look the way I want to, without being dictated by the conforms of society, and withstanding peer pressure. I am really grateful to say that I never had any such experience. Instead of thinking "less" of me, people have supported me, and respected me for following through with something that I believe in. This is one example of what America is all about. I feel proud to live in a society, which celebrates and supports multiculturalism. I was extremely disheartened when I first learned about the backlash against Muslims, and people of Middle Eastern and South Asian descent as a result of the tragic events on Sept 11. At first, this was not my major concern. I, too, along with the rest of America, was utterly overwhelmed and shocked by the horrendous tragedies that occurred that fateful Tuesday morning. I could not believe that anything like this could actually happen. And when I discovered that the perpetrators were "possibly" Muslim, my heart sank even more. I could not, and still cannot, believe that someone who claims to be a follower of Islam could commit such a heinous crime against innocent people. The backlash against Muslims came as a triple blow to me. It really did not hit me that this was occurring until I received an email, advising women wearing "Islamic dress", not to go out in public spaces. And right then I realized that that was me, "a woman in Islamic dress"... it had never occurred to me that I could be labeled the "other" so swiftly, in just one phrase. No one looking at me could see that I am an American too, that I am grieving for nation, just like everyone else. For the first time in my entire life, I was terrified for my own life. Over the next few days, I received a countless number of emails and phone calls from concerned friends and loved ones. Everyone advised me to be careful, not to walk on campus alone, and some even discouraged me from wearing my hijab. But that is jus something that I cannot do. I will not compromise a part of myself out of fear. I will not let this nation compromise one of its defining principles, freedom, out of fear.

This is an overwhelmingly difficult time for all Americans, but I have faith that we will be able to get through this together. I, as well as the entire Muslim community, have received an amazing outpour of support from our neighbors, friends, and community members. I am extremely pleased that through this difficult time, many national officials have also clearly stated that Islam and Muslims are not to blame for this tragedy.

I strongly believe that something should be done to account for the events of September 11th, but not at the expense of the values that we Americans treasure."

10/12/01: San Jose, CA: New Hampshire State Assemblyman Saghir 'Saggy" Tahir and I attended the Peace Rally held in 'Caesar's Chavez Park', in San Jose California. Both of us talked to Brad Williams of WB20, Channel 11. In a response to the query on the attack on Afghanistan Saghir Tahir replied, "Pakistan doesn't want a neighbor to the North that is an enemy. Foreign policy starts with your neighbor."

10/13/01: San Jose CA: Farooq Ansari, former president of ISGW, and I attended the AMA National Convention in San Jose. The event was extensively covered both at a National and International level: including BBC, CBC, NPR, USA Today, Mercury Times, LA Times, CBS, NBC and others.

10/20/01: Worcester, MA: Officials of ISGW and its members were invited to a town hall meeting with US Senator John Kerry at Clark University. Representing ISGW, were Mahmood Awan, Khalid Sadozai, Mohammad Mushtaque, Isa Mujahid, Steven Shakir and Mrs. Aqilah Shakir, Farooq Ansari, Imrana Soofi, Muzzafar Hasan and Mrs. Dr. Aisha (Tahira) Hameed, and other ISGW members. Imrana and I were successful in getting our opinions across to the, otherwise, reluctant senator.

10/21/01: Worcester, MA: Members from various churches attended the regular Sunday Qu'ranic session, conducted by the *Imam* Hamid Mehmood and moderated by myself. The event was well attended. Dr. Saleem Khanani: president ISGW welcomed the guests and distributed English-translated (without the Arabic text) version of the Qu'ran. The guests were very much enlightened by the program and left with the desire to meet more often. This session was then made open to the public and advertised as such in the *Worcester Telegram,* and the ISGW Web site.

October: The ISGW affiliated Islamic full time school Al-Hamra conducted Numerous Interfaith dialogues and lectures given by chairman Dr. Mohamad Lazouni at various institutions: Dr. Lazouni delivered lectures and conducted workshops at the Massachusetts Institute of Technology (MIT), the University of Rhode Island, the Holy Cross college, etc.

October-November: Several meetings in the city hall with Worcester Mayor, Raymond Mariano, along with clerics from churches and synagogues and members of the ISGW; namely; Mohamad Lazouni, Mahmood Awan, *Imam* Hamid Mehmood and myself.

11/04/01: Worcester MA: Members of ISGW visited Greendale People's Church. We discussed Islam and Christianity in a 'living room conversation' style. ISGW was well represented by: Dr. Yasser Najar, Dr. Khaled Abdul-Kader, Dr. Imad, Steven Shakir, Dr. Ashraf Elkrem and their wives.

11/6/01: Worcester MA: *Imam* Hamid Mehmood and I were interviewed on WVNE in Worcester. We wanted to remove some misconceptions about Islam made by the station on an earlier broadcast. We took this opportunity to inculcate and foster a better understanding of the month of Ramadan and Islam in general.

11/7/01: Worcester MA: Worcester Mayor Raymond Mariano calls for a Press conference of interfaith groups. Among those participating were the rev. Michael P. Bafaro of Our Lady of Mount Carmel/St. Ann, the Rev. Dr. Barbara Merritt of the First Unitarian Church Second Parish, the Rev. Dr. Richard Wright of the Emmanuel Baptist Church, the Rev. Jeffrey R. Newhall of the Greendale People's Church, and Rabbi Jordan B. Millstein of Temple Emmanuel. *Imam* Hamid Mahmood and I represented ISGW.

11/9/01: Worcester MA: Students from Anna Maria College visited the Islamic center in Worcester in an effort to participate in the 'learning about Islam' project. Dr. Russell, their professor, had taught them the Qu'ranic verse *Surah Fatiha*. And they recited the verse in Arabic. The students resolved to observe a fast day in the holy month of fasting (*Ramadan*), and to break the fast with the members of ISGW.

11/16/01: Worcester MA: *Imam* Hamid Mahmood, Dr. Saleem Khanani and I interviewed on WGTV Channel 3 News: "Ramadan in Worcester & Afghanistan"

12/6/01: Worcester MA: The members of ISGW attend **Muslim Student Association (MSA)** sponsored Fast for solidarity event. *Worcester Telegram* reported: "More than 50 people including students from Clark University, Holy Cross College, WPI and Anna Maria College, joined area Muslims in fasting on one day in Ramadan."

Worcester Mayor Raymond Mariano in a proclamation declared December 6, 2001 as the "Solidarity 'Fast' Day". MSA's President Randa Saleh and Imam Mahmood of ISGW received the Proclamation.

Imrana Soofi of American Muslim Communication Link (AMCL), Worcester Peace, WOGAN helped organize the event. I was later interviewed on the National Public Radio (NPR), and comments were broadcast repeatedly in NPR daily news the rest of the week. This event was the fulfillment of the November 9, 2001 meeting at ISGW.

12/8/01: Worcester MA: ISGW members (Dr. Saleem Khanani, *Imam* Hamid Mehmood, Zahid Hussain, Fazal Alam, Hanif Balaparia) were invited to discuss Islam and interfaith dialogue at the Unitarian Church in Worcester. The members of the church were very impressed with the discussion and asked a lot of questions. They appreciated the effort and asked for an encore, and we were only glad to oblige.

12/9/01: Worcester MA: Members of the Unitarian Church and representatives of the Muslim Community (ISGW) held small group discussions focused on understanding Islam.

12/12/01: Worcester MA: ISGW members, Dr. Mushtaque along with his nephew Awais Rizzak and his [Mushtaque] son Zeeshan Mushtaque, Steven Shakir and Zahid Hussain attended an interfaith dialogue at the synagogue, Temple Emmanuel in Worcester. Worcester Mayor Raymond Mariano, Jordan B. Millstein senior Rabbi of the Temple, and I on behalf of ISGW spoke at the occasion. The meanings and customs of *Hanukkah* and religious freedom were the main topics of discussions.

12/16/01 Worcester MA: During the holy "fasting" month of *Ramadan* the ISGW executive committee resolved to feed the hungry (175 people) at the PIP shelter on 701 Main Street in Worcester. This activity was to be continued on a regular basis.

GLOSSARY OF ISLAMIC TERMS

A list of commonly used Islamic terms and concepts are included below: (*including those used in the book*)

Adhan
Adhan is way of summoning Muslims to the obligatory Prayers. The *Mauzen* calls the Adhan starting with "Allah is great." Similar, to church bells when they are rung to call Christians to church.

Allah
It is an Arabic word, denoting the one who is worthy of worship. He is the creator of the Universe. God in Christianity or the Jews use for God (Eloh), in Hebrew.
There are many verses in the Qur'an that describe the attributes of God:
 "Say: He is God, the One, the Eternal, Absolute. He does not beget, nor is He begotten, and there is none like unto Him." (Qur'an, 112: 1-4)

"It is He who brought you forth from the wombs of your mothers when you knew nothing, and He gave you hearing and sight and intelligence and affections that you may give thanks." (Qur'an, 16:78)

Al-hamdo lillah
"All praise is due to Allah." These words are usually uttered to thank God. These words are also uttered when one sneezes. Similar to "Bless you."

Al-Qaeda
In Arabic it means the base.

Al-Quds
Jerusalem

EID
The word 'Eid is an Arabic name to mean a festivity, a celebration, a recurring happiness, and a feast. In Islam, there are two major 'Eids namely the feast of Ramadhan ('Eid Al-Fitr) and the Feast of Sacrifice (Eid Al-Adhha).

EId Al-Fitr

'Eid Al-Fitr is celebrated by Muslims after fasting the month of Ramadhan as a matter of thanks and gratitude to Almighty Allah.

Eid Al-Adha

A four-day festival that completes the rites of pilgrimage in Makkah (or Mecca). This feast commemorates Prophet Ibrahim's obedience to Allah by being prepared to sacrifice his only son Ismael (Ishmael)

Fatwa

A religious decree. A legal verdict given on a religious basis, based the Holy Qur'an, and the *Sunnaah* of the Prophet Muhammad (s.a.w.)

The Five Pillars of Islam

1. **Iman:** Faith or belief in the Oneness of God, and Muhammad (s.a.w.)

2. **Salat:** There are five obligatory daily prayers. Their times are:
   a) *Fajr:* Early morning: Prayed after dawn and before sunrise.
   b) *Zuhr:* **Noon:** Prayed when the sun move away from its zenith.
   c) *Asr:* **Mid-afternoon:** Prayed after the time for offering *Zuhr* is over, until sunset.
   d) *Maghrib:* **Sunset:** Prayed immediately after sunset.
   e) *Isha:* **Evening:** Prayed after the time for offering *Maghrib* is over.

3. **Saum:** The Arabic word for "fast". Muslims all over the world, in the month of *Ramadan*, observe fasting from sunrise to sunset, abstaining from any food or water, and sensuous pleasure (with their spouse).

4. **Hajj: *The Pilgrimage to Makkah*.** It is a one-time life obligation for those who are not physically and financially challenged.

5. **Zakat:** The word zakah means "purification" Muslims are required every year to pay 2.5% of their yearly savings to the poor and needy.

Hadith
Reports on the sayings and the traditions of Prophet Muhammad (s.a.w.)

Halal
"That which is lawful and allowed in Islam."

Haram
1. "That which is unlawful and forbidden in Islam." Opposite to "Halal" which means, "That which is lawful and allowed in Islam."
2. Sanctuary or boundary of any mosque (*Masjid*), but usually used with regard to the sanctuaries of the Masjid al-Haram in Makkah and Masjid al-Rasool in Madinah.

Hijab
The root word for *hijab* in Arabic is *hajaba*, which means to conceal from view.

Muslim women accomplish this by wearing garments that covers the head, the hair, the neck and the bosom.

A common misconception, in the West, about the *hijab* is that it is sign of oppression for women because, men force it on them. Muslim women observe *hijab* because *Allah* has told them to do so.

"O Prophet, tell your wives and daughters and the believing women to draw their outer garments around them (when they go out or are among men). That is better in order that they may be known (to be Muslims) and not annoyed..." (Qur'an 33:59)

Imam
Means Leader in Arabic. The term is generally applied to religious leaders, equivalent to a cleric. Any person who leads a congregational prayer is called an Imam. A religious leader who also leads his community in the political affairs may be called an Imam, an *Amir*, or a *Caliph*.

Islam
The word is derived from the Arabic root *salaama* (peace). Islam literally means "submission to the will of Allah."

Jihad

It is derived from the root Arabic word *Jahada*, which means to struggle for a better way of life. The other meanings are: endeavor, strain, exertion, effort, diligence, fighting to defend one's life, land, and religion.

Jihad is often misinterpreted and confused with Holy War; the latter does not exist in Islam, there is nothing holy about a war. Jihad is not be interpreted as a war to force the faith on others. Jihad is not a defensive war only, but a war against any unjust regime.

Madrassa

School where Islam is taught. Often confused in the West with "terrorist" breeding schools.

Masjid

Another name for Mosque or Islamic Center.

Makkah (Mecca)

Also written as Mecca, is a city in Saudi Arabia, where Muslims go every year to offer their Pilgrimage. Muslims face Mecca when they offer their prayers.

Mujahideen

Plural of the Arabic word, Mujahid. One who fights in the way of Allah.

Pbuh

An acronym for 'Peace be upon him' used after the Prophet Muhammad's [pbuh] name. Whenever the Muslims mention Prophet Muhammad by name they pronounce the "may the blessings and peace of Allah be upon him" upon him. It is better to use (s.a.w.) instead of using (pbuh.) after the name of Prophet Muhammad (s.a.w.), as it is much closer in meaning to the blessing in Arabic.

Prophet Muhammad (s.a.w)

The last prophet to mankind.

Muhammad (s.a.w) was born around A.D. 570 in Mecca, Arabia into a polytheistic society. Muhammad (s.a.w.) received his first revelation through the Angel Gabriel when he was 40 years old. The revelation came to Muhammad (s.a.w) over a period of 23 years.

The Qur'an

The holy book of Qur'an was revealed unto Muhammad (s.a.w) from Allah through angel Gabriel for a period of 23 years. There are 114 *Surah* (chapters) in the Qur'an. These chapters and verses in the Qur'an are referenced as: (Qur'an, 6:103) meaning verse 103 in chapter 6.

There are hundred thousands of Muslims who memorize the entire Qur'an, they are called *Hafiz-ul-Qur'an*.

Ramadan

A month that Muslims all over the world observe by fasting from sunrise to sunset, abstaining from any food or water, and sensuous pleasure (with their spouses).

Shahada

Shahada is the declaration of faith. The shahada in Islam is: "I bear witness (or testify) that there is no god but Allah and I bear witness (or testify) that Muhammad is the Messenger of Allah."

Sunnah

The word Sunnah (spelled also Sunnaah), in reference to the Prophet Muhammad (s.a.w.), means his sayings, practices and living habits.

Takbir

When Muslims hear someone utter Takbir, the response is Allah-O-Akbar, which means "Allah is the greatest"

Taliban

Plural of the Arabic word, Talib, which means student.

ACRONYMS

List of Acronyms and Definitions of some of the organizations mentioned in the book:

AAI
The Arab American Institute (AAI) with headquarters in Washington D.C has been in existence since 1985. According to its web site, AAI is a "nonprofit organization committed to the civic and political empowerment of Americans of Arab descent." Some of the famous Arab Americans include: presidential candidate, Ralph Nader; Former New Hampshire Governor John H. Sununu; *"American Idol"* judge Paula Abdul; Cabinet Secretary Donna Shalala; football player Doug Flutie and movie star Salma Hayek.

AMA
The American Muslim Alliance (AMA) is a national civic and political education organization. Its main goal is to organize Muslims in mainstream public affairs and civic discourse. It has over 100 chapters in the U.S. It has its headquarters in Newark, California.

AMC
The American Muslim Council (AMC) before it dissolved was a lobbying and grassroots group. It had its headquarters in Washington, D.C.

AMPCC
The American Muslim Political Coordination Committee (AMPCC) an umbrella organization was established in 1998 to encourage American Muslims to be part of the mainstream American politics, with main focus on year 2000. AMPCC members include the American Muslim Alliance, American Muslim Council, Council on American-Islamic Relations and Muslim Public Affairs Council.

AMT
The American Muslim Task force (AMT) an umbrella organization was established in 2004 with a mission to protect civil and human rights and to encourage American Muslims to be part of the mainstream American politics in 2004. AMT, an umbrella organization

is represented by the following Muslim organizations: American Muslim Alliance (AMA), Council on American-Islamic Relations (CAIR), Islamic Circle of North America (ICNA), Islamic Society of North America (ISNA), Muslim Alliance of North America (MANA) Muslim American Society (MAS), Muslim Public Affairs Council (MPAC), Muslim Student Association – National (MSA-N), Project Islamic HOPE (PIH)

CAIR

The Council on American Islamic Relations (CAIR) a civil advocate with headquarters in Washington, D.C., was established according to its web site "to promote an accurate image of Islam and Muslims in America." CAIR is recognized nationally for its role in documenting and reporting hate crimes carried against the Muslim Americans. CAIR's web site further states "misrepresentations of Islam are most often the result of ignorance on the part of non-Muslims and reluctance on the part of Muslims to articulate their case."

ICNA

The Islamic Circle of North America (ICNA), a non-sectarian, grass root organization was established in 1971 with the goal to seek the pleasure of *Allah* (SWT), and to establish a way of life following the Qu'ran and *Sunnah* of the Prophet. ICNA also offers Islamic education and training seminars.

ICNA has its headquarters in Jamaica, New York.

ICNE

The Islamic Council of New England, according to its web site, was established in 1984 as a non-profit religious organization to serve as an umbrella for many Islamic Centers or Societies in New England. In so doing, it fulfilled the Qur'anic injunction, "and hold fast, all together, by the rope which Allah (stretches out for you), and be not divided among yourselves." Its guiding principle is also derived from the Qur'anic text, "and their affairs are conducted through mutual consultation among themselves."

ICNE serves as an umbrella for the following Islamic Centers or Societies in New England:

Connecticut Islamic Center of Hartford (Hartford, CT), *Masjid Mohammed* (New Haven, CT), Islamic Center of the University of Connecticut (Storrs, CT), Islamic Community of Fairfield County (Norwalk, CT),
Islamic Association of Greater Hartford (Hartford, CT)

Maine None

Massachusetts Islamic Center of Boston (Wayland, MA), Islamic Center of New England (Quincy, MA), Islamic Center of New England (Sharon, MA), Islamic Society of Boston (Cambridge, MA), Islamic Society of Western Massachusetts (Holyoke, MA), Islamic Society of Greater Worcester (Worcester, MA), *Masjid Al-Qur'an* (Dorchester, MA), Society of Islamic Brotherhood (Boston, MA), Islamic Society of Amherst (Amherst, MA)

New Hampshire
Islamic Center of Merrimack Valley (Salem, NH)

Rhode Island
Islamic Center of Rhode Island (Providence, RI), *Masjid Ar-Razzaq* (Providence, RI)

Vermont None
Affiliated Organizations: New England Muslim Sisters' Association (NEMSA), Muslim Youth of New England (MYNE)

ISGW

In early 1980 a handful of Muslims living in the greater Worcester area collected enough funds to buy an abandoned church at 57 Laurel Street in Worcester. That Islamic center or the Islamic Society of Greater Worcester, after a few renovations still stands as strong as ever and to date remains active. The Islamic society of Greater Worcester is a community-based organization.

According to its web site. It provides a wide range of services for the community at large, both for its members and for the community in general. Wherever and whenever necessary, it joins hands with other political and humanitarian bodies to serve the community better. The organization also provides other services such as marriage ceremony, funeral rites etc. according to Islamic traditions. We also sell meat from animals slaughtered according to Islamic guidelines.

The following is an overview of our regular community services and activities. Participation in all of these programs is free Interfaith Activities This services emphasizes ISGW's belief in the historical continuity of divine religions and its effort towards a common understanding and mutual cooperation among members of different faith groups. Over the last few years several interfaith groups, church delegates, students from the local colleges and universities have visited our premises where they have had the opportunity to meet with our members and have open discussions about various aspects of Islam and the common thread that runs through all religions. ISGW conducts many education courses to learn and revive Islam. These courses are designed towards Muslims and non-Muslims as well. Imam and many knowledgeable members of the community conduct these courses. Everybody is encouraged to join these courses.

ISNA

The Islamic Society of North America (ISNA) is probably the oldest Islamic institute in North America. It started out as a Muslim Student Association (MSA) for Canada and U.S. in 1963. Twenty years later, the Islamic Society of North America (ISNA) as an outgrowth of the Muslim Students Association (MSA) was launched.

According to ISNA's web site, it is, "a product of the resolve of the Muslims in North America to live an Islamic way of life. In keeping with its charter, ISNA works for the pleasure of Allah [SWT] to advance the cause of Islam and Muslims in North America." ISNA has a clear mission that state, "to provide a common platform for presenting Islam, supporting Muslim communities, developing educational, social and outreach programs and fostering good relations with other religious communities, and civic and service organizations."

The national convention that ISNA organizes every year draws over 30,000 Muslims from all over the states. The four day "41st Annual ISNA Convention" starting on September 3, 2004 is expected to draw an even larger crowd. The theme of the convention is "ISLAM: Dialogue, Devotion and Development"
ISNA headquarters are in Plainfield, Indiana.
To say ISNA serves as an umbrella for all the Islamic Centers or Societies in U.S. and Canada, is not far from the truth.

MANA
The Muslim Alliance in North America was established in February 2001. MANA was formed to address the concerns of indigenous Muslims, as is evident from its welcome message:
"Welcome to the web site of the Muslim Alliance in North America (MANA) — a new organization, just beginning to grow. We are committed Muslims, pledged to focus our attention on issues and concerns that especially impact indigenous Muslims — issues and concerns that have been largely neglected. With the launch of this web site we are inviting *Masjids* [Islamic Centers], organizations and individuals to join MANA."

MAS
Muslim American Society (MAS), with headquarters in Virginia, was established in 1992, with multipurpose objectives that included, but not limited to: "To present the message of Islam to Muslims and non-Muslims, and promote understanding between them."
With an eye on the future, and "Mindful of the dynamic changes that are taking place within the Muslim community and its surroundings," the MAS message state, "a number of Islamic workers and Islamic movement followers decided in 1992, after a painstaking measured and tedious process of soul-searching and consultation, to launch the Muslim American Society (MAS) in order to comple-

ment the work accomplished over the last three decades, and to lay the ground for the Islamic effort needed to face the next century's challenges."

MPAC

The Muslim Public Affairs Council (MPAC) has a vision statement that says, "To establish a vibrant American Muslim community that will enrich American society through promoting the Islamic values of Mercy, Justice, Peace, Human Dignity, Freedom, and Equality for all." MPAC's vision resonates well with its mission that state, "To effect positive change in public opinion and in policy with the purpose of realizing the vision."

MSA-N

In January 1963 some of the most respected personalities in the Islamic movement established the MSA of the United States and Canada. Over seventy students from across the country, met to discuss the state of Muslims in North America. Organizations like ISNA grew out of MSA, as the students that once had established MSA were no longer students and now professionals in their communities, building mosques and Islamic Centers. Hence, Muslim Student Associations' of U.S. and Canada grouped together to form a combined entity what is known as Muslim Student Association – National (MSA-N).
[Information mostly extracted from the web site of MSA-N]

PIH

Project Islamic H.O.P.E., (Helping Oppressed People Everywhere) has its headquarters in Los Angeles, California. According to its web site it is a "non-profit national civil rights organization, that works collectively with other ethnic and religious groups to stand on the front lines in the war against poverty, hunger and social injustice."

Its mission statement indicates that the Project Islamic HOPE is for developing and improving, "the spiritual, social, mental and physical life of youth and adults in the community in accordance with the Holy Qur'an and the example of Prophet Muhammad (*pbuh*)."

President Bush among supporters at his fundraiser, in
Boston, March 25, 2004.

Andrew Card (White House Chief of Staff) *Center*;
John J. Monahan (Telegram & Gazette) *Right*; and Tahir Ali *Left*
at a fundraiser for President Bush in Boston, March 25, 2004.

Presidential candidate, Sen. John Kerry with Shahid Ahmed Khan, in Framingham, MA.

Presidential candidate Sen. John Kerry talking to Pakistani-Americans at Shahid Ahmed Khan's residence, standing next to the senator on October 18, 2002 in Framingham, MA.

March in Washington D.C. to show solidarity to
Palestinian cause October 28, 2001.
Photo credit: Ahsan Lari

Rally in support of Kosova in front of Worcester City Hall.

Members of Muslim Delegation with Gov. William Weld. (1992)

Gov. William Weld at the hospitality suite during
Republican National Convention, Houston, 1992.

Ambassador Paul Cellucci (former Mass. governor)
spending time with the youth at the hospitality suite
during the Republican National Convention, Houston, 1992.

Tahir Ali thanking Congressman James McGovern
during a meeting in his office on June 22, 2001.

Sheikh Muhammed Nur Abdullah, President of ISNA presenting a copy of the Qu'ran to Dennis Kucinich, US Representative (D-OH).
August 31, 2003

U.S. Representative Dennis Kucinich (D-OH) with ISNA's Secretary General Sayyid Syeed at ISNA convention.
August 31, 2003

Nahla Al-Arian discusses her husband's case with former U.S. Senator Carol Moseley-Braun and AMA's Chairman Dr. Agha Saeed.
August 31, 2003

Panelists at ISNA convention (L to R) AMA Chairman Dr. Agha Saeed, MPAC's Dr. Salam Al-Marayati, Former Congressman and author Paul Findley, and CAIR's Nihad Awad.
August 31, 2003

(Left) *Imam* Hamza Yusuf speaking at the ISNA convention as Ingrid Mattson, ISNA's vice president awaits her turn to speak. (Right) *Imam* Sirhaj Wahaj speaks at the ISNA convention. August 31, 2003.

Former AMC President Abdurahman Alamoud explains AMC's Charter to Hamid (nephew of Malcolm X), Tahir Ali, and Gov. William Weld.

Gov. Weld greets Saghir Tahir (NH -State Rep.), Siddiq Abdullah and Siddique from PAGB of Boston.

President Bush and Muzammil Siddiqi in the Roosevelt office at the White House on September 26, 2001.

Index

Born in Pakistan in 1949, Mr. Ali came to America in 1974. He obtained a Master's degree in engineering from McGill University in Montreal, Canada in 1977. He is married with a daughter and two sons, all born and raised in America. The younger of the two sons died of leukemia at the age of nine. Mr. Ali has affiliations with the American Muslim Alliance, having served as the Massachusetts Chairman, Media and Public Relations Chairman on the national level. As a former Chairman of the Islamic Society of Greater Worcester, he has been instrumental in renovating the Islamic center from an abandoned church to a lively Mosque. He is the author of many articles published in various Muslim magazines, newspapers and websites. He is often called upon as a guest speaker at Muslim national and local conventions and conferences, including MIT and Harvard.

His political activities include fundraising for Hillary Clinton, former First Lady and U.S. Senator from New York; Michigan Congressman David Bonoir; hosting meetings among Muslim and political figures; and 1992 Republican National Delegate/Alternate-at-large from Massachusetts. He has received key-to-the-city from the Mayor of Worcester. He is an active member of the Republican Presidential Task Force. His name is engraved on the founder's wall honoring President Ronald Reagan at the Republican center.